Country Living's
healthy living

DEPRESSION

DEPRESSION

WHAT YOUR BODY'S TRYING TO TELL YOU

SUSAN SKOG

AND THE EDITORS OF *HEALTHY LIVING MAGAZINE*

AN AVON BOOK

The alternative healing methods described in this book are not intended as a substitute for medical advice from your physician. Always consult your doctor before beginning any new regimen that can impact your health. The publisher assumes no responsibility for any result derived from the implementation of the methods described herein.

Grateful acknowledgment is given to Nancy Wood for permission to use her poem "Earth Cure Me" from *Hollering Sun,* Simon & Schuster, copyright © 1972. Used with permission. All rights reserved.

Grateful acknowledgment is given to Dana L.J. Cribari for permission to reprint her poem "If I Look Now."

AVON BOOKS, INC.
1350 Avenue of the Americas
New York, New York 10019

Copyright © 1999 by Hearst Communications, Inc.
Published by arrangement with Healthy Living Magazine
ISBN: 0-380-80649-5
www.avonbooks.com/wholecare

Library of Congress Cataloging in Publication Data:
Skog, Susan, 1955–
    Depression : what your body's trying to tell you / Susan Skog and the editors of Healthy living magaine.
        p.   cm.
    "An Avon book."
    Includes bibliographical references and index.
    1. Depression, Mental Popular works. I. Title.
RC537.S573   1999   99-25037
616.85'27—dc21   CIP

First WholeCare Printing: July 1999

WHOLECARE TRADEMARK REG. U.S. PAT. OFF. AND IN OTHER COUNTRIES, MARCA REGISTRADA,
HECHO EN U.S.A.

Printed in the U.S.A.

OPM   10 9 8 7 6 5 4 3 2 1

CONTENTS

DEPRESSION

INTRODUCTION

Our Collective Angst

"How heavy the days are. There is not a fire that can warm me, not a sun to laugh with me. Everything base. Everything cold and merciless. And even the beloved dear stars look desolately down."

Hermann Hesse struggled to lay down these words to describe his depression. Do they summon a kindred recognition? Do they call to something deep within you? Do they resonate with feelings that envelop you more and more? If health statistics bear truth, Hesse's mournful song stirs something within millions of us.

Part of our shared humanity these days seems to be our collective feelings of depression. In fact, experts say there is now an epidemic of depression in our country. Despite our seeming outer affluence, there is rampant inner unrest. As many as 16 million people are experiencing depression at any given time.

The societal implications of depression are staggering.

Called the common cold of psychiatry, depression leads more people to seek medical attention than even the flu. In addition, hundreds of thousands more may have masked depression, in which vague physical aches and pains are actually undiagnosed depressions, according to Dr. Mark Gold.

Why Are We All So Sad?

What is behind this ubiquitous angst that ranges from melancholy to despair? Why is it such a hallmark of our culture? Why are so many of us feeling so sad? We will examine the roots of our depressions, both individually and culturally, with the help of today's leading mind/body/spirit practitioners, teachers, and authors, from Dr. Andrew Weil to Joan Borysenko, Dr. Dean Ornish to Caroline Myss.

Their words resound with several pervasive truths about depression, truths still grossly ignored in our culture. First, there is no reason for you to suffer alone, forever, in vain, or in shame. Second, we need to radically alter our perception of depression. Like any human experience, depression can be a powerful threshold to greater wholeness and healing. "It can be an opportunity to awaken one's heart and deepen one's connection to life," says psychologist John Welwood.

Over the centuries, we have lost these powerful understandings about the value of depression—and suffered greatly for it. Through all ages and cultures, depression has been viewed as a natural, initiative rite of passage to greater maturity, wisdom, and contentment. As you will see through the stories of people in this book, depression can indeed be a gateway to unparalleled strength—physical, emotional, and spiritual.

A Way to Become More Fully Human

We need to reclaim the ancient understanding of depression as a threshold to greater wholeness and healing. As painful as depression can be, it often is intended to be a wise and perfectly timed messenger, a sentinel warning us when something is amiss in our lives. A prophet pointing to the fact that our choices; lifestyles; spiritual, physical, and psychological well-being may be seriously out of balance.

The signs of depression—the heaviness, insomnia, sadness—are often our entire being's way of getting our attention, telling us that it needs something. Our body's heaviness might literally be intended to stop us so it can tell us that it feels sad, that it needs nurturing, variety, change or something more. That it doesn't want to pretend that everything is OK when it really isn't.

Our feelings, finds researcher Candace Pert, have a profound effect on the chemistry of our bodies. "No system in our body operates in isolation," says Pert. "Whether it's the brain, the heart, the digestive tract or the liver, they're all in constant communication." Pert has studied the body chemistry underlying the body/mind/spirit connection for more than twenty years. She is a former chief of the section on brain biochemistry at the National Institutes of Health.

As you will see through the stories of dozens of people who have journeyed through depression, if we can heed its messages, depression can become a natural, illuminating gateway.

"Depression wells up and encompasses us for a time in a state of painful, dream-saturated formlessness, but its true purpose is to provide the opportunity for healing insight, renewal and reintegration," says Dr. Jonathan Zuess, author of *The Wisdom of Depression*.

I hope this book will help you see that depression, like the state of contentment, fear, or anger, is natural, universal, and can provide powerful insights into our natures and our purpose on earth. Albeit painful, depression can be an acute source of empowerment, intuition, and transformation. It often allows us to finally understand: What is my purpose here on earth? What did I come here to do?

Depression is one way we become more fully human. But it is not easy or pain free, and this book doesn't profess to glorify or romanticize being depressed. It's unsettling, scary, and can rattle your spirit like no other state. The descent into the dark night of the soul can be more desolate than we ever imagined. The land of tears can be a cold landscape indeed.

Dark Nights of the Soul Can Bring Light

But as this book will help you see, you don't need to stay in this landscape forever. Nor are you alone in this often unfamiliar terrain. As statistics show, it's a mighty crowded landscape after all! Most of us—at least one in five of us—journey to despair from time to time, often overnight when we lose a relationship, a child, a parent, a job—or our way. It is a place of deep grief—but hopefully fertile insight.

The dark nights of the soul have much to teach us,

indeed. As Theodore Roethke eloquently wrote, "In a dark time, the eye begins to see."

By signaling us of our soul's deepest desires, our heart's yearnings, our body's needs, depression can be a catalyst, albeit a painful one, for long-needed change. If we heed the messages of depression, we can heal and build a richer, more resilient life. If we ignore the messages, our depressions will just escalate, our whole being will get weaker.

"Depression is part of our intuitive guidance system. It is a warning bell that tells you something in your life is out of balance," says Dr. Mona Lisa Schultz, author of *Awakening Intuition*.

"Usually you need to fully feel an emotion and make a change, often in a relationship, your job, or your perception of where you are. If you don't make that change, your depression will continue unabated and raise the incidence of disease in your body. The warning bell will just get louder and louder if you don't hear it."

This book will help you heed the warning bell, listen deeply to what your depression has to tell you, and find effective, healing treatments that honor body, mind, and spirit. It is full of hopeful stories and choices from people who peered deeply into the root of their depression and found greater inner strength and outer vibrancy through complementary therapies.

Activating the Healer Within

Today's top holistic practitioners share powerful meditations, diets, writing and art exercises, breathing and movement techniques, prayers, visualizations, and other lifestyle choices to help you reclaim your true nature.

This book will guide you to examine your lifestyle, daily routines, choices, and support network to see if they support optimum health. You will learn of new research into the healing effects of cognitive therapies, herbal and homeopathic remedies, spirituality, bodywork, exercise, and service to others.

All of the choices explored in this book are aimed to help you activate your own innate healing powers. They are designed to allow you to be an active participant in your own recovery from depression. That participation alone is supremely important if you are to become whole again. "On some level people possess within themselves the drug to cure every ill," says Candace Pert. I hope this book helps you find your unique prescription for your own inner healing.

May it bless you with the peace of mind that depression, as messenger, can usher you, admittedly often with deep suffering, to the next stage in your journey. Like all life experiences, depression is one way we become more fully human, more aware of our amazing inner power and deep compassion for others' suffering.

Sophy Burnham says, "As you evolve spiritually, you become more sensitive and possibly more touched not only by your own suffering, which you can name, but by that of others and the compassion you feel for them. . . . If there was no pain, what would you do? How would you care for one another? How would you love one another? We don't love only in pain, but we find our humanity in this suffering."

We can also find more seasoned compassion and insight. Joseph Campbell once said there are two ways to gain wisdom. One being zapped with instant insight. The other, through great suffering. For millions of us, the way we gain wisdom is by being plunged, often overnight, into depression. It's as simple and as complex as that.

I hope this book allows you to see that you can descend into the depths of your being and emerge a more whole, resilient, and vibrant human being. If you understand it and work with it, depression has the potential to open your eyes to your true greatness and power. It has the potential to show you your innate magnificence—and how that magnificence is intended to be displayed. From the darkness can come the light. As Albert Camus wrote, "In the depth of winter, I finally learned that within me there lay an invincible summer."

ONE

Understanding the Face of Depression

We all get the blues. We all feel out of sorts, restless, and sad from time to time. As human beings, we're supposed to. It's part of the light and dark, the yin and yang of our nature. But occasional days of melancholy don't add up to being depressed. The overwhelming grip of sadness, heaviness, and often hopelessness that accompany depression is a level of suffering far greater.

How can you know if you are truly depressed and need professional help? How can you distinguish between intermittent sadness and chronic depression? It helps to listen deeply to the voices of those who have journeyed through the many stages of depression.

Writer William Styron referred to his own depression as a "black tempest." He said it exposed him to "the dungeons of my spirit." He also movingly captured how depression and anxiety are often intimate partners that robbed him of once-deep pleasures.

He wrote of walking through the woods one bright fall day and seeing a flock of Canadian geese honking above the colorful trees. He knew he normally would have been exhilarated by the sights and sounds, but instead, "the flight of birds caused me to stop, riveted with fear, and I stood stranded there, helpless, shivering, aware for the first time that I had been stricken by no mere pangs of withdrawal but by a serious illness whose name and actuality I was able finally to acknowledge."

Dr. Kay Redfield Jamison, too, chronicled her own haunting depression in her memoir, *An Unquiet Mind*. The heaviness and self-loathing she felt vibrates in her voice: "Everything—every thought, word, movement—was an effort. Everything that once was sparkling now was flat. I seemed to myself to be dull, boring, inadequate, thick-brained, unlit, unresponsive, chill-skinned, bloodless, and sparrow-drab. . . . It seemed as though my mind had slowed down and burned out to the point of being virtually useless."

Hold a Mirror up to Your Moods

Ask yourself: Do these portraits of depression mirror my own life and experience? Am I feeling as these people did? How can I tell if I am really depressed—and need comprehensive treatment?

Find a comfortable chair, keep the world at bay for a bit, and give yourself a health quiz to see if your feelings and behaviors might tally up to a signature of depression. You want to see if these symptoms are the pattern of your life. If you have four or more of the symptoms below, for two weeks or longer, or that regularly interfere with your work or family life, this is the criterion for a diagnosis of clinical depression, according to the National Institute of Mental Health.

OK, time to check in with yourself. Do you experience:

- Persistent sad, anxious, or "empty" moods?
- A loss of interest or pleasure in activities, including sex?
- Restlessness, irritability, or excessive crying?
- Feelings of guilt, worthlessness, helplessness, hopelessness, pessimism?
- Sleeping too much or too little, early morning awakening?
- Appetite and/or weight loss or overeating and weight gain?
- Decreased energy, fatigue, feeling "slowed down"?
- Thoughts of death or suicide, or suicide attempts?
- Difficulty concentrating, remembering, or making decisions?
- Persistent physical symptoms that don't respond to treatment, such as headaches, digestive disorders, and chronic pain?

Now, shift gears to your office. Continue your quiz and ask yourself how often in your workplace you have:

- Decreased productivity
- Morale problems
- Lack of cooperation
- Safety problems, accidents
- Absenteeism
- Frequent complaints of being tired all the time
- Complaints of unexplained aches and pains
- Alcohol and drug abuse

Physicians familiar with depression also note that many of their patients display a "lack of assertiveness, oversensitivity to rejection, or excessive shyness," which can be hidden forms of depression, says Dr. Burton Goldberg, who wrote *Alternative Medicine Guide to Women's Health 2,* along with *Alternative Medicine* editors.

People who are depressed often withdraw from society, even view it in a negative, dangerous way. Other people seem hostile, not to be trusted. They may be unable to plan for the future—"What's the use?"—and explode or break into tears at the slightest provocation. Others have irrational fears and thoughts of death.

As you sit with yourself and examine whether you truly may be depressed, also look at the stuff you may be addicted to. Many people who are depressed also become addicted to and try to self-regulate their moods with alcohol, cocaine, food, and other forms of addiction.

Men, especially, will become addicted to anger, rage, alcohol, and drugs to avoid looking into their darker side, says Dr. Harold Bloomfield. "Men are the ones who jump off bridges shouting all the way, 'I'm not depressed.' They externalize their depression. They become rage-aholics, alcoholics, cocaine-aholics. Unfortunately, they take out their pain on the women and children in their lives."

Men and women both rely on these behaviors and addictions to erect elaborate defenses. For women, many of the common addictive defenses can be excessive dependency on a man to meet their needs and solve their problems. They are addicted to blaming other people in their lives for their problems—and crediting others for their happiness.

"Dependency is a state in which you assume that someone or something outside you will take care of you because you cannot take care of yourself," says author Anne Wilson Schaef.

Anything can be used addictively, from work to shopping to chronic busyness to having the perfect face and hair. "This is because the purpose or function of an addiction is to put a buffer between ourselves and our awareness of our feelings," points out Schaef. "An addiction serves to numb us so that we are out of touch with what we know and what we feel."

Jungian analyst and author Marion Woodman has long explored the addiction to perfectionism and other addictions that prevent people from being in touch with their essence. It's as if people "put pins into themselves to put themselves to sleep and refuse to wake up."

One of the biggest issues in our civilization now, say Woodman, is to take the pins out, to deal with life, suffering, warts, illusions, and all. "Keeping our eyes open and dealing with the pain. And the joy of living in this century now. Developing the eyes and the ears to live happily. We just have to make the very most of it while we're here and live it to the fullest."

Knowing When to Get Help

OK . . . how did your self-check go? Are you living life to the fullest—or did some disturbing patterns emerge? Are these symptoms a mirror of your daily existence? If so, it's time to seek help. Treatment is available, and you don't need to stay in the troubled place you find yourself.

Contrary to popular opinion—still stubbornly clinging to our consciousness even today—depression typically can't be willed away, at least not deep-seated depression. Positive thinking is powerful, but marshaling our intellectual power and ordering depression to go away and leave us alone falls far short for most people. Some of the most dynamic people couldn't will their depression away. Abraham Lincoln and Martin Luther King certainly couldn't. Realize that asking for help may be the wisest, most conscious choice you could make.

Main Messages

- Depression is far deeper than occasional melancholy or the blues.
- Take the self-check in this chapter to determine whether a pattern of depression emerges.
- As you look deeply at your life, examine whether addictions to alcohol, drugs, work, even shopping or compulsive busyness may be masking pain and depression.
- If you are depressed, get help. You can't will away your depression. Some of the most dynamic people—past and present—couldn't and can't.

TWO

The Source of Our Discontent

Now the question that has captivated physicians and healers since the beginning of time and still holds us in its sway—what causes depression? The basic theme of this book is that like all medical conditions, depression arises from a complex dance between physiology and consciousness, body and soul.

It's true that many people are more genetically predisposed to depression. But we are far more than our bodies, than our brain chemicals. The medical and psychological practitioners interviewed for this book said that to understand why some people get depressed and others don't we have to broaden our understanding of depression and of its genesis.

Triggers for Depression

Depression can be caused by:

- A genetic predisposition
- Birth and childhood trauma
- Life losses and disappointments
- Personality
- Poor nutrition
- Hormonal imbalances
- Stress
- Silencing our voice
- Failure to express emotions
- Sense of powerlessness and loss of control
- Substance or sexual abuse
- Social isolation
- Sensitivity to chemicals
- Food allergies
- Spiritual impoverishment
- Toxic thought patterns
- Disconnection from and destruction of the earth

Depression can spring from a complex mixture of any of these factors. The biology of depression and its physiological causes, like dramatic hormonal swings after the birth of a child, will be more fully explored in the next chapter. But beyond our physiology, depression is often directly related to what happens to us in life—and how we respond to it.

Root of Depression Often Overlooked

Yet many doctors don't even explore whether other medical conditions, such as low thyroid, or emotional and spiritual issues exist and fuel the depression. Instead, they often automatically put patients on prescription antidepressants without examining the many other factors that cause depression. If left untreated, these factors can endanger your health and erode your quality of life even further.

Which is why just taking antidepressants to address one aspect of depression—namely brain chemistry—is often just masking symptoms that may arise from past emotional trauma, an abusive childhood, poor nutrition, hormonal imbalance at midlife, or negative thought patterns. Prozac alone can't address these other factors that give rise to depression. A chemical "cure" can't heal emotional wounds.

Dr. Mona Lisa Schultz says we should think of low serotonin levels in the brain—one physical marker of depression—not as the root cause of depression, but as a surface symptom of deeper unrest, just as gas emitted during an earthquake is symptomatic of the earth's plates shifting underground.

Because depression can be caused by a whole array of deep-seated factors, it should be addressed with a comprehensive regimen that targets health issues that affect your entire being.

That is the overwhelming theme of this book. If you seek treatment for your depression, work with trained and experienced medical practitioners who will address your physical, spiritual, psychological, and emotional health.

Don't settle for a quick fix. There is none.

Demand a complete biochemical workup to make sure you have no other physical illness, like an underactive thyroid or chronic fatigue syndrome, masquerading as depression. Ask for a urine analysis, thyroid tests, and blood chemistry profiles to determine your nutritional condition. Make sure your liver is functioning properly. Check for allergic reactions to certain foods, chemicals, and dyes—often overlooked in our culture.

Examine Your Biology

Gather your own family history from both side of your family. How many family members, including aunts and uncles and grandparents, suffered from depression? How many had alcohol or other substance problems which could indicate masked or untreated depression? How many were addicted to or compulsive about specific routines or behaviors? Share this picture with your therapist.

If you believe you are depressed, please seek help immediately. Don't assume you can buck up if you just try harder. Depression is a stubborn match for perseverance. These are all the misguided messages we get about mental health in our culture. If you or a loved one is seriously depressed, you need immediate intervention, which may include psychotherapy and antidepressant medications. Without treatment, about 30 percent of seriously depressed people try to kill themselves.

And an important note of caution about this book: We are not advocating that the prescriptions within, some of which include alternative therapies, substitute for your conventional antidepressant prescriptions. Many people need medication—at least in times of crisis. Pharmaceuticals have proven powerfully effective in alleviating depression, if accompanied by psychotherapy. A more thorough discussion of traditional antidepressants and how they work is found in the next chapter.

Get Professional Support

The truth of the matter is, if you suffer from serious, debilitating depression, you may not have the motivation and ability to even try some of the lifestyle changes explored in this book until you feel better.

Nor may they be effective enough. For instance, most holistic practitioners do not consider the herb hypericum, or St. John's wort, a first-line treatment for serious depression.

If you are seriously, chronically depressed, the strategies and ideas offered in this book can be powerfully effective and help you heal your depression. But they are a complement to, not a substitute for, your ongoing work with qualified, trained medical practitioners.

If you have mild to moderate or intermittent depression, on the other hand, you may find great success in treating your depression with many of the suggestions and ideas explored in this book and may not need to take traditional medications. As with all the choices offered in this book, these are issues to be discussed and managed by you and your doctors and health-care practitioners.

Finally, there are no instant elixirs offered in this guide. You can't do a body scan and melt depression away over your lunch break. Popping Prozac or St. John's wort without examining the source of your depression is just a Band-Aid approach.

If, for instance, you're chronically stressed and pushing your body to function like a machine that never shuts down, your depression will likely be a tenacious companion unless you change your lifestyle.

Medication Is Never the Only Answer

If your depression finds its genesis in choices that poison body, mind, and spirit, in past or current abuse, or a lack of love and spiritual sustenance, you need far deeper change than that afforded by medication. Medication may help dull those jagged edges of your existence, but they remain raw, sharp, and hungry for attention and healing. "A drug fails to move us through the expansion of consciousness that would ultimately bring us out of this circular impasse," says Rudolph Ballentine in his book *Radical Healing*.

Many people find antidepressants like a bridge during a crisis that helps them span the transition from heaviness and sadness to lightness and joy. But when their depression has lifted, they're afraid to stop taking their medications for fear that their moods will again plummet. Some people also experience undesirable side effects when they taper off their meds. Work with your doctor and therapist to determine if and when it's best to discontinue your antidepressants. Many of the people you will meet in this book were successfully able to do so after healing on numerous physical, emotional, and spiritual levels.

The therapies explored in this book are intended to be part of an in-depth, ongoing approach that can help you reach greater health. They are part of a lifestyle, a shift in the way you manage and live your days, to promote optimal vibrancy. As you create this way of being, there are many choices available to you. As Bill Moyers points out: "Health becomes the freedom not to react to things but to respond and have many different options—not to be trapped by an old belief about life."

Main Messages

- Depression is much more than occasional melancholy or intermittent blues.
- Take the questionnaire on page 10 to see if you're depressed.
- Depression must be treated. It can't be willed away by our mighty intellects.
- Depression can spring from dozens of factors, from childhood trauma to hormonal imbalances to chronic stress.
- Demand a complete biochemical workup to rule out any other physical illness.
- Seek professional help as soon as possible, especially if you are seriously depressed or even suicidal.
- There are no quick fixes. Easing depression involves a comprehensive spectrum of disciplines and life-style choices.

THREE

The Chemistry of Depression

The majestic mind has much to do with our moods. But it's no prime dictator. You are far more than your brain chemistry. Your choices, passions, moods, and behavior are shaped by more than your neuronal circuitry.

Yet they play a critical role. Scientists do know that your neurotransmitters, chemicals used to send messages from one area of the brain to the other, are affected by and, in turn, affect your emotions.

The part of the brain that regulates your emotions is the limbic system, which lies deep within your brain below your cerebrum. The limbic system controls your appetite, body temperature, hormone levels, sleep, blood pressure, and behavior, in addition to your emotions.

When Our Neurotransmitters Are Low

In the 1950s, researchers began to explore how depression is caused by low levels of certain brain chemicals, namely the neurotransmitters serotonin, norepinephrine, and dopamine.

These neurotransmitters are a wonderful mirror of your emotional health. When your emotional equilibrium wanes, they fall. Scientists further concluded that when these neurotransmitters are low, the nervous system slows down, the brain's functions are depressed, and depression often manifests.

For example, serotonin helps you feel relaxed and mellow. It helps you feel more content and at peace with yourself and the world. When serotonin levels drop, you may feel more agitated, anxious, impulsive, sad, and confused. You find it more difficult to say "No" even though you are already overloaded.

Take a closer scan at what happens inside your brain as you get stressed. You are at work and have to turn in your project results to your boss by day's end. Unexpected snags hit. As you feel yourself getting anxious, a small amount of serotonin floats across from one brain cell, or neuron, to another receiving cell, which has thousands of receptors to catch the serotonin.

When the serotonin hits the neuroreceptor, it passes along the message that you should remain calm. But your serotonin level is too low, so the signal is not strong enough. You remain too stressed, irritable, and anxious as your deadline looms closer.

Scientists know now that many people have a family history of chemical imbalances that contribute toward depression. But this is equally key: Researchers also have discovered that many people with a genetic predisposition don't become depressed. "Low serotonin apparently is more of a vulnerability factor, causing depression only when other conditions exist," maintains Dr. Michael Norden, author of *Beyond Prozac.*

Since the 1950s, doctors have used many new antidepressant medications to treat depression by boosting neurotransmitter levels. These new antidepressants include Prozac, Paxil, and Zoloft. They work by allowing the serotonin molecules released by your brain to stay in the space between your neurons longer so your receptor cells can absorb and use the serotonin longer and more efficiently.

When these drugs came into vogue, researchers heralded them as breakthrough drugs. But many more cutting-edge discoveries about brain chemistry continue to give us a clearer window into depression. "Progress," says Dr. Steven Hyman, director of the National Institute of Mental Health, "is just moving faster and faster."

For instance, as new clues are uncovered in our neuronal map, new medications are being developed. Now researchers are developing new drugs that target "substance P," a compound found throughout the human body. Substance P appears to affect our perception of mental anguish and play a major role in controlling our moods. New antidepressants that affect substance P levels may be on the market early in the next century.

Hormonal Imbalances Often Ignored

In our culture, depression brought on by chemical imbalances in the brain has seized center stage. The lucrativeness of the new serotonin antidepressants has certainly fueled much of this visibility. But our glands, not our neurotransmitters, are an often overlooked and undervalued physiological cause of depression in women, says Gillian Ford, hormonal educator at the Center for Hormonal Health in Roseville, California.

"Women with hormonal problems, particularly those who experience depression and fatigue as a result, often have great difficulty in finding a physician who will affirm and treat their problems sympathetically," writes Ford in her book *Listening to Your Hormones*. Even if physicians are sympathetic to hormonal depression, many don't know what to do, she adds.

Yet many women are vulnerable to depression brought on by many of the major hormonal "events," from premenstrual syndrome to menopause. Even less attention has been given to women who suffer from the dramatic postpartum hormonal shifts, claims Ford.

She points to work by Dr. James Alexander Hamilton, who believes that postpartum depression is a polyendocrine disorder, occuring because of the dramatic drop in estrogen, progesterone, B-endorphins, and cortisol within a few days of delivery. As these hormones plummet, the pituitary can become sluggish, and thyroid levels drop. In such cases, hormonal treatment may be more effective than antidepressants, which are commonly given to women who suffer from postpartum depression.

Dr. Jamie McGregor, an OB/GYN professor at the University of Colorado and Denver Health Center, has also studied postpartum depression and how new mothers' health is affected after delivery. The placenta makes several substances that affect the central nervous system, such as corticotropin-releasing hormone, or CRH.

"CRH in the normal brain plays a role in modulating mood and anxiety," McGregor says. "It's kind of an evolutionary substance associated with fear and reaction to fear."

Dr. Doris Gundersen, an assistant psychiatry professor

at the University of Colorado Health Sciences Center, says postpartum depression, or PPD, affects 10 to 20 percent of women and usually appears about three to four weeks after delivery. New mothers who are especially vulnerable are those with a past history of depression, marital discord, incest, an inadequate support system, unrealistic expectations, or ambivalence about motherhood.

Symptoms include profound sadness, crying spells, despair, pessimism, feeling overwhelmed, sleeplessness, severe anxiety, difficulty bonding with the baby, thoughts of inadequacy, and shame.

About 30 to 80 percent of all women become anxious, sad, moody, and suffer from sleep problems shortly after the birth of their child. "A woman may feel as though she is walking through wet concrete," says Ford, "But this feeling usually goes away with time. It is not accompanied by the terrifying emotional problems of serious PPD."

And the so-called baby blues typically subside after several weeks.

PPD, on the other hand, may linger for months. If you feel you are suffering from postpartum depression, seek immediate help. Explore with your caregiver whether a combination of hormonal treatment, antidepressants, and therapy can be used.

As with PPD, researchers are scrambling to unravel the relationship between hormonal changes and midlife depression. Why do so many women develop full-blown depressions at two distinct points of their lives—after childbirth and, again, at menopause? The physiological link is still under intense investigation, but to many women, midlife depression is all too real.

Connie Zweig, editor of *Meeting the Shadow* and *To Be a Woman,* wrote of her midlife depression in the book *Sacred Sorrows: Embracing and Transforming Depression.*

"When I turned 40, the solid ground beneath my feet cracked open. I dropped through a fissure, down, down and disappeared into a great blackness. I lived for a long while at the bottom of a dark hole looking up. Nothing had prepared me for such an eclipse."

When she turned 40, Zweig says it was as if the earth "yawned open, a long hand rose up from the depths of the underworld, grabbed me by the foot—and stopped my dancing."

Certainly midlife depressions and their capacity to offer both spiritual incubation and great regeneration have been explored in archetypal terms by ancient philosophers and psychologists on through Carl Jung and Joseph Campbell. But the changing female physiology and the hormonal link to depression need much greater scientific scrutiny so women don't have to spend more time in the deep underworld than is necessary. Midlife rejuvenation and wisdom is great; unrelenting misery is anything but.

Again, as with postpartum depression, explore with your doctor whether your midlife melancholy and mood swings could indeed have a hormonal basis. Syd Baumel, author of *Dealing with Depression Naturally,* reports that in about a dozen clinical studies, depressed women not responding to antidepressant drugs were also given a small dose of thyroid hormone. Usually 50 to 75 percent improved or recovered within two weeks. Additional studies have shown that depressed women who take progesterone and estrogen find significant relief.

"In depressed men, testosterone levels tend to be low—the deeper the depression, the lower the testosterone," says Baumel. Perhaps, suggests Baumel, testosterone will soon be given to depressed men.

If you even suspect your hormones are contributing to your depression, demand a complete endocrine gland workup. Make sure your doctor explores the possibility of hypothyroidism. The physical symptoms of hypothyroidism include depression, fatigue, cold intolerance, thinning hair and eyebrows, and dry and thick skin.

Blood tests are not always accurate in detecting low thyroid levels. The basal temperature test may be even more accurate, many doctors feel. Menstruating women should take their basal temperature only during the first two days of their cycle. As soon as you awaken, put the thermometer under your armpit for ten minutes, advises Gillian Ford. "The normal temperature under the armpit should be above 97.2. If your temperature taken this way is consistently well below 97.2, you may have low thyroid activity."

Again, we are much more than our neurons and our endocrine glands. But brain or hormonal imbalances make us more vulnerable when stress, loss, trauma, or crisis come into play. Don't let your doctor downplay or overlook any possible physiological clues. Your quality of life depends on it.

Main Messages

- We are far more than our brain chemistry, but low levels of the neurotransmitters serotonin, norepinephrine, and dopamine can make us more vulnerable to depression.
- Newer antidepressants, like Prozac and Zoloft, act on and improve serotonin levels.
- Hormonal imbalances—often overlooked—can also lead to depression.
- For postpartum depression and midlife depression, hormonal treatments can be very effective.
- Use blood and basal body temperature tests to rule out hormonal imbalances.

FOUR

Valuing the Message of Depression

Why is it that only one-third of those who are depressed seek treatment? Part of the problem is that depression is sometimes hard to detect, especially when it presents itself as low energy, irritability, moodiness, and insomnia. But a big part of the problem is the stigma that still clings to depression.

In our feel-good, go-for-perfection, full-tilt, success-at-all-costs culture, feeling sad or lost isn't OK. Being vulnerable, confused, and uncertain are not states we fully accept—in ourselves or those around us. They make us squirm, judge, avoid, bolt.

We still view depression as a sign of personal weakness and professional failure. We are afraid to admit our psychic pain for fear of judgment and rejection.

"We still, even in the 1990s, have a medieval mentality when it comes to emotional illness. We're afraid what people will say, what they'll think, and how they'll feel about us. So we remain silent, suffocating in isolation under our burdens," observes Elaine Fantle Shimberg, author of *Depression: What Families Should Know.*

Updating Our Understanding of Depression

As touched upon in the introduction, to fully understand and ease depression, we have to bust these antiquated stigmas and misunderstandings. If we are going to heed the messages of our depressions and truly heal, we have to dramatically shift our cultural and individual perception of depression.

Know this, sit with it, remember it as you drive to work or brush your teeth: Depression wasn't always viewed as "bad" or something to scour away as quickly as possible, like a bad stain. In ancient times and up to the Renaissance, depression was simply viewed as one of many states of being, as normal and natural as mirth or anger.

Depression was an initiation, a threshold into the depths of the psyche and a deeper way of living in the world. Five hundred or six hundred years ago, melancholy was associated with the Roman god Saturn, points out Thomas Moore, author of *Care of the Soul.* To be depressed was to be "in Saturn." Traditional texts and medical books from that time refer to Saturn as the "old man" who presides over the golden years, the god of wisdom and philosophical reflection. A successful statesman and poet, Ficino refers to Saturn as a "unique and divine gift."

Depression as Doorway to Next Level

Depression, then, was often viewed as one face of the soul, as a gateway into greater wisdom and growth. As Thomas Moore writes, "melancholy thoughts carve out an interior space where wisdom can take up residence." Peering into, embracing, accepting our depressions, will allow our souls to expand and tell us what they really need.

Moore's sentiment is echoed by Dr. Jonathan Zuess in *The Wisdom of Depression*. When he graduated from medical school, like many in our society Dr. Zuess viewed depression solely as an illness. "As I began to work with depressed people, though, I was struck by the way that a period of depression was often followed by a kind of personal renewal, a deep-seated transformation that enabled the individual to cope at a higher level than ever before."

Dr. Zuess found that, for some people, breaking down was necessary "in that it allowed a truly meaningful reorganization and reintegration to occur on many levels of their lives."

Dr. Chris Northrup refers to this as Breakdown to Breakthrough. Like the immune system's innate response to fighting a virus, depression might be a "built in" response in the human system to help you overcome and creatively solve problems in your life. The fatigue and irritability associated with depression may be a prod to make you take a break from your activities, spend time on your own. Your appetite and sleep might wane so you can focus more on your inner work, to specifically prevent you from being distracted by the outer world.

"As in many of the conditions we call illness, the

symptoms are actually caused by your own protective healing forces in action," points out Dr. Zuess.

Depression, though, if unresolved, can escalate into chronic, serious debilitating illness that does require serious treatment and can even prevent this kind of introspection and inner seeking.

Listening to the Messages

How do we begin to heed the message of depression, especially when we first become distressed? How can we seek its guidance so we can deal with it, process it, and become stronger? Instead of pathologizing or ignoring our depression, get more familiar with it, says Moore. When Saturn comes knocking, invite him in.

"Some Renaissance gardens even had a bower dedicated to Saturn—a dark, shaded, remote place where a person could retire and enter the persona of depression without fear of being disturbed."

Perhaps, Moore says, depression has its own angel, "a guiding spirit whose job it is to carry the soul away to its remote places where it finds unique insight and enjoys a special vision."

If we instead, in this culture-of-perpetual-feel-great, try to snuff out our dark moods, we run the risk of dulling all of our senses. If we don't fully feel our darker moods, we don't fully feel joy, hope, contentment. The colors of nature, skies and leaves, will be less brilliant. Our passions blunted.

"The ability to feel is indivisible. Repress awareness of any one feeling, and all feelings are dulled. . . . The same nerve endings are required for weeping and dancing, fear and ecstasy," says Sam Keen, author of *Fire in the Belly: On Being a Man.*

Plus, the energy spent to avoid feeling your dark moods drains and depletes you of energy you could be using for positive purposes in the world. Again, depression is not something you can push or will away, like an unwelcome interloper. You can't shelve it or file it away until a more convenient time arises. When depression beckons, it beckons for a reason. It wants to be listened to. It wants your full attention and acceptance.

If you are feeling sad, heavy, overwhelmed with unrelenting grief, begin to look at your moods, sit with them, respect what they may be trying to say to you. Your feelings may be a powerful signal from your inner guidance system that something is amiss. Something is out of balance in your life and is calling out to be addressed.

When the dishes are done, the phones turned down, the faxes are quiet, and the kids in bed, what still pulls at your soul? Or what calls to you and stirs you from a sound sleep?

Don't turn away. Take the opportunity to see what's there. This time, says John Welwood, is "an opportunity to see depression not merely as an affliction, but as an opportunity to relate to one's life situation more honestly and directly."

Depression as Note of Caution

Sometimes we are depressed because our spirits are telling us that our choices aren't nourishing, our thoughts aren't positive, our past wounds haven't healed, our lives are draining away as we avoid fully living them.

"Depression, like all psychopathology, is not merely a

disease to be quickly eliminated. Instead it can be an opportunity to awaken one's heart and deepen one's connection to life," Welwood says.

Begin to see your dark nights of the soul—maybe by now they are full days—as windows into the depth and magnificence of yourself. As guides into the next, full chapter of your life. "I love the dark hours of my being in which my senses drop into the deep," wrote Rainer Maria Rilke. "I have found in them, as in old letters, my private life that is already lived through, and becomes wide and powerful now, like legends. Then I know that there is room in me for a second huge and timeless life."

Like Rilke, there is hopeful room in you for a huge and timeless life. May this book help you make your way into what lies ahead.

Main Messages

- We need to shift our cultural understanding of depression. It is not something to be ashamed of, but a threshold to greater wisdom and growth.
- The fatigue and heaviness of depression may intentionally slow you down so you can closely examine your life.
- If we ignore and avoid feeling our darker moods, we dull the sensation and experience of all our moods, including joy and euphoria.
- Depression signals us as to what's amiss. Maybe our thoughts are too negative, our past wounds not healed, our lifestyles not nourishing.
- View your dark nights of the soul as new windows into the depths of yourself.

FIVE

Tracing the Roots of Our Unrest

When Joan sank into her deepest depressions, her appearance and environment reflected the extent of her misery. She wore only black or gray clothes. All day long, she kept the curtains drawn so no light could pierce the darkness. She avoided leaving her apartment because the world seemed too animated, bright, and overwhelming.

There are far too many Joans among us today. And many more men—maybe more than we've ever thought—whose own darkness refuses to abate. Across cultures, genders, and races, depression is soaring. The shadows that fall on our days appear to be lingering and lengthening.

We suffer from depression ten times more often than our grandparents, according to Martin Seligman, a leading depression expert at the University of Pennsylvania. Researcher Myrna Weissman and her colleagues examined medical records since the beginning of the century and found that each successive generation has doubled its susceptibility to depression.

Throughout the world, depression is on the rise and appearing at early ages than ever before.

These are some of the sobering facts:

- At least one in five of us will be depressed at some time in our life.
- Women are two to three times more likely to be diagnosed with depression than men.
- Another study found that one in three women 18 to 24 is significantly depressed.

Male Depression Not Appreciated

But recently, more experts wonder if men aren't suffering from depression at the same rate as women. Maybe it's just that men are more adept at suffering in silence and hiding or denying their depression. Maybe in our win-at-all-costs culture, we haven't allowed men to be depressed, or to admit it if they are.

Psychotherapist Terrence Real believes that male depression is highly underestimated. Because men so often deny and are ashamed of their depression, much of their suffering is under-reported and under-treated, says Real, the author of *I Don't Want to Talk About It: Overcoming the Secret Legacy of Male Depression.*

"Traditionally, we have not liked men to be very emotional or very vulnerable. An overtly depressed man is both—someone who not only has feelings but who has allowed those feelings to swamp his competence. A man brought down in life is bad enough. But a man brought down by his own unmanageable feelings—for many, that is unseemly."

Because they can be ashamed about being depressed,

men often push their pain deeper and deeper from view. They struggle to manage and camouflage their disquiet in excessive work and other addictions, like alcohol or sex. They often distance themselves emotionally from others—or become addicted to others to bolster their self-esteem and self-worth.

And, as our crime statistics show, when men can no longer stuff their pain any longer, they "act out distress" in violent, self-destructive ways, Real says. "Men are less used to voicing emotional issues, because we teach them that it is unmanly to do so." No accident, then, that men make up 93 percent of the prison population.

Real contends that, as we look at the breakout of depression in our country, if we factor in male personality disorders and chemical dependency, the incidence of depression between men and women is equal.

Our Lust for Outer Riches Breeds Inner Depression

So why in the world are we so depressed? What is behind all this angst? Tracing the root of these questions in our daily lives will lead us to insights about the source of much of our individual depression. The answers, say those who contributed their wisdom for this book, aren't that hard to find. They are all around us, woven deeply into our days.

In many ways, our culture at this time is prime, fertile loam for the seeds of depression to take root. It's sad, but not surprising at all that depression is epidemic.

Consider the fact that in our society we base much of our lives on expectations and beliefs that can only disappoint us and lead to depression. Take, for instance, our belief in the power of material stuff to make us happy. Those who get the goodies feel good and happy, right? Sated and successful, isn't it so?

But our voracious appetite for outer trappings has not made us happy. In many ways, it's made us miserable and even more depressed, says Joan Borysenko.

"People kept looking for the carrot. 'Oh, the American Dream is out there.' We will soon have a chicken in every pot, a *Chicken Soup for the Soul* in every library, two cars in every garage, and then we will be happy. But as more and more people have actually moved into that economic bracket and been able to achieve those things, lo and behold, they turned around and said, 'We've been had. We're still not happy.' "

Even Webster's dictionary, points out author Susan Jeffers, defines success as "the attainment of wealth, position, honors or the like." Sounds good, even noble, says Jeffers, author of *End the Struggle and Dance with Life.*

But there are big flaws in that definition. Is it success, she asks, when we have given up a balanced and full life to pursue wealth, position, and honors?

"Our present-day ladder to success ignores the attainment of inner riches—peace, joy, caring, love, appreciation, and gratitude—all of which are necessary for ending the struggle and dancing with life. Making it is painful when we are spiritually bankrupt and unable to enjoy any of our rewards."

Our materialistic, outer-directed culture "breeds depression by promoting distorted and unattainable goals for human life," says John Welwood. "In a society such as ours, where the motivating ideal is to 'make it' through social status and monetary success, depression is inevitable when people fail to find the imagined pot of gold at rainbow's end."

Our Crazed Lifestyles Isolate Us

Beyond our lust for stuff lies our appetite for life in the fast lane. Our crazed, full-tilt high-stimuli days can't help but set us up for emotional meltdown. Trying to balance everything on our plates is not only exhausting—it depresses our spirits, bodies, and minds. Our non-stop rhythms also isolate us from nourishing, sustaining relationships, says stress management consultant and humorist Loretta LaRoche.

"As a society, we live from crisis to crisis. And there is a high degree of depression and isolation to this crisis mentality. In our businesses, we've lost our connections to others," says LaRoche, also an adjunct faculty member for the Behavioral Institute of Medicine, an affiliate of Harvard Medical School.

"There is no time to hang out with those we like and love, with our families. So we are really living in this state of aloneness, which creates depression."

Our isolation from one another only increased with the World Wide Web invasion. In the first concentrated study of the social and psychological effects of Internet use at home, researchers at Carnegie Mellon University found that people who spend even a few hours a week online experience higher levels of depression and loneliness than they would have if they used the computer network less frequently.

Those who used the Internet reported a decline in interaction with family members and a reduction in their circle of friends that directly corresponded to the amount of time they spent online.

"It's ironic," wrote R. L. Stine, author of the infamous *Goosebumps* series. "Somehow our age of satellites, faxes, e-mail, cell phones and beepers has brought people into closer contact, but not necessarily closer communication."

Speed Blurs Joy

We are also an extremely frenzied culture. No news there. We are so fast-paced we often only skim the surface of any experience. A recent study conducted at the National Zoo in Washington, D.C., found that the average time visitors spend looking at any individual exhibit was just five to ten seconds. Larry Dossey, a Santa Fe physician and author of *Healing Words,* calls this addiction to speed "time sickness."

As we continuously weave more time-saving devices from cell phones to mega-computers into our lives, time sickness nears epidemic, he believes. We are obsessed with the idea "that time is getting away, that there isn't enough of it, and that you must pedal faster and faster to keep up. The trouble is, the body has limits that it imposes on us. And the body will not be fooled if we try to beat it into submission and ask more of it than it can deliver in a twenty-four-hour day. It will let us know."

One way it lets us know, says Dossey, is by becoming depressed.

Other cultural characteristics that fuel our depression epidemic? More people are more depressed today because we are so outer focused we totally ignore our inner passions, says Dr. Mona Lisa Schultz, author of *Awakening Intuition.*

Quite simply, if we suppress our life force, we get sick. If we are on fire and passionate about making an impact in the world, but beat down those inner flames, we get sick. Often extremely, debilitatingly ill.

If we instead focus on what the world—or others—require of us instead of tuning inward to our heart's desire, we signal depression to come near. "We become detached or unbonded from the things we want to do in the world, the things that will feed our hearts. So we become dispassionate and depressed."

Many people so want to live up to the media and advertising-hewn image of material success, that they take jobs purely for money and abandon their real passions. Refusing to act on what is in our hearts, ignoring our soul's cry, abandoning our purpose in life, can easily lead to some form of depression, says Dr. Schultz. It creates a form of self-imposed impotency and powerlessness.

"We feel, 'I can't assert any authority or power over my existence in the world. What's the use? I have no impact on my environment.' That is a lethal feeling that leads to depression."

This sense of powerlessness and futility might explain why women are three times more likely to become depressed than men. Borysenko points out that forty studies have found the same preponderance of depression in women in thirty different countries. While research provides no specific answers, one theory is that because of cultural conditioning around the world, women have a harder time expressing anger than men and are then sometimes less honest about their feelings.

"Since some forms of depression are thought to be related to keeping anger in—turning it against oneself—one would expect women therefore to be more depressed," Borysenko says.

Also, more than a third of all women are sexually or physically abused during childhood, infusing them with a sense of powerlessness, Borysenko adds. In *A Woman's Book of Life,* she cites research by sociologist Diana Russell, who in 1980 studied a group of nine hundred women, chosen randomly. In this group, one woman in four had been raped and one woman in three had been sexually abused in childhood.

"One of the most compelling behavioral models of depressions is based on helplessness. If we feel unable to control the world around us, changing those things that impinge negatively on the quality of life, we soon lapse into self-blame, hopelessness, and become less able to appreciate our own strengths. This makes us less resilient in the face of stress and more likely to become depressed when faced with life challenges."

Women More Programmed to Feel Relational Loss

Researchers also have found that women are more prone to depression because they rely more heavily on relationships for their sense of well-being. If their key relationships founder or are lost, women often feel alone, helpless, and depressed.

This relational theory was studied by researchers at the National Institute of Mental Health. They looked at PET scans of brains as the subjects recalled episodes of sadness or loss. The area of the brain that lights up in response to sadness was eight times larger in women than in men.

As early as the 1970s, neurobiologist Jerre Levy, while at the University of Chicago, discovered that the female right cerebral hemisphere is more attuned to emotion and the understanding of facial expression. Further research also finds that women are also more adept at empathizing with others' sadness, partially because they are more encouraged as young girls to discuss emotions. They are also more encouraged to engage in imaginative play, which allows them to empathize with how others may feel. If more of us in our culture are depressed, maybe women are neuronally wired to tune into this collective suffering.

Still another theory about why women are more vulnerable to depression is that they have a heightened sense of their relative powerlessness in a male-dominated society, which has created more aggressions toward humanity and great destruction of the earth. "I have a feeling that, even if they don't articulate it, most women feel this, at least on some emotional level," says Borysenko. "You see the earth being destroyed. It's the womb in which we live and move and have our being. We are literally children of mother earth, and you see, my God, the smokestacks going up and the land being paved.

"You see the power structures sending our sons off to war. A lot of women are saying, 'The world shouldn't be in these situations. We shouldn't be sending our sons to war, where they will potentially be killed. We shouldn't be killing mother earth.'

"There is a sense that, 'My God. No one has asked the women.' These are things that have happened because of the excess male energy in our culture, from the imbalance of the male and female. You look at our world and you just can't help feeling very deep grief over it."

Mourning the Annihilation of the Earth

Deep grief. This is exactly what many experts think we are feeling. Increasingly, many mind-body-spirit researchers are questioning how much our rising rates of depression are tied to our literal biological and spiritual connection to a changing earth, an ecosystem we largely squander instead of honor.

If we are part of the earth as a living, connected organism, how can we not be depressed by the fact that species leave the earth every year due to our actions? How can that not weigh on our hearts, minds, and spirits and make us grieve in ways we can't even begin to understand or articulate? No wonder we feel deep grief.

The loss of biodiversity in the world is "a holocaust on a scale we cannot imagine or comprehend," says Terry Tempest Williams, author of *Refuge* and *Unspoken Hunger*. As we lose our connection with the land, as we lose animals and plants from our earthly garden, who knows the toll on our psyches.

"What kind of inconsolable loneliness are we experiencing on a conscious and unconscious level?" asks Tempest Williams. "I think this is the grief we intuitively feel. This is our unspoken hunger."

Rabbi Zalman Schachter-Shalomi says that "on some deep, inchoate level we feel so grief stricken about the destruction of the rain forests. . . .We feel saddened and depressed by the toxic poisons that clog her bloodstream, the planet's lakes, rivers, and oceans."

Though we have systemically altered and changed the natural perfection of the earth, we haven't hesitated to seek perfection in our material world. There is a rampant pursuit of perfectionism in our culture that is immensely toxic.

Addiction to Perfection

Our society places enormous value on youth, beauty, and material success. Women, especially, are given the message that they must be thin, beautiful, charming, pleasing, and nurturing, especially to men and their families.

Our culture's obsession with thin women has fueled many women's depression. *Glamour* magazine recently surveyed 27,000 readers about body image, eating disorders, and other topics. Fifty-two percent of women surveyed said they were dissatisfied with their bodies. More than two-thirds say they "feel too fat" and more than half say they feel "resigned" and "upset" when they look in the mirror. Any wonder women lack in self-confidence and are more depressed than before?

Harvard University psychologist and researcher Carol Gilligan and her colleagues have done groundbreaking research into the loss of confidence girls suffer as they approach adolescence. The same girls who at 9 and 10 were outspoken and sure of themselves begin to respond, "I don't know." Suddenly, the girls' knowledge and authentic voice goes underground.

On the other hand, men in our society still get the message that they must make lots of money, secure material stuff for their families, vault the ladder of success—and become more caring, nurturing, sensitive males. They feel increasingly torn between their jobs and their families, as discussed in a recent *Business Week* article.

Toxic Parenting Takes a Toll

In tracing the root of our depression we shouldn't overlook the fact that many people were raised in emotionally constrictive, if not emotionally abusive, homes, says Dr. Harold Bloomfield.

"This doesn't blame parents, but a generation ago the model for child rearing was that children should be seen and not heard. Parents felt they should mold children in their image instead of discovering their children for who they are."

Psychoanalyst Alice Miller is a pioneer in tracing the origins and impact of emotionally—and spiritually—constrictive parenting. In her book *For Your Own Good,* she describes "poisonous pedagogy," the process of breaking a child's spirit so the adult can have easy control—all supposedly done out of affection and concern for the child's welfare. Children raised in this fashion are trained to believe from early on that adults are godlike masters who determine what is right or wrong. Any life-affirming feelings pose a threat to the autocratic parent.

If you were parented in this fashion, Miller found, you may have consciously or subconsciously absorbed the damaging impression that you were undeserving of respect and tenderness. You were conditioned to believe that responding to your needs wasn't important and that a high degree of self-esteem and strong feelings are harmful. You probably learned to believe that the way you behave is more important than the way you really are. You may have been trained to view your body as something dirty and disgusting, Miller says.

It's not hard to see that any variation of this poisonous childhood predisposes you to depression. But even if your childhood was, on balance, loving and nurturing, if your passions were downplayed or ignored, you, again, are more vulnerable to depression. Let's say your childhood dream was to become an artist, but for years your parents exerted their will until you went into advertising. That stifled, invalidated passion can certainly lead to depression as an adult, says Dr. Bloomfield.

But many researchers, including Dr. Mona Lisa Schultz, who is also a medical intuitive, believe we often

need to go even farther back than childhood in un-
earthing the cause of some depressions. The connection
between mother and child begins in utero, reasons Dr.
Schultz. So what happens if that bond is never established, if a mother does not want or anticipate ever loving
that unborn child? What happens when the child is born
and neither parent bonds with or abandons the child?

"If you were predisposed to a distant relationship with
a caregiver, prematurely weaned, or initial contact wasn't
made with your mother, the biological modifiers innate
in that connection are not present. You will have a lifelong predisposition to depression and possibly cancer because our mothers help entrain our cortisol levels, heart
rate, blood pressure, eating, and sleeping."

If a child is weaned too early or never bonds with his
or her mother, the biological regulations of these factors
is always somewhat vulnerable through life, Dr. Schultz
says. "So later on in life, if we lose something important
to us, we have a predisposition to being weak in that
area, we again have the symptoms of first being weaned
from our mother, which are the symptoms of depression,
decreased activity, changes in our body temperature and
eating patterns, and other symptoms."

Scientists have theorized that isolation and not belonging to a family are stored in a person's early childhood
memory and predispose him or her to feelings of isolation, a lack of meaningful relationships, "which give rise
to a sense of hopelessness, helplessness and despair,"
says Dr. Schultz in her book *Awakening Intuition*.

This sense of vulnerability carries over into our adult
lives, making us vulnerable to depression and anxiety,
says Dr. Schultz.

Finally, in our culture, we don't have a healthy, accepting attitude toward the natural state of grieving. After

a major loss, we still expect people to buck up and get on with it. What's the matter? You took a couple days off of work—why don't you feel better now?

Many medical practitioners featured in this book said they saw patient after patient experiencing full-blown depression because they never fully grieved losses that happened years, even decades ago. As we will explore later in the book, prematurely halted, the grieving process only goes underground to fester and later manifest as serious depression.

After reading this chapter, you may conclude, "My God, no wonder we're all so depressed." But that recognition is an awakening; illumination opens up hope. Recognizing that we as a culture are far too depressed allows us to begin to finally take powerful steps toward our individual and shared healing.

We can't help ourselves until we fully see, without downplaying or shrinking from, the reality we have created. Until we fully understand and address depression for what it truly is—a warning sign that our beings are out of balance—can we make lasting change and find vibrant, long-term health.

With this level of awareness about depression, you can then begin to take concrete, active steps toward bringing yourself back into greater physical, spiritual, and emotional balance. A big part of the distress that accompanies depression is the lack of control and the confusion about where to turn or what to do next. Knowing you have viable choices to relieve your suffering is empowering and comforting.

Hopefully, you will find great comfort in this book. May you find some practical answers, some peace of mind, some healing strategies that help you reach a place of greater wholeness.

Main Messages

- Depression is on the rise. At least one in five will be depressed at some point in his or her lifetime.
- Our excessive reliance on accumulating stuff has not made us happy. It's diverted us from true, inner joy.
- Our outer-directed, success-oriented culture breeds depression by promoting unrealistic, and often unfulfilling, goals.
- Isolation from meaningful relationships fuels depression.
- The stress of non-stop motion and trying to cram too much into one day can lead to depression.
- To avoid depression, we must live out our life's passion and purpose.
- Women are more prone to depression because they rely on relationships more than men for their sense of well-being.
- The patriarchal culture has left many women feeling powerless, which is fertile ground for depression.
- Deep grief over the destruction of the earth is universally shared in our world.
- An addiction to perfectionism of any kind breeds depression.
- Weak early bonds with our parents or emotionally abusive childhood environments lead to adult depression.
- We are uncomfortable with grief in our culture. Unexpressed grief goes underground into depression.

SIX

Expressing the Full Range of Emotions

This particular vignette from Allison's life was all too depressingly familiar, all too humiliating. As she waited for her husband to come home, she suspected he was otherwise occupied with another woman. For months they'd been arguing about the colleague from his office he admitted he'd become involved with.

Even though he vowed the relationship would end, his absence night after night belied his promise. Around midnight Allison forced herself to try to sleep. Instead, she lay seething. "What does that bastard think he's doing? Doesn't he realize what this does to me?" she screamed inwardly.

Long after midnight, her husband came into their darkened bedroom. Putrid waves of smoke, alcohol, and perfume came to bed with him. But not wanting to rock the boat or go to bed mad—all the things she'd been conditioned never to do—Allison didn't confront her husband. She didn't say a word. Instead, she feigned sleep.

The pattern continued the next morning as they both got ready for work. Not wishing to provoke an argument, Allison was sullen but mute. "Why are you so quiet? Is something wrong?" her husband asked. "It's nothing, really. I'm fine." Allison shrugged, forcing her lips to form in a tight, artificial smile, even as her stomach roiled with anger and sorrow.

Emotions Can't Be Buried

How many times have you said the equivalent of those words? Maybe your version is: "Don't worry about me. I'll be OK," or "It's just a little something. I'm sure it will go away."

But nothing could be further from the truth—and our psyches know it. Our emotions, especially strong emotions, don't just go away. Unexpressed, they escalate, build, and lay embedded in our psyches and bodies, like a talisman of our unspoken experiences.

Our feelings aren't "nothing." We won't be fine if we deny, stuff, ignore them, and wish them away.

Anger, sadness, fear, grief, disgust—all the emotions Allison is likely experiencing—can't be just banished from our minds, says Dr. Alice Domar, author of *Healing Mind/ Healthy Woman*. Left unexpressed, they can fester, burrow deeper into our consciousness, make us vulnerable to depression and other illnesses, she says.

"When we try to wish away primary emotions such as sadness, fear, and anger, they don't disappear; they go underground where they cause chronic states of unhappiness that drag us down."

Researcher Candace Pert, author of *Molecules of Emotion: Why You Feel the Way You Feel*, has studied how buried feelings left to ferment can run amok in the body. "If the outward response to an emotion does not match the chemical changes going on inside of you—for example, if you feel angry but put on a smiling face . . . then you're setting up conflict in your body. And that drains energy away from your vital organs."

And if, like Allison, you fail to grieve the loss of a loving relationship or other disappointments in life, you set yourself up for a visit from Saturn, from the messenger of depression. In fact, depression may actually be the body's normal response to unhealed grief and emotional loss, says Dr. Andrew Weil. Depression may look like illness but actually be a progressive stage of the grieving process, he feels.

Expression Blocks Depression

Expressing our emotions, releasing suppressed feelings and grief, can be a powerful boost to our health. But how do we do so if many of our authentic feelings have been so ignored they barely swim below the surface of our consciousness? Do you relate to author Melody Beattie's observation years ago when she wrote: "I have stuffed my emotions so long, they have freezer burn"?

The first step in unfreezing—and releasing—our emotions is to honor them. Realize you have a right to feel and fully express your own emotions. A radical thought for many women, especially those of us over 40 who have often been conditioned like Allison to avoid "rocking the boat." To suppress or deny our emotions so they don't upset others. Far better to slam a door, scrub an already clean floor, or scream and rage inwardly than assertively and naturally expressing the full range of our emotions—with our voices.

Maybe as a little girl, you weren't allowed to fully feel and express your emotions. Were you expected, trained even, to "make nice" and "be sweet" or "act like a good girl." "Good girls don't get angry" was the hidden message.

In your family, it may not have been safe to show anger, disgust, frustration, or sadness. But keep remembering: Suppressing our emotions and keeping silent will not make us whole. It will only weaken and diminish us. "Keeping silent doesn't make us feel more safe. . . . It makes us feel more vulnerable. It gives the pain and problems and fears more power," says *Essence* magazine publisher Susan Taylor.

Many body/mind/spirit teachers also point out that if we have an emotional block in expressing our feelings, we invariably draw to ourselves the very situations that help us to learn how to express our pent-up feelings. For instance, if you had a hard time expressing your feelings of anger with your parents, as an adult, you may find, lo and behold, that your relationships with your spouse, boss, coworkers, or children constantly force you to process and express your unresolved anger.

"We are unconsciously drawn to situations that repeat the pain we haven't healed. As long as you have unresolved pain from your past, the future will repeat the past. Your soul needs to heal," says author John Grey.

Once we express our feelings, it's amazing how they can be released. They no longer have any power over us. It is like opening up the steam valve; the interior pressure dissipates.

As you do so, know this: Expressing your so-called negative emotions is not bad. "The only bad emotion is a stuck emotion," Dr. Rachel Naomi Remen reminds us.

Done constructively, expressing our anger, rage, and frustrations is natural and healing. It is not only OK to express the full range of emotions—it is a way to feel fully alive. It is a way to be fully human, a way to claim our true power in the world as we are intended to do.

Know that this feeling process may take a long time. It might hurt so much you'll just want to numb your feelings with drugs, alcohol, social whirls, or other distractions. But try to stay with the process. It may take lots of practice, like learning any new skill.

Becoming Intimate with the Full Range of Feelings

"There is no quick fix for emotional turmoil," writes Judith Sachs in *Nature's Prozac.* "Sometimes it's a stage you have to go through, sometimes it's simply your darker side coming up to the light that begs to be acknowledged. You can do so much more for yourself than mindlessly taking a pill to cheer up. If you rely on a 'magic bullet,' you will be shortchanging yourself from learning how to take charge of your feelings and just, well . . . feel them."

The alternative to feeling? Compromising your life and health. Not fully acknowledging how upset you are over your husband's abuse, your unsatisfying job, your stress, the state of our country, or whatever bothers you will take its toll on your emotional, spiritual, and physical health. You just needlessly prolong your internal agony. "If you don't heal the wounds of the past, you just bleed into the future," says Oprah Winfrey.

The key is to name, validate, and release our emotions, says Dr. Mona Lisa Schultz. "Instead, if we say, 'Nothing is wrong,' or 'I'm not upset. I'm just tired,' this denial held over time about anything, whether you don't like your boss, you career isn't shaping up, you don't like the way you look, anything held over time and not expressed fully, expressed vaguely, will lead to depression."

Dr. Schultz says we need to be able to say, "What you did makes me angry." We need to honor our feelings as worthy of recognition and expression. We need to stop censoring ourselves.

"If I were to extinguish any words from a woman's vocabulary, they would be 'Oh, I was just upset. Never mind.' Your vagueness equals lack of emotional expression equals lack of emotional resolution equals depression."

So how do we more fully name our fears, pain, and hopes? How do we better express the full range of emotions, from fierceness and anger to tenderness and gratitude? How do we reclaim our inner voices in ways that not only nurture our own health, but allow us to go outward in the world, voicing our frustrations and needs, expressing our pain and joy, or speaking out against injustice, lack of compassion, or cruelty?

Finding Your True Voice

If speaking your truth is so uncomfortable you habitually cringe away from doing it, explore your discomfort with a therapist. (How to find the right therapist for you is explored in Chapter 8.) Seek assertiveness training to strengthen your confidence in expressing yourself so it begins to feel natural and instinctive, as it should. Visualize yourself, over and over, saying the things you really want to say.

The more you practice expressing yourself, the more confidence you will build to go outward and relate to people with greater assertiveness and honesty. The easier it will be to speak your truth without worrying about the consequences. After all, if someone disagrees with your opinions, it's only their opinion.

After decades of being silent on many levels, women, especially, are being called to develop their voice. To speak out when something needs to be said. To develop endurance and stamina in speaking forcefully and truthfully when something is wrong in their lives and amiss in the culture. To gloriously bring forth what has been buried within.

But, admittedly, this can be daunting. Expressing anger can trip many of us up. If you find it difficult to express anger, psychologist Ellen McGrath recommends you create a space in your home where you give yourself permission to get angry. "This is the nineties' version of *A Room of One's Own,* which Virginia Woolf described as essential to a woman's mental health. . . . Not only do we need our own physical space, we also need a private emotional space to express and understand intense negative feelings," says McGrath, author of *When Feeling Bad Is Good.*

Your Anger Space should not be in your house, if possible, she advises. Maybe it can be in your car where you go for a drive and scream your anger. It might be a corner of your garage where you punch a punching bag. Pillow, darts and dart board, angry red pens, might be supplies to store in your Anger Space, McGrath says.

Another McGrath anger-busting strategy that I find particularly endearing and effective: Thaw your rage by taking a bag of ice cubes and smashing the ice against the wall of your house or a nearby sidewalk. (It's probably most prudent that these be your own buildings!)

Again, the idea is to feel and then release your anger to reach a higher state of calm.

"If you give yourself the time necessary to express your anger fully, you won't need an Anger Space for long. But we all need a temporary sanctuary for a while in order to rid ourselves completely of the anger that so easily converts into depression."

But McGrath includes a note of warning: As you release this anger, especially if it's been repressed for years, be prepared that your "negative Traditional Core" may send suppressing messages like: "Just shut up, will you?" or "It's not ladylike to be so angry," and, "You have it so good—why are you complaining?"

But keep remembering that expression, not suppression, is the name of the anti-depression game. The next chapter explores some more anti-depression strategies for emotional expression, namely journaling and art therapy. Both are extremely effective at unleashing pent-up feelings and accelerating emotional healing.

Main Messages

- You can't get rid of your emotions by ignoring or denying them. Unexpressed emotions can become full-blown depression.
- If you bury your feelings, they set up conflict in your physical body and drain energy from your organs. You put your health at risk.
- The first step to releasing emotions is to honor them, including your anger.

- Once we release our emotions, they no longer have any power over us.
- Work with a therapist, get assertiveness training, practice expressing your feelings and using your true inner voice.
- If necessary, create a physical space in your home where you can express your feelings. An Anger Space can be a place where you are safe and free to scream out your anger and pain.
- Expression, not suppression, is the name of the anti-depression game.

SEVEN

Releasing Emotions Through Pen and Paint

When Dana Judy became depressed during college, she did what came naturally to her. Since nature had always been a source of solace to her, Dana went deep into the grasslands and plains of Colorado to "be alone with the wind and the sky and expose myself as a person."

And words started pouring out of her. She filled pages with poems and images that had been buried deep in her core. Writing about her depression, Dana found, was a way to describe her feelings, so she could work with and process them. The language and emotional power of poetry became a channel through which Dana could trace the root of her anger, grief, and depression.

"That's the power of language. It's a way of connecting with what's happening inside. It's also a way to access our inner power. I used to internalize my anger and feelings. That's what a lot of my depression was about.

"I used to let my feelings drag and pull me down and

cover me like a wet blanket. Expressing myself became a way for me to take that energy and turn it around and use it in a positive way."

Writing Unlocks Floodgates

Dr. Alice Domar has seen the power of journaling and writing countless times in her patients. She says one of the most powerful mind-body approaches to fully accessing emotions is deceptively simple. In her groups, she hands participants a blank piece of paper and asks them to sit quietly and write about the most traumatic event associated with their health.

"Write about your deepest thoughts and feelings about that event. Write nonstop for twenty minutes, keep your pen moving on the paper, and don't worry about grammar or spelling."

Over and over, participants report they release grief, fear, or anger that had long been locked in their mind and body, Dr. Domar says. Floodgates opened to emotions and conflicts they didn't even realize they'd harbored.

The powerful healing effect of writings about fears, traumas, and hopes has been extensively documented by Dr. James Pennebaker, a professor in the psychology department at Southern Methodist University. He asks people to write about their deepest thoughts and feelings—and often brings them back four days in a row to repeat the procedure.

A Boost to the Immune System

Pennebaker finds that writing about traumatic events not only boosts our moods, it improves our physical health. He and his colleagues find that our T-cells—immune system cells that help us fight off disease—are still higher six weeks after we fully write about and release our emotions. Pennebaker said four other studies also found similar immune system boosts in subjects who underwent writing therapy.

Pennebaker, author of *Opening Up: The Healing Power of Expressing Emotions,* has found the same outcome with a wide range of people, from university students to Holocaust survivors. "Just putting upsetting experiences into words has profound psychological and physical benefits for our participants," he says.

Recently, Pennebaker worked with a woman who saw her husband die in a freak accident. She was just a few feet away when it happened. "Most people who knew her thought she was coping well. She went back to school, she was very upbeat and positive. Her friends were able to talk with her.

"But when she went on a vacation alone, she became extremely depressed. She had never talked about her loss with anyone."

Pennebaker recommended the woman write twice a day for five consecutive days. Through her writing, she saw the profound loss she'd experienced. "She hadn't realized the impact this had on her entire world."

Through writing therapy, Pennebaker's client experienced "profound" improvements in her outlook and physical health.

Only Twenty Minutes a Day

If you are truly motivated to explore your deepest feelings in writing therapy, Pennebaker recommends, at a minimum, you write for twenty minutes each day, four days in a row. "This can make a huge difference in some people's lives."

Dr. Domar has found that to be true. Journaling not only helps ease depression but it effectively wards it off, she says. One striking example of this was one of her patients, Brenda, an office manager. Brenda found it difficult to handle conflicts in her marriage and in her job. As her stress levels mounted, she also began to suffer from headaches and severe menstrual cramps. After only a few writing sessions in which she described how she felt about her problems, she got substantial relief from her stress and physical symptoms.

Writing is an alchemy for the self, *Chicago Sun-Times* writer Hank De Zutter wrote. "Writing can slow us down, forcing us to examine the events of our lives so that even bad or boring days can be transcended and transformed into something unique."

If you write only a little each day, you will find it indeed allows you to transcend your problems. It's almost as if once they are placed on the page, their power over you is diluted.

Natalie Goldberg, author of *Writing Down the Bones,* honors writing's ability to "explore the rugged edge of thought," to plumb the depths of the soul. Come to your writing, she advises, "not with your mind and ideas, but with your whole body—your heart and gut and arms. Begin to write in the dumb awkward way an animal cries out in pain, and there you will find your intelligence, your words, your voice."

Write, Goldberg advises, without worrying about spelling, punctuation, logic, grammar, or social politeness. "Go for the jugular. If something comes up in your writing that is scary or naked, dive right into it. It probably has lots of energy."

If you find it difficult to express your emotions, try this journaling technique. Spend twenty minutes for at least four days in a row, writing about the most stressful events in your life today—or the most traumatic circumstances in your past.

Write poetry, a journal, or whatever becomes your own private way to feel free and safe to illuminate whatever is inside, says Dana Judy, who now plans to publish a collection of her poetry. "Your writing can become a powerful discovery process. The heart of your poems will take you to the heart of yourself. I would write and say, 'Oh My God,' as these nuggets of truth and revelation would blow me open into a whole new level of understanding, a whole new place."

The following is a poem Dana wrote to express her feelings and heal her depression. Read it out loud and discover its power to stir something deep within you.

If I Look Now
  desertedness lies not upon my soul
  and coming down from the mountains
  I am curling across the plain.
  There is a rise and turn within me
  that I seldom hear mentioned in words before.
  It is a knowingness, a richness, a ripeness.
  It carries me without question.
  though that is what brought me to it—
  Here upon the brow of my hill
  to spread my arms and be carried by wind.

It is my choice to fly
though I know not where I go till I arrive.
And even then I don't stay long.
It is my choice to sing
though I know not the song
til the melody rises out of me.
If I look now
be it genesii.

Expressing Feelings Through Art

Art therapy is another proven way that deep feelings can finally be accessed, honored, and released. Art therapy pioneer Lucia Capacchione first discovered the power of art to "make sense out of mystery and chaos" in the 1960s. In the wake of President Kennedy's assassination, she countered the violence she felt in the culture by creating hope-filled, loving images of flowers, meadows, mountains, and butterflies. This natural ability to channel her psyche's longings for harmony through art proved to be life-saving when years later a full-blown depression rocked Lucia's life.

As a young mother in the 1960s, Lucia was trained in the Montessori education method. She was a successful child-development supervisor, and later a toy designer. "As a wife, mother, and busy professional woman, I led an extremely active life. But there was no time for the inner life, for introspection, or for listening to my deeper thoughts and feelings."

Then one day, Lucia's life collapsed around her. Her marriage and business partnership ended, just as her parents' marriage began to crack open, largely due to her father's manic depression. She and her children moved, and she developed mononucleosis.

"I had no idea what hit me. It was worse than any earthquake I had ever known while growing up in Los Angeles, and it shook me to my foundations."

She developed a debilitating condition that would years later be diagnosed as a disease of her collagen, the connective tissue in the body. It was as if she had become unglued, she wrote in her book *The Picture of Health: Healing Your Life with Art.*

"I experienced a tremendous lowering of self-esteem. Here I had been an extremely energetic, productive person and all of a sudden I was staring into space. I would sit at my desk for hours and not know what I had done. I had anxiety attacks, a couple of car accidents. I wasn't in my body."

Art and journaling became an immediate, powerfully soothing way for Lucia to begin her journey into healing. She began to unearth fear, anger, and grief that had been buried for years. Her body began to speak to her through her art. Often drawing or writing with her nondominant hand began to bring up messages from her inner world. It began to yield guidance to what she needed to get well.

"The great thing about art therapy is it really reaches to the deepest level of the unconscious the same way dreams do. Our images come from the deepest level of the unconscious. That is where our real wisdom lies."

Tapping the Physician Within

Now one of the foremost authors and lecturers in art therapy, Lucia has helped hundreds of people tap their own inner messages and heal from within using imagery.

One client, Jason, was a workaholic who suffered from chronic low-back pain. He believed he had to do everything himself, so was in the habit of carrying "back-breaking responsibilities."

It was only when Jason drew pictures of his back pain that he got the message. The picture included captions that said, "Help! I need rest." Jason heeded his body's signals and started delegating some work to others. He went away to a spa in the desert and finally learned how to relax.

Jason made the valuable discovery that each of us has an inner artist and an inner healer deep within us. That is the message of Dr. Michael Samuels and Mary Rockwood Lane in their book *Creative Healing: How to Heal Yourself by Tapping Your Hidden Creativity*.

"The inner healer is the part of you that balances your body perfectly and sets your blood flow, your immune system, and your killer T cells to be in harmony. Art frees the healer within so you can heal yourself of an illness. . . . Art helps you conquer disease by freeing your inner healer to work at its optimum."

Dr. Samuels has used art and guided imagery with cancer patients for more than twenty-five years and is the founder and director of the Art as a Healing Force project. Mary Rockwood Lane is an R.N. and cofounder and codirector of the Arts in Medicine program at the University of Florida.

Mary became a healing artist after she became extremely ill and depressed. She was going through a difficult divorce and felt as if "all the resources in my life had collapsed and I was drowning."

In therapy, she was told that she must do something different with her rage and grief. At that moment, Mary decided to abandon her fears of being a painter. She had always dreamed of being one but had never given herself permission to do so because she never felt good enough.

Mary began to paint feverishly, producing a series of self-portraits that helped her experience her pain—and finally let it go. When outwardly expressing her feelings in an image, she released herself from the cage of despair. "The first painting I called 'Cut Out My Heart.' It was my pain, a deeply intense and dying pain. The figure was broken, distorted, diffuse, cramped, and bleeding. I painted 'her.' And in the moment I released this image."

Any creative form of expression, from cooking to making pottery, helps you put your life into perspective. As you stir a pot or work with clay, you create a space in yourself for the promptings of the soul to be heard. You can finally be sensitive to what feelings are waiting to come to the surface.

I know a woman who makes beaded necklaces as a form of meditation and quiet contemplation. Sometimes, each bead represents a challenge she has met and triumphed over. Even coloring in a coloring book, tending to a collection of orchids, or weeding in your garden, are ways to silence the outer distractions and tune into what wants to be discovered within.

Know that there is no right or perfect way to express yourself. That is the beauty and magic of it. What works for you, may not work for someone else. Play with your artistic side and intuitively see how it feels. You will find a freedom you've been longing for. And your Inner Artist—and highest self—is sure to emerge, says Lucia Capacchione in *The Picture of Health.*

"As you transform the raw materials of life's experiences into precious gems of insight and wisdom, your Inner Artist will emerge. And it is through embracing this Inner Artist that the secrets of healing will be revealed to you. Love, the divine power that can heal your life, resides in your very own heart. It has always been there, waiting only to be liberated."

Main Messages

- Writing releases unexpressed feelings and emotions.
- Writing helps us process and release the impact of traumatic events.
- Writing therapy can boost your immune system.
- To transcend and release your problems, spend twenty minutes a day for four consecutive days writing about the most stressful events in your life or a traumatic circumstance from your past.
- Art therapy also accesses and releases pent-up emotions. It helps you tape your inner healer to strengthen body, mind, and spirit.
- Cooking, gardening, pottery, and other creative forms of expression also help balance the psyche.
- There is no right or appropriate way to express yourself. That is the beauty of it.

EIGHT

Unearthing Buried Trauma and Crisis

A hip, fun art teacher, Lisa joined a therapy group to resolve issues she previously medicated with drugs and alcohol. But whenever other group members touched upon their feelings of loss, Lisa always jumped up and got a drink of water or visited the ladies' room.

In individual therapy, Lisa was sometimes so overcome with such intense emotions, she was unable to talk. She cried often but seldom understood why. What her psychologist Tian Dayton slowly uncovered is that when she was a child, it was never safe for Lisa to fully express her powerful emotions. Plus, whenever tension or anxiety surfaced in her family, Lisa, who had a fabulous sense of humor, became the person who would relieve the tension with a joke. But this role backfired when it eventually made Lisa the family scapegoat, a problem child.

"In the confused emotional container of Lisa's family, where her role had been to act out everyone else's pain, she had little time to feel or understand her own," writes Dayton in her book *Heartwounds: The Impact of Unresolved Trauma and Grief on Relationships.*

Because of her painful childhood experience with intimacy, for the adult Lisa, emotional closeness always triggered anxiety. It always rekindled a fear of rejection and distance, so she would distance herself first, Dayton discovered.

"She had, in her repertoire, a thousand ways of distancing people. It was her childlike way of protecting herself. . . . Because Lisa had not had a parent who could tolerate her powerful feelings and needs, she was left yearning and searching for a feeling of closeness that, when she attained it, made her feel anxious and frightened."

Draining Inner Wounds

Dr. Dayton helped Lisa begin the hard work of building the inner self she had been denying. She guided her to "sit" with her raw feelings rather than venting them through outbursts of anger and blame, one of her many distancing strategies.

When Lisa learned to fully face some of the grief and shame from her family of origin, she became remarkably stronger. She ended an unhealthy relationship and later became engaged to a man with whom she built a stronger partnership. By experiencing her pent-up bitterness and hurt, Lisa removed blocks that had earlier prevented love from coming into her life, says Dr. Dayton.

"Until the pain was drained, each little hurt threw her back into her hidden past, which made the current daily problems feel huge and unsolvable."

Healing our deepest wounds, from the loss of a child to childhood incest, may require even more intense work than the emotional expression through journaling and art therapy we've just described. It may require "sitting in the wound," says Dayton, a trainer and practitioner of psychodrama and a faculty member at New York University.

"This can be scary because you may be afraid you will never get out of it. You are afraid the pain will over-whelm you. You have these voices in your head saying, 'Don't be a cry-baby. Don't feel sorry for yourself.' "

But we need to remember that cutting off our grief is like amputating part of the self, says Dayton. It also helps to fully understand that our humanity, our powerful inner self, doesn't spring full-grown. "Instead, it is earned through the contests and challenges of daily life, pounded and chiseled on the blacksmith's white-hot furnace. . . . Facing grief gives the self the freedom it needs to breathe, and that breath is necessary to sustain life."

Revisiting Trauma

For many people to "sit in the wound" means revisiting and fully looking at the pain inflicted by a specific trauma that occurred in their childhood or later in life. Many people can remember the exact hour their life was shat-tered and the once comforting fragments of their exis-tence flew around them in chaotic shards, like emotional shrapnel.

In healing those traumas, the path to cultivate is "somewhere between being a stoic, a non-feeler, unable to feel either deep pain or joy, and being a victim of the trauma," says Dayton. "The key is to learn how to be stoic enough to keep yourself in the game without falling apart, without flipping into a victim role where you perceive the world in a negative way and don't have the strength and optimism to move forward."

Finding the Right Therapist

If you are ready to do some of the deeper work with a therapist, finding one you can trust and feel safe with is critical. It's also important to find someone who is skilled at helping you examine and process your pain without being consumed by it, says Jessica Saperstone, a Fort Collins, Colorado, psychotherapist. "The therapist's job is not to keep clients from looking into the abyss, but to help create some bridges so they can cross it. From then on, they will be able to see but not fall into the abyss, whether it is low self-esteem, grief and loss, childhood abuse, spiritual emptiness or something else."

Find a therapist who is not afraid to go into your interior with you. Use your intuition as you interview prospective therapists, advises Saperstone. If you look at your life from a spiritual perspective, find someone who can honor that, she adds.

"The role of the therapist is to serve as the priest or priestess at the altar of the client's soul, extending your hand. Your job is to help gently unveil the soul of the client, providing safety and love."

You will share the most intimate, revealing aspects of yourself to your therapist, so make sure you feel valued and respected. Remember that you are in charge of your own well-being. Come empowered with criteria and questions and interview prospective therapists. Don't settle with the first person you talk with.

Check with trusted friends, family, and colleagues and find out who they see. Be up-front about your values and your beliefs.

Any therapist who comes off as dispassionate, cold, or arrogant is obviously not a therapist you want to share your life, pain, and dreams with. Also steer clear of anyone who tries to "diagnose" you on the first visit.

If you are more experiential in your self-growth, it also helps to find a therapist who is willing to use some affirming and imaginative exercises, dramatization, even rituals.

Saperstone created a new ritual that turned out to be very powerful when she was working with a client, Diana, who needed protection and inner strength during a combative domestic violence court battle.

"I wanted to help Diana call upon the support of those around her, gain a sense of her own inner strength, and build her energy as she went into her court sessions. I led a ritual in which her friends brought blessings and readings that showed their support and their recognition of her strength. As they went around the circle, each added a bead to a necklace with the intention of blessing Diana and sharing their strength and energy with her."

From then on, Diana wore her necklace in court and in other situations to remind her of her own inner strength and that of the women in her life.

Using exercises and rituals that go beyond traditional psychotherapy can be astonishingly powerful. In her book *Heartwounds,* Dayton offers wonderful exercises to heal your deepest wounds. For instance, she suggests creating a "Time Line" of the traumas and loss in your life since birth to help you to understand patterns of your loss or incomplete mourning. Creating a "Loss Chart" can help you understand how a present loss might be affected by or resonate with a past loss. You record a current loss and then you fill in any past life incidents or feelings that arise as you think about this loss.

You may find that the loss and depression you feel about your child going off to college may lead you to uncover and look at the feelings of loss you felt when your parents divorced, holidays changed, your home dynamics shifted, and you were, again, lonely.

When You Feel It, You Release It

Even when this process yields raw, painful feelings, keep remembering. Healing can only occur when we allow ourselves to release these long-suppressed emotions. Dr. Christiane Northrup likens this process to the treatment of an abscess. She calls it emotional incision and drainage.

"Any surgeon knows that the treatment for an abscess is to cut it open, allowing the pus to drain. When this is done, the pain goes away almost immediately, and new healthy tissue can re-form where the abscess once was. It is the same with emotions. They too become walled off, causing pain and absorbing energy, if we do not experience and release them."

As you begin to release more and more of the pain you may have walled off, you may literally feel the need to release that pain further in your voice, in your body. Work with therapists, go to support groups, play music to elicit feelings that want to be expressed. And as indigenous peoples have shown us for ages, wailing and crying and physically expressing your grief is a powerful release. So are drumming and dancing, channeling your grief in your voice as you do so.

"When you feel something, you release it from your

body," says scientist Candace Pert, who has pioneered work on how cellular memories and feelings are stored throughout our body.

That was certainly the case for Elizabeth, who struggled with infertility for years. Month after month, she had painful and invasive tests, procedures, and surgeries. And month after month, her period came predictably like an emotional blow to her psyche.

Often it would begin when she was at work, in the middle of a crowded meeting with her colleagues. As she sat there and tried to appear focused and calm, she would instead feel the grief pool up in her body like waves of trapped water. Her body felt sad and defeated by her inability to conceive.

Sometimes the tears would begin before she even left her office parking lot. When she got home she would go straight to her bedroom, wail and cry, pound her pillow, and kick the bed as hard as she could. She screamed about the unfairness of it all, and cried out her anger at a universe that wouldn't grant her a child.

By expressing her grief in this manner, Elizabeth still felt sad and melancholy many months, but she was able to avoid a full-blown depression.

If we are encouraged to honor our feelings, go into our pain, make the sounds we need to make, and to cry or yell as long as we need, we often discover that our bodies have the innate ability to heal the most painful events, says Dr. Northrup. "When we have allowed ourselves a full emotional release, the body, mind, and spirit feel cleansed and free."

EMDR/Thought Field Therapy

An amazing technique for processing trauma that is rapidly attracting professional respect and success stories is EMDR, or eye movement desensitization reprocessing. Developed by Francine Shapiro, a California psychologist, EMDR has been used with victims of the Oklahoma City bombing and war-torn Bosnia, Vietnam War veterans, plane crash survivors, and thousands of others suffering from post-traumatic stress disorder, anxiety, and depression.

Usually when we experience something traumatic, or merely unpleasant, we use our internal information-processing system to process the upsetting events so we can stay balanced, says Shapiro. We talk and think about the event, even dream about it. We learn from the experience and store in it our brain with the appropriate emotion so it can guide us in the future.

But sometimes this internal processing goes amok. "Our perceptions of the terrible event (what we saw, heard, felt, and so on) may be stuck in our nervous system in the same form as when we experienced them. These unprocessed perceptions can be expressed as the nightmares, flashbacks, and intrusive thoughts of PTSD (post-traumatic stress disorder)," Shapiro writes in *EMDR: The Breakthrough "Eye Movement" Therapy for Overcoming Anxiety, Stress, and Trauma*, co-written with Margot Silk Forrest.

EMDR stimulates our information-processing system so traumatic experiences can be appropriately processed, or digested, says Shapiro. EMDR works like this: Your therapist identifies a traumatic event or moment that disturbs you. As you concentrate on that trauma, he will start leading your eye movements. He will hold his fingers about twelve inches from your face and move them rhythmically back and forth across your field of vision. Without moving your head, you will track this movement with your eyes.

When Shapiro does EMDR therapy, she continues with this movement for about a minute or so, for what she calls a "set," and then stops and talks with her patient. If the anxiety hasn't changed much, she asks the person to concentrate on a different aspect of the unsettling event, and then they do another set.

"With gratifying regularity, people reported that their thoughts had changed for the better or their disturbing mental images had disappeared completely, along with the anxiety that had accompanied them. . . . Unexpected memories frequently came up as the procedure quickly got people to look at the root of the problem, not just its leaves and branches."

In Colorado, Jessica Saperstone has marveled at EMDR's ability to help many clients ease their depression and find new joy. One such man was Benjamin, who not only had a history of serious depression but who was diagnosed in his late 50s with a form of leukemia. Benjamin said when he was on antidepressants, he had never felt better than just "OK." He felt no joy in his life. Anticipating future health complications, Benjamin had retired from his job.

After about five sessions of EMDR in which Saperstone had Benjamin focus on some childhood issues, he remarked, "I can honestly say I am not only not depressed, but I am experiencing what I think is joy."

Interestingly, Benjamin also reported a tingling sensation all over, almost as if joy was once again circulating throughout his entire being.

More than 23,000 therapists from fifty-three countries

are now trained in EMDR, says Shapiro, of the Mental Research Institute in Palo Alto. She has been publishing her EMDR research since 1989, and now many colleagues are reporting similar success.

In the 1997 issue of the *Journal of Psychotherapy,* clinicians from Kaiser Permanente, the largest HMO in California, compared EMDR to the standard care that trauma victims receive at their centers. The patients were traumatized by assault, sexual abuse, rape, traffic accidents, earthquakes, and other events.

Steven Marcus and his colleagues reported that virtually all patients who suffered from a single trauma got better after six fifty-minute EMDR sessions compared with only half of those in regular psychotherapy treatment.

Sadness Is a Normal Side of Life

Above all, in any form of grief and trauma processing, whether talk therapy or EMDR, gently remind yourself that it is extremely cathartic to occasionally visit the Land of Tears, says author Susan Jeffers. "Much of our depression is when we don't allow our tears to come out. We allow our pain to weigh us down. Sometimes we need to do what our mothers and grandmothers talked about, have a good healthy cry."

For years, she tried to avoid going into the Land of Tears, believing that life should always be happy. "I became such a pseudopositive thinker that I became detached, disconnected from my own pain and disconnected from other people's pain as well."

Entering the Land of Tears helps us ease our own pain and reconnect with all that is beautiful in the world, she says in *End the Struggle and Dance with Life.* "Having made the Land of Tears an integral part of my life so many years ago has had enormous benefits. In the first place, I've joined the human race. When I watch the struggle of others, I can now connect with my own struggle, and we are no longer strangers.

"Now when the deep sadness comes over me, I can let it be there like a warm blanket. I don't have to push it away. It feels so good to just let the tears flow freely. When I let the tears wash over me, I feel cleansed and healed. And when the river of tears is empty, I am freer to enjoy the delights the world has to offer, without a layer of sadness dampening my joy."

Once we process and learn to cope with, not suppress, our pain, we build inner strength, says Tian Dayton (see page 68). Then the next time a difficult challenge arises, we are better able to cope because we know we have greater resilience. When you process your past pain, you have greater optimism that you will be able to deal with whatever comes your way in the future. "It's the equivalent of lifting more weights. As you build more emotional muscle, you can handle more complex circumstances and not feel them as deeply because you have more emotional strength. You are emotionally toned, like you are physically toned."

The more emotionally toned you are, the better able you are to cope the next time a traumatic event happens. You can be more able to say, "No matter what life decides to hand me, I'll handle it," writes Jeffers.

Being able to say those words is key to your emotional freedom, she insists. "Do you see the peace this assurance of our inner power brings us? . . . We can never control life in any other way. Yes, life is filled with surprises. But with the inner knowing that we can handle anything life hands us, we don't have to worry about the future any longer. We can get on with our life with a feeling of freedom and adventure. . . . Wherever life takes us, we'll be okay!"

Forgiveness Heals

Finally, explore the power of forgiveness as you heal. Learning to forgive those who traumatized you may be one of the final blocks to lifting your depression. For instance, when children who have been neglected or sexually abused are able to forgive their parents, they have decreased depression and anxiety and a better outlook on their future, shows research by educational psychologist Robert Enright of the University of Wisconsin at Madison.

Forgiveness doesn't condone the bad behavior, the mistreatment. It doesn't mean you want to invite someone who abused you back into your life. It means you halt the dangerous, depressing flow of negative chemicals churning through your body, which you previously used to maintain your anger, grief, or hostility. It means you restore your sanity.

All the things we've talked about so far, from journaling to therapy to art therapy, can help you learn to forgive. Start in small steps, try to forgive the person who has hurt you today for one minute. Tomorrow for two minutes. Be patient with yourself. It takes as long as it takes.

Service is what helped Richard heal and forgive the man who raped and killed his daughter years ago. Over the years, his anger faded, but he still felt "a hole in my soul."

Richard became a volunteer at the Alternative to Violence Project in New England, which helps rehabilitate prisoners and their family members. Though he acknowledges that his healing took a long time, service helped hasten the forgiveness process, he says.

"With the help of these programs and groups, I have come to forgive the man who was convicted of killing my daughter. . . . I seek to honor and respect the memory of my daughter by doing positive things inside and outside of prison that may in some way lessen the incidence of violence and loss in people's lives."

Try to empathize with the pain and hurt that led someone to inflict pain on you. Visualize the person you are now, comforting the person you were when you experienced the trauma. Visualize yourself then turning and forgiving the person who traumatized you.

Again, forgive today for one minute. Tomorrow for two.

And if you've been weighted down by the pain you caused someone else, forgive yourself. Own your behavior, make no lies or excuses. Accept responsibility for what you did.

Only when we fully acknowledge what we have done, with no "but's" and other qualifiers, can we really begin to heal, says psychologist Marilyn Mason. "There's a mean, cruel part of each of us. It's our shadow self, and it's part of being human."

Life is too short and too precious to let lack of self-forgiveness make you sodden with bitterness and despair. Once you truly forgive yourself, it's almost like taking off a layer or unloading debris you've carried for too long.

Forgive yourself. Today for one minute. Tomorrow for two. Set yourself free. Forgiveness is truly one of the first steps on the path to liberation, says Stephen Levine. "Forgiveness allows us to let go of some of our grief—the curtains of resentment and the fear which filters all but the shallow and desperate in the mind. Forgiveness lessens clinging and allows the agitated mind to sink a bit more deeply into the healing heart."

If forgiving others or yourself is an issue in your life, Levine's meditations for forgiveness are brilliant. One is found in his book *Guided Meditations, Explorations, and Healings.* I will close with just a small part of this beautiful meditation, a reminder that we all should sit with from time to time: "See yourself as if you were your only child; let yourself be embraced by this mercy and kindness. Let yourself be loved. . . . How unkind we are to ourselves. How little mercy. Let it go. Allow you to embrace yourself with forgiveness. Let yourself be loved. Let yourself be love."

Main Messages

- If you've unresolved pain and trauma, you may need to "sit in the wound" or "look into the abyss" to finally process and heal your grief.
- Cutting off grief is like amputating a part of the self. Facing grief gives you the freedom to breathe and become stronger. It sustains your life.
- Create a Loss Chart of current and past losses. Write how you feel as you record your losses.
- When you feel something, you release it from your body. It is like literally draining an incision.
- Sadness is not to be avoided. It is a normal part of a full life.
- Processing and learning to cope with life's pain is a way of building emotional fitness. The next time something traumatic happens, you are more emotion-

ally toned. You are better able to deal with whatever life hands you.

- Forgive those in your life you need to. This is healing for body, mind, and spirit. It stops the flow of dangerous chemicals produced by hate and animosity.

- Forgive yourself. Take responsibility for what you did, but forgive yourself.

- Start small. Forgive today for one minute; tomorrow for two.

- Do a forgiveness meditation, such as found in Stephen Levine's book *Guided Meditations, Explorations, and Healings*.

NINE

Banishing the Inner Critic

In many ways Jennifer, a corporate CEO, was at the top of her career. But even though she loved her work and knew she should be content, something still gnawed at her confidence. No matter how much she accomplished outwardly, inwardly she couldn't stop hearing her father telling her, "You are just a girl. You will never amount to anything."

Like Jennifer, we all have negative tapes running repeatedly in our head. The average person, researchers say, has about ten thousand random thoughts each day. Three-quarters of these are anxious concerns about the future or regrets about the past.

Many of the negative messages we send ourselves are ones we received in childhood, buried in our consciousness, waiting to sabotage us as adults, says Dr. Alice Domar. "Half of our negative self-talk is made up of things from our childhood we don't even realize made such an impression."

Cognitive Therapy Stops Negative Tapes

Cognitive therapy is a powerful method of banishing the inner negative narration that drains our energy, even leading to depression. Largely pioneered by Dr. Aaron Beck and Dr. David Burns, cognitive therapy helps to identify negative self-talk and patterns, question their truth, and replace them with more realistic and nurturing thoughts.

Cognitive therapy eased Olivia's depression and helped her finally move forward with her life. Olivia was drained and dispirited from years of infertility treatments that still left her unable to conceive a child. If that wasn't stressful enough, a toxic internal message planted by her doctor kept circling through her mind. He once said, "There is no way you will ever get pregnant using your own eggs."

What a blow to her spirit. Olivia also sent herself the message that she would never be a mother unless she conceived a biological child.

So by the time Olivia came to see Dr. Alice Domar, she was dispirited and severely depressed. Dr. Domar directs the women's health programs at Harvard Medical School's Division of Behavioral Medicine. She is an assistant professor of medicine at Harvard and is a staff psychologist at the New England Deaconess Hospital.

Tuning in to Your True Desires

Domar introduced Olivia to a whole buffet of treatments—including cognitive therapy. She showed Olivia how she could stop her negative internal dialogues and get to the root of her real desires. "We focused on what it meant for her not to conceive a biological child. We talked a lot about what being a mother meant to her," says Domar, author with Henry Dreher of *Healing Mind/ Healthy Woman*.

"What were her fantasies about the kind of mother she would be? What did she like about her relationship with her own mother?"

Olivia's depression really started to lift when she realized her thoughts constantly centered on getting pregnant—just what a doctor told her she could never do—without asking why a pregnancy was so important to her. "She began to think about what it meant to mother versus what it meant to reproduce."

In cognitive therapy, Olivia realized that what she really wanted to do was to mother a child. She didn't care if the child looked like her or was her biological child. With her own child, she wanted to express the kind of unconditional love she had received from her mother.

Exercises and Actions

To search for what is really true, to silence the false negative tapes within, we can actively work to end our negative thought patterns. Dr. Domar asks her patients four questions:

- Does this thought contribute to my stress?
- Where did I learn this thought?
- Is this thought logical?
- Is this thought true?

"Before you can restructure an automatic negative thought, you must first honestly confront that thought, discover its origins and effects, and put it to the test of logic."

It also helps many patients to undergo some relaxation techniques prior to cognitive therapy because their thoughts are more logical when they are calmer, she advises. "Relaxation helps to clear the mind and body of excessive tensions that work against your effort to think and feel with clarity. Thus the relaxation response and cognitive restructuring can work together in a synergistic fashion."

Cognitive restructuring is what many experts refer to as "mental rewiring." It may also include rewiring, or removing your inaccurate and counterproductive beliefs about your depression and replacing them with more accurate, supportive ones. For instance, cognitive therapy can help you go from thinking: "I am always so depressed. I will never get well," to "There are steps I can take that will definitely improve my mood."

Many of us also harbor irrational, inaccurate fears about our health and hardiness. We fear that we may get cancer, have a heart attack, develop a debilitating disease. We fear that we may lose our relationships, job, or financial stability.

We worry that if all of the above happens, we would fall apart, not be able to cope. One innovative technique you can use to neutralize your negative thoughts and anxiety is a strategy called Freeze Frame, developed by Heart-Math Institute in California.

Freeze Frame works like this: When you feel stressed, step back from the moment. Shift your focus to the area around your heart and imagine that you are breathing through your heart. Hold your heart focus for at least ten seconds. Now, recall a positive experience or a happy time, like a wonderful holiday with friends or a relaxing walk along the beach. By calling forth feelings of love and appreciation when your worries are in overdrive, you can neutralize your inner conflict.

Cognitive therapy also brings our irrational fears to the surface so we can begin to confront and banish the inner saboteur.

Record Your False Thoughts

Often, as with processing any feeling, it helps to process and examine our distorted thoughts, often called cognitive distortions, by writing about them. Some of the most effective ways to process cognitive distortions come from Dr. David Burns, a pioneer in cognitive therapy and author of *Feeling Good: The New Mood Therapy*. Dr. Burns recommends keeping a daily "Mood Log."

In the log, you describe an upsetting event that happened to you or automatic negative thoughts you harbor. Then you examine these thoughts for their distortions. For instance, George, a mid-level manager at a telecommunications company might write in his Mood Log, "I know my boss will yell at me today. I just know he's planning to hold back my raise because he's not pleased with my work this month."

In his Mood Log, George can record his job-related fears and then examine the twisted, skewed reasoning behind his worries. George is tortured by a spectrum of cognitive distortions we all fall prey to, like "jumping to conclusions" or "mind reading," points out Dr. Burns.

"You assume that people are reacting negatively to you when there's no definitive evidence for this." Another common distortion is "fortune telling"—"you arbitrarily predict that things will turn out badly."

Still another distortion is "overgeneralization" when we "view a negative event as a never-ending pattern of defeat."

After you process how you have been lapsing into distorted thinking, use the Mood Log to record your rational response. Substitute more realistic thoughts and estimate your belief in each one.

Then, "after a few weeks' practice with the Mood Journal," a similar record-keeping technique advocated by Dr. Richard O'Connor in *Undoing Depression,* "you should begin to see the connections between your mood changes, external events, and internal processes. Once you can see that mood changes are caused by what's happening to you, you can stop pretending that they come 'out of the blue.' You'll also find that your moods are more closely connected to 'normal' feelings than you think they are. When we take the trouble to investigate, to get underneath our own defenses, we usually find that there are perfectly good reasons for feeling the way we do. Understanding that is the first step toward doing something about it."

In her book, *On the Edge of Darkness,* Kathy Cronkite wrote about her depression and that of other high-profile persons. She described how her negative thoughts swirled ominously around one another, like a spiraling funnel cloud. "I saw the world through dark-tinted glasses—my house was a wreck, my children monsters, my marriage in trouble, my body fat, my wardrobe ugly, my work without merit, and on and on."

Other effective tools for dissolving your counterproductive beliefs and connecting to more supportive, empowering thoughts are found in *The Depression Book: A Guide for Living with Depression and Manic Depression* by Mary Ellen Copeland. Like Dr. Burns, Copeland includes a step-by-step process for examining your negative self-talk, but guides you to write about your feelings and thoughts and alternatives to your distorted perceptions.

Recording your automatic thoughts may be the most powerful step you can take to curb and modify them, says Dr. Burns. "You will eventually discover that the thoughts that upset you are nearly always quite unrealistic, although they seem completely valid when they are running through your mind. Your Automatic Thoughts are deceptive.

"They create the illusion of truth, even when they're extremely illogical. When you write them down, it will be easier to put the lie to them. The moment you see how unrealistic and pessimistic they are, you will feel better."

Negative thoughts only drive you deeper into depression. Cognitive therapy can help you out of it. A National Institute of Mental Health study showed that after sixteen weeks of cognitive restructuring training, 51 percent of those with mild to moderate depression reported significant improvement.

You don't have to be trapped by your old beliefs about life. You can choose new ways of thinking. Replacing your rigid thought patterns and use of the words "never" or "always" with "sometimes" can be empowering and make life more livable. With your therapist, you can explore the difficulty and blocks to more positive thinking.

Someone who knows this intimately is Kay Redfield Jamison, who wrote movingly in her books about her struggle with manic depression. In *An Unquiet Mind,* she describes how psychotherapy helped banish her negative thoughts and put life in a more accurate, brighter perspective.

"Ineffably, psychotherapy heals. It makes some sense

of the confusion, reins in the terrifying thoughts and feelings, returns some control and hope and possibility of
learning from it all."

The Power of Humor

Beyond therapy, an extremely useful way to melt your
distorted thinking is through humor. Stepping back and
looking at the ludicrous catastrophic thinking we fall prey
to shifts our perspective just enough to lift our mood, at
least for a while.

Laughter and mirth have been hailed for their curative
powers since at least the time of the ancient Greeks. As
seventeenth-century physician Dr. Thomas Sydenham
said, "The arrival of a good clown exercises more beneficial influence upon the health of a town than that of
twenty asses laden with drugs."

But looking at life in a more humorous tint may take
some practice. We are not great humor masters in our
society. As author Matthew Fox says, "Our civilization
has not done very well with the energy called delight
and play."

Master humor teacher Loretta LaRoche describes humor's ability to dissolve toxic thoughts, or what she calls
"stinking thinking" in her book *Relax: You May Only Have
a Few Minutes Left*. Her stress-management specials have
aired on PBS.

When we start "awfulizing" it often helps to move
from common sense to nonsense, LaRoche has found.
"Our minds are so cluttered with things we have to do,
we don't witness our own comedy."

In her book, she relates how she used this strategy
when she was on a business trip and her flight was can-

celed. By the time they got a new flight, the passengers were complaining and moaning. "As I went down the aisle, I decided to liven things up. I said 'Hi, great to see you' to three men sitting in one row."

When she saw how tightly squeezed in the men were, she said, "Isn't this exciting, now you can bond!" They just stared at her and by the time LaRoche got to her seat she started singing, "If you're happy and you know it. . . ." Soon everyone on the plane joined in. "I lightened the load of a lot of people who'd have spent the whole time on the flight complaining, and all it took was a few silly comments and a little song."

Humor is now so recognized for its ability to dissolve stress and depression that it is the subject of burgeoning research. There is even an organization, the American Association for Therapeutic Humor, consisting of more than six hundred doctors and health-care professionals, that researchs the impact of humor on our bodies.

Two of the associations's researchers, Dr. Stanley Tan and Lee Berk of Loma Linda University School of Medicine in California, found that laughter lowers stress hormones in the body and boosts the immune system's natural killer cells.

"The biochemistry and the physiology in the body associated with laughter, lightness, and joy are precisely the chemical soup our bodies need to function optimally," points out Dr. Chris Northrup. She recommends making a list of all the things you find funny. Go on a humor search. Watch children, who laugh on average four hundred times a day. Listen to humorous tapes.

"You have to develop an attunement to the absurdity of life while simultaneously believing that your life and work do make an enormous difference," Dr. Northrup reveals.

Another way to substitute negative thinking with positive thinking is gratitude. When you feel a stinking thinking coming on, supplant it with a joyous one. From Loretta LaRoche to Susan Jeffers, many contributors to this book advocated keeping a gratitude journal.

Gratitude Transcends Problems

"Without gratitude, we shrink from life and live a diminished existence," insists Jean Houston. "I've always found in my life that being grateful and thankful are key to returning to what is really fundamental."

Begin each day by writing down ten things you are grateful for at day's end. Take gratitude breaks throughout the day to say thanks. The things you are grateful for may be as simple as feeling blessed that your car started, that the kids weren't sick, that the sun shone, that you had a productive day, and that a leftover pot of chili waited in the fridge at dusk.

Like many of the strategies in this book, the act of being grateful helps you transcend your problems. It inspires you to get in touch with your spirit and can immensely shift your thinking and become habit forming. It also shifts your energy from a lower state to a higher, more energetic one.

Sometimes, though, even therapy, gratitude, reframing, and humor aren't enough to purge our inner critic. For many of us, talking things out just doesn't go deep enough. "It's easy to get locked into 'thought addiction'— a kind of gerbil wheel in the brain that keeps us going around in circles," says Dr. Chris Northrup.

Sometimes we have to go deeper and literally help cleanse our bodies of stored negative energy from our toxic thoughts. As with unhealed grief, we store many of our chronically toxic messages in our muscles and other body parts, says Dr. Northrup. The many forms of bodywork, from rolfing and massage to reiki and acupuncture, can often help release old energy blockages and chronic messages and pain we've held in for years.

In the next chapter we will discuss the many forms of bodywork and breathwork and their ability to lift your moods as they deliver peace of mind.

Main Messages

- Cognitive therapy can help you examine your negative thinking patterns. It helps you substitute those toxic thoughts with more accurate, affirming ones.
- Cognitive therapy also helps you tune in to your real desires and passions that may be buried under other's expectations.
- When you have a negative thought ask yourself:
  1) Does this thought contribute to my stress?
  2) Where did I learn this thought?
  3) Is this thought logical?
  4) Is this thought true?
- Keep a daily "Mood Log" to record your cognitive distortions. Then substitute more realistic thoughts for your distorted thinking.
- Practice looking at life, even the so-called bad stuff, in a more humorous light. Humor dissolves "stinking thinking."
- Be grateful for your blessings. When you feel a negative thought coming, zap it with a joyous one.
- Begin each day by writing down ten things you are grateful for.

TEN

Strengthening Body and Breath

As we explored in the previous chapter, much of our depression is linked to unresolved trauma and grief. Strengthening both our breath and body, commonly known as breathwork and bodywork in holistic circles, can be dramatically therapeutic.

They can also alleviate the distress that comes from trying to manage too much in our lives. Both breathwork and the many forms of bodywork, such as yoga, massage, or reiki, can bring us back to our centers, to the calm, strong epicenter of our being. They can transform us to a timeless moment when we're not replaying the tape of our past, regretting what's happened or plotting the future.

Gay and Kathlyn Hendricks say they have worked with several hundred patients who were able to get off traditional medications by learning breathwork and other natural methods. The Hendrickses authored *At the Speed of Life: A New Approach to Personal Change Through Body-Centered Therapy.* They predict that breathwork will come to be considered "first-line treatment" for depression and anxiety in the next twenty years.

Breathwork Supports Nervous System

Our breath, through all cultures and times, has been viewed as the source of life and vitality. In many languages, the words for *spirit* and *breath* are the same: Sanskrit, prana; Greek, pneuma; Hebrew, ruach; Latin, spiritus.

"If breath is the movement of spirit in the body—a central mystery that connects us to all creation—then working with breath is a form of spiritual practice. It is also one that impacts health and healing because how we breathe both reflects the state of the nervous system and influences the state of the nervous system," writes Dr. Andrew Weil in his bestseller *Spontaneous Healing.* Dr. Weil offers many wonderful ways to improve your health by consciously changing the rhythm and depth of your breathing.

One "spiritual tonic" for the nervous system that he says he cannot recommend too highly is this way to take a relaxing breath: You can either sit with your back straight, lay down on your back, or even do this breathing standing or walking. Place your tongue in the yogic position, which means touching the tip of your tongue to the back of the upper front teeth, then slide it just above the teeth until it rests on the alveolar ridge, the soft tissue between the teeth and the roof of the mouth.

"Exhale completely through the mouth, making an audible sound. Then close the mouth and inhale quietly through the nose to a (silent) count of four. Then hold the breath for a count of seven. Then exhale audibly through the mouth for a count of eight. Repeat for a total of four cycles, then breathe normally."

Dr. Weil recommends doing this breathing exercise twice a day. If it's tough exhaling with your tongue in place, try pursing your lips. After one month, if this breathing exercise agrees with you, Dr. Weil recommends increasing it to eight cycles twice a day.

During his residency at the Karl Menninger School of Psychiatry in Topeka, Kansas, psychiatrist David Nichol researched the therapeutic effects of meditation on clinically depressed patients. "Often depression is fed by a series of negative thoughts," he says. "If a person can focus attention on something other than her own negative life story and find some relief, then there's the possibility of change."

A Guided Meditation

Many ways to invoke the relaxation response have been pioneered by Dr. Herbert Benson, who wrote *The Relaxation Response*. Dr. Benson is the head of the Mind/Body Medical Institute at Deaconess Hospital in Boston. He suggests listening to the following guided meditation, which you can tape with your own voice:

"My breath is calm and effortless . . . calm and effortless. Repeat the phrase as you imagine waves of relaxation flowing through your body; through your chest and shoulders; into your arms and back; into your hips and legs. Feel a sense of tranquility moving through your entire body. Continue for several minutes."

Continue feeling the warmth, heaviness flowing into the rest of your body, from your hands to your feet.

Benson's research group has found that invoking the relaxation response, along with exercise and good nutrition, has eased the depression of hundreds of patients.

In her book, *Healing Mind/Healthy Woman,* Dr. Alice Domar includes nine different approaches to eliciting the relaxation response, which she uses with her patients. One powerful method she has found is the body scan relaxation, in which you use your mind's eye to scan your body, becoming aware of any tensions throughout it, from your taut forehead muscles down to clenched stomach muscles. "You use your breath to focus on these tensions, and to gradually, gently let go of them."

Body scan relaxation can be especially helpful if you find your mind wanders with other forms of relaxation or meditation. In her book, Dr. Domar shares the success story of one of her patients, Lorrie, a 40-year-old career counselor. Lorrie had irritable bowel syndrome, anxiety, and depression. She developed toxic hepatitis from one of her IBS medications and eventually had gallbladder surgery. For several years she was constantly hospitalized and became suicidal.

When Lorrie joined Dr. Domar's mind/body group, life finally began to take on more hope. After learning several relaxation methods, including the body scan, Lorrie learned how to release the tension in her stomach. Relying on relaxation responses to control her physical symptoms gave her such a sense of empowerment, Lorrie's anxiety and depression dramatically improved, as did her moods, relationships, zest for living, and religious faith.

If her pain occasionally crops up, Lorrie manages it herself. "Wednesday morning, I woke up at three a.m. feeling like I had an elephant on my chest. The nausea and pain probably stemmed from something I ate that I shouldn't have. I stayed home from work, and I used the body scan tape. I returned to work the next day, just a bit sore. This may be the best I've ever done after an attack. I was able to manage it without medication."

Coupled with breathwork, any form of bodywork, from therapeutic touch to reiki or massage, can be incredibly healing when you are depressed. And those who are depressed often feel unworthy, antisocial and may pull away from touch, when touch is what they really need to feel loved and valued.

Miriam Jacobsen, who calls herself a "cuddly hugger" described the benefits of touch. "Touch demonstrates caring for another person, aliveness, bonding, compassion, warmth, and tenderness. It softens and relaxes the body, releases tensions and emotions. It enables a person to open up and allows you to feel."

Touch Releases Emotional Buildup

The magic of touch and its sweeping ability to unearth buried feelings cannot be underestimated. When we suppress and store negative emotions and energy in our bodies, a therapeutic massage can sometimes effectively release that unwanted emotional debris.

Such is the case for patients of Ilana Rubenfeld. The founder of the Rubenfeld Synergy Method, Rubenfeld combines compassionate touch with psychotherapy, breathing, visualization, and other strategies to access stored emotions and memories in the body, which may result in energy blocks, tensions, imbalances—and depression.

Rubenfeld practitioners, called Rubenfeld Synergists,

use gentle touch and movement to detect areas in the body of emotional holding and tension. The Rubenfeld Synergist then talks with the client to evoke and help release the unconscious emotional issues stored in the body.

Ilana Rubenfeld, whose story is powerfully told in the book *Bodywork: What Type of Massage to Get and How to Make the Most of It* by Thomas Claire, studied at the Julliard School, where she began her career as a musical conductor. But she hadn't bargained on how physically demanding her career would be.

Because she had been standing for hours at a time, hunched over a music stand, her arms in constant motion, her spine and back became painfully strained.

Rubenfeld consulted Judith Leibowitz, a teacher of the Alexander Technique, who introduced Ilana to the idea that her body, mind, and spirit were all connected. After weeks of bodywork, Rubenfeld sometimes erupted in intense crying, laughter, or anger during the sessions. "I discovered that my body had many stories that needed to be heard and that it was connected to early childhood feelings."

But Leibowitz told Ilana, "I can help you with your physical problems, but not your emotional ones." Rubenfeld then went to an analyst, who said, "I can help you with your emotional issues, but I can't help you physically, and I definitely can't touch you." How ironic, she realized, that one healer talked and wouldn't touch; the other touched and wouldn't talk.

Rubenfeld saw the glaring gulf that stood between bodywork and psychotherapy. For thirty-five years, she has worked to develop and practice a new method to integrate body, mind, emotions, and spirit. Now there are more than five hundred certified practitioners of Ruben-feld Synergy throughout the world.

Though touch is one of the most ancient forms of heal-ing, our culture is just beginning to fully recognize the power of touch in healing, Rubenfeld believes. "We're en-tering a time of spirituality and feelings through the body. The body is our instrument—the house we live in—and we need to listen to its song when we deal with emotional and spiritual issues."

The University of Miami School of Medicine's Touch Research Institute brings together researchers from Duke, Harvard, Princeton, and other universities to study the role of touch in healing depression. One of their stud-ies showed that a thirty-minute back massage given daily for five days to hospitalized, depressed and adjustment-disorder children reduced their depression, decreased stress hormones, and improved sleep.

In another study of parents who massaged children with diabetes, both the parents and their children re-ported fewer levels of anxiety and depression. Following regular massage, another group of bulimic adolescent girls showed improved body image, decreased depression and anxiety symptoms, decreased stress hormones, and increased levels of serotonin.

Magic of Aromatherapy

Combining aromatherapy with your massage is yet an-other step you can take. In inhaling the correct essential oil, you can shift your moods and help dissipate your stress. Ask your massage therapist what essential oils he or she recommends. Geranium and ylang-ylang are re-ported to be effective in treating depression. Also consider jasmine, neroli, melissa, and citrus oils like grapefruit, lime, mandarin, or bergamot.

"Touch, like smell, bypasses the logical mind and plumbs the depths of the soul," writes Nikki Goldstein in *Essential Energy: A Guide to Aromatherapy and Essential Oils.* Goldstein also recommends trying clary sage, patchouli, or rose as essential oils to ease depression and balance your energy. You can add three to four drops of oil to a tissue or six to ten drops to your bath.

Yoga Restores Harmony

The three-thousand-year-old practice of yoga is by far one of the most time-tested methods for regaining balance and inner peace. And Western medicine is finally recognizing yoga's combination of postures, meditation, and deep breathing as an effective balm for depression and the anxiety it brings. Among many other benefits, yoga helps you reach a state of greater calm and tranquility so the stresses and pressures in your life can be put in perspective, even banished.

Diane Roberts, a California yoga instructor, experienced the power of yoga in her own healing. When she was the director of a yoga school in California she developed a bulging disc in her lower back. She realized how some forms of yoga were too extreme for our western bodies, not accustomed to the practice.

Diane refined her understanding of the anatomy of the spine by studying with orthopedic surgeons, yoga instructors, personal trainers, chiropractors, and cranial sacral therapists.

Cranial sacral therapy was first developed by osteopath John E. Upledger. He discovered that we each have a regular, rhythmic pulsation of cerebrospinal fluid, which helps the brain and spinal cord to function optimally. Disturbances in the craniosacral rhythm can cause dysfunction, including depression. Dr. Upledger developed a light touch technique for restoring the natural craniosacral rhythm.

By weaving together these various disciplines, Roberts began to practice a different form of yoga known as Foundation Yoga, which she credits with helping heal her spinal problems and chronic fatigue.

Foundation Yoga is a hatha yoga system of postures and breath that strengthens and revitalizes the spine and core muscles in the body. Based on a deep reverence for the body's intuition, it encourages listening deeply to the body's wisdom for guidance with each pose, modifying the postures to suit individual needs.

As Roberts healed, she saw with new eyes the power of yoga to heal a whole host of mind/body/spirit illnesses, such as depression, by allowing tension to leave the body and the nervous system to be nourished.

"When you are in a crisis, your whole body immediately tightens, which diminishes the entire functioning of your system. Your spinal disc faces are compressed, your muscles are pulled tight, there is less nerve and blood supply to your organs and brain. So your whole body undergoes a depletion in the nourishment it needs to perform optimally. And we know that if the brain doesn't perform optimally, it doesn't create the neurotransmitters it needs."

The liver, which is key to handling emotions, and the pancreas, which helps us stay balanced, become stressed. All these combined reactions, over and over, in our bodies can easily lead to depression, says Roberts. She has repeatedly witnessed yoga's ability to improve her clients' moods, stress, and quality of life.

Yoga relieves tension in the muscles, which allows the spine to elongate and be better nourished, which allows the whole body to be better nourished, she says. Yoga also nurtures the entire being with its concentration on the breath.

"Breath is now being recognized by scientific researchers as the master system of the body. The West is proving what yogis have known for thousands of years. When you calm and slow the breath, the heart rate, mind, and emotions also calm and balance. Our emotions, thoughts, and bodies are so intertwined, you can't affect one without affecting the other."

Yogis claim to have mastered the art of calming their breath to the point of remaining breathless for long periods and slowing the heart until there is no longer a perceptible beat, Robert says. "Although most of us will not aspire to such extremes, the breath is a powerful tool we can use to restore our well-being whenever we need it most."

Yoga Exercises

One tool Roberts uses extensively in her classes and recommends for those who are healing from depression is a technique known as Alternate Nostril breathing. It is an ancient method that balances the right and left hemispheres of the brain by switching the breath from one nostril to the other. It flips the nervous system from the fight-or-flight response of anxious, fast shallow breath and racing heart, to its restorative, calming response of meditative, relating, healing and relaxed.

To practice alternate nostril breathing:

1) Sit comfortably where you will not be disturbed for several minutes. Close your eyes.
2) Raise your right hand and press your thumb against your right nostril just enough to close off the airflow.
3) Inhale a full, slow breath in through the left nostril.
4) Hold the breath by pressing the right ring finger against the left nostril so both nostrils are closed.
5) At the first sign of strain, release the thumb and exhale a long, slow, full breath through the right nostril.
6) Inhale through the right nostril.
7) Hold the breath with the ring finger at the left nostril and the thumb at the right.
8) Release through the left nostril. Continue inhaling, holding and exhaling through opposite nostrils until your body calms.

Here are two simple yoga exercises Roberts recommends:

1) The Cat Stretch. Sit on your knees and bring your upper body down until your chest and belly rest on your legs and your buttocks rest on your heels. Place your forehead on the floor—you can place a pillow here to support your neck—and extend your arms out in front of you. Either press your palms together and cross your thumbs or just keep your hands palms down on the floor.

Begin to take slow, deep breaths, feeling your belly press against your thighs with each inhalation. As you inhale, gently pull the tailbone toward the wall behind you and reach your fingertips out in front. On the exhalations, focus on your belly, chest, throat, and spine softening deeper with each breath.

2) Fetal Position/Breath Control. Starting on your back, draw both knees toward the chest and roll to your right. Count slowly to the count of eight, drawing the breath for the full count. Feel your lungs fully inflated. Hold the breath and count to four. Then exhale to the count of eight. Feel your lungs empty completely, pulling in your abdominal muscles to complete the exhale. Hold the exhale and count to four. Inhale again and repeat the breath sequence at least ten times. Then switch sides.

Many healthcare practitioners are eagerly sharing their yoga success stories. Dr. Alice Domar finds yoga dramatically healing for many patients.

Yoga helped one patient, Marta, begin to make big leaps in her healing. As Domar describes in *Healing Mind/Healthy Woman,* Marta suffered from intense PMS symptoms. The week before her period she always had lots of dark depression, anxiety, and underground anger.

Marta, who was working to heal from emotional abuse as a child, was often depressed the entire month. A film editor, she had headaches, burning sensations, and severe menstrual cramps.

After Marta joined Domar's mind/body group, she began to do yoga five days a week. Many buried truths surfaced to her consciousness. "Marta discovered that her burning sensations were directly linked to early physical abuse. Her depression, anxiety, and sense of vulnerability originated in a family environment where she never felt safe. As she began to heal emotionally, she used relaxation and yoga in a different way—to cultivate peace of mind."

New Attention on Acupuncture

Finally, as you explore the many forms of bodywork, check out acupuncture. It is rapidly gaining attention as a safe and effective way to heal depression. Acupuncturists also attest to its value to relieve the insomnia that often accompanies depression. Even the United Nations World Health Organization endorses acupuncture as a treatment for depression.

Acupuncture is a nearly five-thousand-year-old Chinese therapy in which very fine needles are inserted into specific points in the body. As the needles enter these points, they gain access to the circulation of the body's blood and ch'i, or our vital life energy. The ch'i runs through the body's meridians, which are regarded as the circuits or pathways for our life force.

Chinese doctors feel that all illness, including depression, stems from an imbalance in the flow of ch'i and acupuncture helps re-balance the body. It is thought that acupuncture promotes a sense of well-being by stimulating the body's production of the biochemicals it needs.

Western scientists are now beginning to understand why acupuncture is effective. Among other things, it apparently triggers the release of neuropeptides known as beta endorphins, the natural opiates in the brain that alleviate pain and provide a sense of well-being.

Acupuncture also helps lift depression by shutting down our body's ability to experience pain, says Judith Sachs, author of *Nature's Prozac*. Sensory thresholds for pain and pleasure lie close together in the brain, so when the "pain gate" is closed, only pleasure can be experienced, and vice versa. "Needle stimulation shuts down the gate and prevents the transmission of pain from the brain to an affected organ," Sachs says.

Research data now supports what Eastern practitioners have long known. At the University of Arizona, John J. Allen, an assistant professor of psychology, and acupuncturist Rosa Schnyer, did a sixteen-week experiment on the value of acupuncture with thirty-four women diagnosed with major depression.

The women were not being treated with antidepressant medication. A third of the women who received tailored acupuncture on the depression points showed a 43 percent reduction in their symptoms. More than half of the women no longer met the criteria for clinical depression after just eight prescribed acupuncture treatments, says Allen.

Acupressure

Acupressure also is something you can practice yourself, advises Michael Reed Gach, director of the Acupressure Institute in Berkeley and author of *Acupressure's Potent Points*. Dr. Gach suggests using acupressure on a point known as B38, which is located between the shoulder blade and the spine at the level of the heart.

To apply pressure on these points, you should lie on your back, place two tennis balls on the floor underneath your upper back and below your shoulder blades, suggests the book *New Choices in Natural Healing*. If you wish, you can place a thick towel folded in half over the balls. Close your eyes and breathe deeply a few minutes.

As with all the therapies offered in this book, your personal prescription of bodywork and breathwork will be unique, just as the source of your inner turmoil is unlike no one else's.

Breathwork and Bodywork as Bridges to Healing

Teena Leben Slatkin enjoyed the power of breathwork and bodywork when she experienced an internal struggle that came upon her like an "uninvited emotional fog." A thick and oppressive vapor that surrounded her almost overnight.

"It beat me with its unfamiliar icy, wicked breath, haunted me with its opaqueness, and suffocated me with its dense and heavy weight." Before her emotional storm seized her spirit, Teena had been busy raising four children with her husband, a kind and generous man, a respected attorney. Her life seemed blessed, calm, perfect, even.

Then, suddenly, she lost her footing. She began to feel burnt out, unsure of everything she once knew about herself. Teena felt the woman she had been for twenty years was fading from sight.

"Why after twenty years of raising a family, knowing who I was, my purpose and direction in life, why did I wake up in this terrible dense fog of bewilderment? I was groping with outstretched arms, trying desperately to find my way through this dark, mysterious, and uncharted course. I began to ask myself the same questions I had asked myself thirty years ago during my teenage years. Questions like, 'Who am I? What am I? Where am I going?' "

In the middle of her search for clarity and direction, Teena met a woman who had been teaching yoga for thirty years. This gentle and spiritual woman became a guide for Teena as she coped with this tumultuous mid-life passage. "She helped me realize I wasn't even breathing correctly. In fact I discovered that I had been holding my breath during stressful times."

Teena learned how to breath so she could slow down and release the negative stressful energy raging inside her. She realized that in neglecting her breath, she had neglected her spirit. In neglecting her spirit, she had lost her once-fierce passion for life. "Without breath, one has no life. One's breath is one's life or one's spiritual energy."

Teena also began to use her breath in meditation, which also brought her in greater harmony with her soul. She also began to do yoga. "Yoga helps me find the quiet place inside of me. I began to observe and learn how to be in the 'present moment' and appreciate how centered I then felt. I learned how to just 'be.'

"I had to learn to crawl before I could walk again to find my way out. This blinding emotional storm caused great confusion within my soul. My inner wisdom and vision were being questioned or taken away. As difficult as this struggle was, I came to realize it was the beginning of my profound spiritual journey. It was the beginning of an awakening that required an intense struggle before I could comprehend its true meaning."

Both breathwork and yoga helped Teena develop a vision, an awareness about the source of her struggle. She saw that as her children matured and separated from her, a void opened up in her life.

She also realized that she was tired of all the community and school work she had been involved in. She felt she had been constantly racing back and forth, trying to keep everything in control. Mediation and yoga restored Teena's equilibrium and lifted her.

"As I observe my life now with this new insight and vision, I realize I am able to see, appreciate, and comprehend so much more than I could before the fog rolled in. The positive outcome of my internal storm was a new vision filled with wisdom from my heart, soul, and mind, not just from my head.

"Learning to be at peace in the present was a tranquilizing experience for me. I no longer held on to the regrets of the past or constantly planned the future. I felt as though I was seeing my life for the first time with sacred eyes. I felt a holiness I had never felt before."

Main Messages

- Use breathwork, such as meditation, to bring you back to your center. It will strengthen your nervous system.
- Try Dr. Andrew Weil's breathing exercise, Dr. Herbert Benson's guided meditation, or Dr. Alice Domar's body scan relaxation.
- Get regular massages or other bodywork, such as acupuncture, to release unwanted emotional debris and unblock your energy.
- Treat yourself with aromatherapy to lift your moods and calm your spirit.
- Sample the power of yoga to restore and renew your whole self.
- Try Diane Roberts's yogic exercises.
- Practice acupressure on yourself using the guidelines on page 107.
- Experience forms of breathwork and bodywork as powerful and effective bridges to your next level of consciousness, to a place of greater strength and vibration.

ELEVEN

Creating an Affirming, Balanced Lifestyle

"We live in a culture where whirl is king . . . Ulcers, migraines, nervous tension, and a dozen other symptoms mark our psychic overload. We are concerned not to live beyond our means financially; why do it emotionally?" asks Richard Foster, author of *Freedom of Simplicity*.

In large measure we have become a people whose lives possess an uncontrolled, impulsive, frenetic quality. Many people often feel just one crisis away from a major emotional meltdown. Life just seems too much, too often.

"Every woman I know, without exception, is exhausted to the point of no return. We're worn to a raveling. We're unsteady in our gait, asleep at the switch, shouldn't be driving cars, sending E-mails, or having telephone conversations," writes Sarah Ban Breathnach in *Something More*.

In examining the root of our depression, individually and culturally, we have to examine how much our lifestyle contributes to that malaise. Many experts are increasingly saying that our overextended, full-tilt lifestyles may very much be at the root of our suffering and epidemic depression.

"Despite their seeming affluence, many people have exhausted their biological and psychological resources. They are almost like rats on a treadmill running faster and faster in pursuit of cheese and yet really feeling crazed by the complexity of the maze," says Dr. Harold Bloomfield.

Becoming Junior Males Breeds Depression

In addition, our culture's denigration of and hostility toward the feminine, especially in the workplace, is also a formula for disaster, a sure prescription for depression. From early on, women are still expected to be pleasing, smiling, placating creatures. They are conditioned to serve, sacrifice and become martyrs, especially for their families and men.

At the same time that we are placating, serving and working tirelessly, our bodies should look luminous, waif-like, yet sexy and inviting. We are molded into consummate consumers who crave only the best designer stuff. Our hair color, breasts, and buttocks are never quite good enough. Little girls get these messages earlier all the time. Witness the new anorexic-wannabe doll on the market: Diet Debbie, who comes with her own treadmill and scales.

Again, no wonder depression is epidemic. When you're addicted to living up to cultural perfectionism, how can you know who you really are if you are too busying perfecting the "you" the media and others expect? When you're constantly looking and acting the part so you can remain on the stage, there's little time left in the wings to know your true self. Easy for amnesia and denial to set in.

Yet it gets worse. When we move into the workplace, all that hyper-femininity, sexy packaging, and nurturing of others is expected to grind to a halt as we adopt men's tougher ways. There, to become "successful," we must become junior males-in-training. The minute our heels hit the office parking lot, the masculine model damn well better kick in. Our emotions must be suppressed, our killer instinct inflamed.

A women's magazine article I read—just a few years ago—was the epitome of the anti-feminine hostility in our workplaces. The article was targeted to pregnant working women. At all cost, it cautioned, you must hide any sign of your swelling abdomen. Your clothes should mask, as much as possible, any evidence of your growing child, the article stressed. And never, ever, if you're in a business meeting and feel any twinges, or even deep pain, reveal your discomfort.

The denial of self, the lack of compassion for the feminine, the suppression, even revulsion for natural feminine essence, sets up a brutal battleground between the inner psyche and outer expectations. It creates a dark shroud over women that obscures our innate brilliance and thrusts us closer to the painful state of depression.

Such damaging messages also keep us separate from, even mistrustful of, other women. When you are busy trying to be a man all day, what time, energy, or interest is left for the life-giving sustenance that female friendships afford?.

T'ai chi instructor and East Coast therapist Judith Duerk explored the impact of the blurred-motion, anti-feminine lifestyle in *A Circle of Stones: A Woman's Journey to Herself.* Her premise is that women have so adopted the male definition of success and so severed nurturing connections with other women and times of solitude that depression is inevitable. "If a woman is caught in an over-extended lifestyle and achievement-oriented values, depression or illness may offer the only opportunity to allow her to be with herself."

Take a Deep Look at Your Life

If this is true, it's happening to both men and women. Men, too, often don't have time or energy for friendships with other men. Ask yourself, "Have I let life become crazy? Does the continuous motion of my days push me perilously close to—or even over the brink of—my psychological and physical breaking point?" If so, the level of anxiety and stress you experience can clearly lead to chronic depression, experts says.

It can also lead to deep despair from not living the life you desire. And there you go—more depression. A recent Gallup Poll found that half of all Americans say they lack enough time to do what they really want. Fifty-four percent of parents surveyed say they spend too little time with their children. "We're wearing ourselves out trying to have it all," concludes Elaine St. James, author of *Living the Simple Life*.

Joan Borysenko sees this sense of despair in more and more people. "Everyone I know says, 'There's no time. There's no time. I don't have enough time for me, for my family or to explore those things that might be deeply meaningful.' That's depressing to people."

If that's true for you, then how do you lighten your

load, take stuff off your plate, lower your stress? How can you find the time to do what is soulful and meaningful?

Soulful work that makes your heart and spirit sing is one of the most powerful antidotes to depression. If you have a compelling reason to get out of bed each morning, if you are on fire, even occasionally, with the sense that your work serves others and makes their lives better, depression finds little soil to root in your psyche.

But if you're really depressed and don't feel capable of getting out of bed, you would do well to think about how work works, according to Dr. Richard O'Connor in *Undoing Depression*.

Best-selling author Alexandra Stoddard has long written about the power and fulfillment of soulful work. Such work is necessary to keep our creative spirits alive. And soulful work is highly individual, Stoddard says.

"You have to listen to yourself and do what your muse tells you. It's simple advice, but very difficult for many of us to follow. The key to our sense of well-being is to be guided by our heart, which yearns to choose the challenging, original path," writes Stoddard in *Making Choices: Discover the Joy in Living the Life You Want to Lead*.

What kind of work absorbs you? What is absolutely fascinating to you? If you follow your muse, you become self-motivated and dedicated to excellence. You also tap into your "art-spirit," explains Stoddard. "If you bring the art-spirit to everything you do, you will not only empower yourself, but you will help others to empower themselves."

And this reduces your stress, lifts your spirit and moods, floods you with high energy, and banishes depression.

Also critical to keeping depression at bay is to find a balance between work and home, obligation and pleasure. Clearly, we Americans must make major lifestyle changes if we intend to live healthier, less stressed and depressed lives—and take less of a toll on our environment.

Tread Lightly

One of those lifestyle changes is to live more simply and walk more lightly on this earth. Our insatiable appetite for outer stuff and possessions is often a sign of our inner yearning for greater peace, security, and equilibrium. How many times have you promised yourself, "I can't relax and stop working so much until X is paid off?

Too often we've sacrificed real peace and pleasure for the material things we hope and pray will deliver the same thing. "We have learned to seek external solutions to signals from the mind, heart, or soul that something is out of balance. We try to satisfy essentially psychological and spiritual needs with consumption at a physical level," write Joe Dominguez and Vicki Robin in their popular book *Your Money or Your Life*.

Many of us are now realizing that "stuff" can't deliver happiness, love, or hope. Possessions can't fill that void within us, no matter how shiny, sweet-smelling, fast, or sleek. It is often the simpler things in life, like talking with good friends around the kitchen table until the candles burn down or reading a good book as the snow sifts around outside, that deliver the deep psychological happiness we crave.

When you're crazed with gathering material stuff, if you count T.J. Maxx as your closest companion, there's precious little time left for soul-satisfying moments with real friends. When was the last time you spent time with people you love—and who love and accept you? When did you last share a hot meal, laugh deep into the night, share something of yourself you'd never revealed before?

Is there time in your days for such moments? If there never is, could you be addicted to incessant motion? Is it possible that you are intentionally busy, crazymaking busy, so you can avoid getting intimate with others—or yourself? You don't have to risk being vulnerable if you don't slow down long enough for you or them to even peer into your being.

But the whirling-dervish life is too painful, says Dr. Dean Ornish. Fear of being hurt may cause us to create inner walls around our heart, he says. "But you pay a big price for having the walls up all the time. When you put a wall around your heart, when you wall off the ability to feel pain, you also shut down the ability to feel pleasure," says Dr. Dean Ornish, in his bestselling book *Dr. Dean Ornish's Program for Reversing Heart Disease.*

Let the pleasure, the decadent pleasure, of friends back in your life. Reach out, even if to only one other person. As I discuss further in Chapter 13, intimacy and social support from other people not only keeps depression distant, it prolongs your life.

Other ways to ward off depression: Simplify, simplify, simplify. I can't stress this enough. "For fast-acting relief, try slowing down," quips Lily Tomlin. But it works.

This month, try eliminating four activities from your normal routine that no longer nourish or improve your life. This week, get rid of four possessions that weigh you down and clutter your life. Start small and work your way up. Maybe it's that unused rice steamer today. Tomorrow, dig deeper into your cache of stuff—especially if you're still paying it off.

Next week, drop several obligations off your plate. Don't cave in if people clamor that "You just can't do that!" Sure you can. And you just did.

Decluttering your life will be one of the greatest gifts you give yourself. Such is the message of former entertainer, now mind/body author and teacher Naomi Judd, who became depressed after her diagnosis of hepatitis. She was often paralyzed by fear, knowing that her life hung in the balance.

Pampering Ourselves

But Naomi didn't stay suspended in panic. She retreated from the outside world, spending almost two years of relative isolation on her farm in Tennessee. She slowed life way down and experienced the healing power of simplicity, prayer, meditation, and humor.

In my book *Embracing Our Essence: Spiritual Conversations with Prominent Women,* Judd reflected on the insights she had during this time of solitude: "There tends to be this headlong rush into seeing how many appointments we can cram into our calendar and how many balls we can juggle at once . . . and I am so strongly against that because until we can truly enjoy what my friend Deepak Chopra calls 'life-centered, present-moment awareness,' we are missing the whole point.

"The reason women are trying to rush headlong into hectic schedules is they think that will somehow make them more fulfilled or self-realized, when instead it has the opposite effect."

Naomi says one of the greatest gifts we can give ourselves is to simplify and organize our lives. "Get rid of the daily clutter and distress that takes time away from those things that matter most in life: faith, family, and friends."

Specifically, she recommends you spend one day—or at least a few hours each week—on yourself. "Read an inspirational book, soak in a hot bath surrounded by aromatherapy candles, take a long walk in nature absorbing the fresh air and beauty, or learn different breathing, relaxation, and meditation techniques."

All of these strategies can counter today's epidemic of "distression," a term coined by Harriet Braiker, author of *Getting Up When You Are Feeling Down: A Woman's Guide to Overcoming and Preventing Depression.* "Being in a state of distression can mean merely that you are depleted, exhausted, and overloaded but not that you are necessarily unhappy."

For those of us who are in the sandwich generation—tending young children, careers, and elderly parents—taking care, good care, of ourselves isn't a luxury anymore. Relaxation techniques, doing things we enjoy, renewing our overtaxed spirits and bodies should be as natural and routine as brushing our teeth.

Instead, many of us follow Janice's pattern. She became totally overwhelmed when she tried to care for her mother, who has Alzheimer's, her father, recovering from bypass surgery, and her son, who has multiple sclerosis.

Janice became understandably depressed. Depression—or at least distression—is a normal response to such a moment in one's life.

But Janice's depression lifted when she began to better care for herself—and ask for and receive assistance from other caregivers. We all have to learn how to ask for help. We're not machines that can go on tirelessly. Our bodies, minds, and souls operate best when we allow ourselves long, regular periods of rejuvenation and self-nurture.

So begin first with a very powerful rule of thumb to eliminate stress and depression in your life. Eliminate those activities, people, obligations in your life that no longer nourish you or feed your soul. That may mean cutting back on work hours, the number of activities you carpool your kids to, business travel, endless evenings of surface socializing with people who don't build, but only deplete, your energy. Step away from friendships that have run their course.

Create Your Own Firm Boundaries

Try to allow only those people and activities into your life that amplify your energy and sustain your spirits. Do you really need to surf so many social functions? Do your children really need to be steeped in all those music, sports, and artistic activities? As kids' stress and mental illness rises, increasingly experts are asking what's more important—that they be super achievers or in super emotional health?

Create your own firm boundaries. Your threshold is entirely different from someone else's. Learn to say "No" to people who push you to do more when you know you can't without sacrificing your sanity.

Say "No" without feeing guilty or excusing yourself. You don't need to offer an explanation. As Oprah Winfrey asserted on a recent show: " 'No' is a complete sentence." That can become your new mantra. " 'No' is a complete sentence."

Saying "No" shifts your state of mind. It "frees us from the habit of stuffing our schedules with everything that comes our way, everything under the sun, as though quantity brings quality of life. Who ever feels really terrific when they overeat? Isn't overdoing just as depressing?" Alexandra Stoddard asks.

Saying "No" implies you have the inner resources to withdraw for a time from the world, she says. Saying "No" gives you confidence and serenity. It gives you time to ponder on your own vision of your life, not blindly following others.

Keep remembering whatever you take on, whatever you commit to, directly affects your body, mind, and spirit. If you agree to do a volunteer or office project that you detest, that brings you no joy, your being is flooded with that disgust, that lifelessness. It becomes depressed by your inability to simply and powerfully say "No."

Create boundaries, so toxic people or events, like violent news images, don't flood your life with negativity. In a time of healing and strengthening, Dr. Andrew Weil urges you to go "media free." Naomi Judd goes weeks without watching TV. Does the average American really feel nurtured, loved, and sated after watching a weekly average of sixteen hours of TV anyway? Join forces with the organization TV Free America.

As we've lost our sense of extended family and rootedness, many of us have become more dispirited. Many experts feel we are trying to find substitute families on TV. But get real—do Ally McBeal, Drew Carry, or Felicity really care if your last check just bounced or that you're sad, tired, needing a new job, or fighting a cold today? Of course not.

We need to reach out to real people who really care about us. This gets tough. It may mean cutting from your life toxic people who no longer nourish and support you.

Also try to banish perfectionism from your life. Try to

free up more time, even if it means hiring more domestic and other help and lowering your standards.

When you are depressed, it's often extremely hard to muster the energy to finish projects at home and work. Ask for help when you need it. Set your own internal expectations of what needs to be completed. Make small, manageable goals that you can accomplish each day for a sense of mastery and satisfaction.

Realize a clean house or an immaculate workspace doesn't add up to a happy life. If you can live with more dust and dirtier kitchen floors, you have more time to weave art, music, friends, natural beauty, dancing, story-telling into your life—all of which bust depression.

When indigenous people were depressed, says anthro-pologist, author, and educator Angeles Arrien, they would ask themselves, "When did you stop singing your soul? When did you stop dancing? When did you stop allowing yourself the comfort of silence?"

Make Time for Still Moments

Ask yourself those same questions. Listen deeply to the answers that surface. Silence—or the loss of silence—has a profound impact on our health. Being bombarded con-stantly with stimuli contributes to our depression. Unless you have some still moments, you only skim the surface of your life. If we are preoccupied with being busy and achieving, we may not allow ourselves time to descend into our deeper natures, to touch our true strengths, says Judith Duerk.

Learn to practice the art of solitude. Give yourself at least thirty minutes each day to just be still, think, medi-tate. Ask yourself, "When did I stop sinking into moments of hushed and motionless sweetness that allow my thoughts and soul to stretch and unspool?"

When you make time stand still, nothing, nothing matters as much. Nature is the consummate serenity guide. When you sit long enough to watch snowflakes silently cover a bush, flake by flake, or when you watch streaks of magenta, orange, and crimson purple flare across the sky at dusk, any inner turmoil is eased by the outer majesty. Awe always eases angst.

Make time for these transcendent moments. Schedule solitude in your appointment book, if you need to. Don't expect it to be easy at all. You will have to fight for your quiet time. Others, especially family members, may try to make you feel guilty or selfish for carving out some downtime. Through the ages, women with young children especially have lamented the difficulty of finding time purely to please themselves.

"It is a difficult lesson to learn today—to leave one's friends and family and deliberately practice the art of solitude for an hour or a day or a week," wrote Anne Morrow Lindbergh in *Gift from the Sea*. "Parting is inevitably painful, even for a short time. It is like an amputation I feel and yet once it is done. I find there is a quality to being alone that is incredibly precious. Life rushes back into the void, richer, more vivid, fuller than before."

Redecorate the Crowded Room of Your Mind

It was on her fiftieth birthday that Kathy realized she needed to spend more time alone, in solitude, to replenish and better care for herself. With five hundred other women, she attended a women's mind/body/spirit conference, based on my book *Embracing Our Essence.*

The conference and being surrounded by the energy of the women around her "shocked her soul" into trusting, loving, and honoring herself, says Kathy.

She realized how much she let others' expectations of her guide and dominate her life. So Kathy began to spend more time by herself—thinking, reading nourishing books, being still. The result was powerful and healing.

"I redecorated the crowded room of my mind in the comforting color of 'me.' Looking within my very own soul for purpose and direction has replaced needing the approval of the dozens of others who once lived in that room—my parents, siblings, spouse, friends, coworkers, society, neighbors, the driver of the car next to me, and on and on. It was a very crowded room, wasn't it?"

"Today, every day, I honor my uniqueness of thought, appearance, value to others, creativity, and spirituality. No longer do I strive to be perfect. I strive to be perfectly me."

Main Messages

- Deeply look at your life. Are you overextended, chronically stressed, and not finding enough meaning?
- Ask yourself whether you are living the life you desire. Are you spending time with the people you love and enjoy?
- Begin to lighten your load. Acquire fewer possessions.
- Empty your plate. This month, eliminate four activities that no longer feed your soul.
- This week, get rid of four possessions that weigh you down and clutter your life.

- Next week, drop several obligations from your schedule.
- Spend a minimum of several hours every week nurturing yourself.
- Make room in your life for only those people who nourish and sustain you.
- Create firm boundaries against toxic people, events, news programs.
- Say "No" without feeling guilty.
- Reach out to others who care for you.
- Banish perfectionism at home and work. Set small, attainable goals.
- Schedule solitude and still moments into your life on a regular basis.

TWELVE

Balancing with Sound and Music

Many of our depressions are directly linked to our life-style, to an overwhelming bombardment of stress and stimuli coupled with a lack of meaning. If that is a picture of your life, you may find the therapy discussed in this chapter especially potent.

As long as we've existed, since handmade instruments were first rattled in fire dances, sound has been used to balance and heal. And now the therapeutic power of sound and music is gaining ground as a mainstream therapy for anxiety, fear, and depression.

Music as Vibrational Relaxant

Don Campbell, a trained classical musician, composer, and author of groundbreaking books on music and healing, attests to the connection between sound and internal harmony. He cites studies, such as that at Saint Agnes Hospital in Baltimore. Patients in critical care units there listened to classical music and "half an hour of music produces the same effect as ten milligrams of Valium," said Dr. Raymond Bahr, director of the coronary care unit.

To fully understand why sound is so effective, we must look at the "energy inside of sound," says Campbell. Within our bodies, "vibrating sounds form patterns and create energy fields of resonance and movement in the surrounding space. We absorb these energies, and they subtly alter our breath, pulse, blood pressure, muscle tension, skin temperature, and other internal rhythms."

Music therapy, whether through sacred music or reggae, is a kind of "vibrational nutrition," concludes Campbell. In recent years, the music of Wolfgang Amadeus Mozart has become the preferred sound used by many researchers to ease anxiety, learning disorders, and autism.

The Tomatis Method

Dr. Alfred Tomatis, a celebrated French physician, has studied for more than fifty years how Mozart calms listeners, improves their spatial perceptions and concentration, and allows them to express themselves more clearly.

Dr. Ron Minson, head of the Center for Inner Change, a Tomatis center in Denver, Colorado, has found listening to Mozart particularly helpful for those who are depressed because they have no meaning or significance in their lives, people who have failed to listen to their inner motivations and dreams.

"We often have been conditioned to listen to others at

the exclusion of listening to ourselves, to what the Quakers call 'the still voice within,' " says Dr. Minson. "It is listening to this inner voice that can bring about an awakening of consciousness and the actualization of our potentials."

Listening to Mozart helps many clients improve their abilities to listen to themselves and their inner wisdom, which all can ease depression. "The energizing high-frequency filtered music of Mozart and the relaxing Gregorian chant is conducive to the therapeutic process being more focused, present and forward looking. With this combination it is truly possible to break through the fog of depression and to move into the lives that we want to live."

When he trained personally with Tomatis, Dr. Minson learned that the ear is a "battery" to the brain. When properly stimulated, the ear converts sound into electrical energy, which the brain uses as food. The most energizing sounds are at the high frequencies. Dr. Timson finds that depressed patients often hear low-frequency sound much better than higher frequencies, signaling that their brains aren't receiving the energy they need from high-frequency sounds.

"Most of us think of energy as coming from food and air which the body metabolizes. We pay little attention to sound and the critical role of the ear in converting it into an energy source on which our brain thrives."

Nothing in his thirty years of medicine prepared him for the advances he's seen in sound therapy, Dr. Minson says. Nothing prepared him for the patient after patient who proved the Tomatis method works. One such patient was Mary, who had been depressed since she was a teenager. She felt cut off from her body, isolated, and fatigued. She had little interest in food and had foggy thinking.

When Mary came to Dr. Minson she was extremely depressed, triggered by the stress of a major move and coping with her child, who had a host of developmental disorders.

"Realizing her loss of energy, joy and enthusiasm, Mary wanted to reconnect with her own sense of aliveness first to better support her daughter."

Mary also desperately wanted to recapture a lifelong dream. She had a deep passion for opera and music. Singing at the Metropolitan was one of Mary's dreams. But she felt constricted and tied up, especially in her neck, throat, and chest. She also felt "trapped in my body," which caused her to swallow her sounds.

So Mary began the Tomatis therapy, which wasn't without its own struggles. Like many of the therapies in this book, as you move into understanding and uncovering your depression, waves of unresolved issues from your past often surface. That was the case for Mary.

Painful dreams, memories and images from her childhood spiraled through her consciousness. But Mary was committed to continuing with her therapy, which included art therapy, to heal. "For deep change to occur, one must be wiling to be uncomfortable for a while," she said.

After only one week of allowing these raw feelings to surface and be processed, Mary felt much better. She further moved her healing along by drawing out her feelings. Her sadness and grief seemed to flow away from her as the color flowed onto the page, says Dr. Minson.

Mary's energy also began to come back. She felt more focused and on task. After two months, she said she was not only no longer depressed, but she was able to make quantum leaps in her singing. "I'm getting a whole new idea of my identity. There is a lot more to me than what you see."

Mary also felt more confident and grounded in a way she had never experienced. "I was at the mercy of whatever was happening in life. Now I've grown strong roots. I'm like a sea plant that can move with the tides."

She also began to make amazing breakthroughs in her singing. "Her voice teacher said, 'Mary has been with you for only several months, and she is doing things with her voice that she shouldn't have been able to do for years.' "

Rediscovering New Joy Through Sound

Dr. Minson has treated from three hundred to four hundred people for depression. "I have gotten 80 to 90 percent of that group off their medications. They become more animated, creative and discover a sense of joy."

One such patient was Wayne, a retired university professor from Arizona. Wayne had Epstein-Barr syndrome and obsessive-compulsive disorder, and was severely depressed. He also was paralyzed with agoraphobia and couldn't leave his house. He was on Prozac and other medications. "His doctors were just barely keeping him out of the hospital."

After trying the Tomatis method for only fifteen days, Wayne was able to come off all of his medications except Prozac. By the end of the program, he was able to discontinue this as well. "This man who couldn't leave his house now started working in an art gallery."

A year later, Wayne wrote Dr. Minson a letter. It said, "You were nervous about using the word 'energy' to describe our method. It is about energy. I have energy mentally to stay focused and concentrate. My wife says she is having an affair with a strange man who is myself."

If you would like to explore the Tomatis Method further, seek out a program in your area. Though there is limited research data on the effect of music on healing depression, studies are underway and early results look promising. For instance, a South African researcher, Wynand F. du Plessis, studied the Tomatis method with twenty women with anxiety. The women received an anxiety reduction program that included sixty half-hour sessions of filtered music and regular therapeutic interviews.

The anxiety of the women decreased significantly, while the control group had no change. The women who received music therapy said they were using their time more efficiently and were heeding their inner needs and motives more.

Beyond structured music therapy, if music isn't part of your life, give it a more prominent role. All forms of music, whether classical, New Age, jazz, or sounds of nature, activate our own healing power. Gregorian or Tibetan chanting also create a resonance within us that balances body, mind, and spirit. Many people say they gain great comfort and strength from the ancient sacred songs. Hildegard of Bingen's music, for instance, is particularly powerful.

Select music to create the mood you desire. If you want to feel more energized and upbeat, don't listen to haunting Vivaldi, but maybe go with some Rod Stewart or Alanis Morissette. If you are working with your therapist to heal some childhood issues, it may be soothing to listen to some timeless lullabies.

Whether it's the Beatles or Bach that may be most soothing to you, many people do seem to find vibrational kinship with Mozart, concludes Campbell. By imparting energetic balance, music may do what many other healing systems strive to do, Campbell says. "Whether through acupuncture, herbal medicine, dietary planning, or assorted other measures, many systems of health care seek to help the patient find energetic balance. Mozart's music may be energy-balancing extraordinaire. It's not too fast, or too slow. Somehow it's 'just right.' "

Main Messages

- Sound therapy can effectively create internal harmony and ease depression and anxiety
- Try listening to music, such as Mozart, to step away from outer distractions and better listen to yourself.
- If desired, seek out a Tomatis Center or other sound therapy program in your community for more in-depth sound therapy.
- Even if you don't go with formal music therapy, weave music into your day. Choose music that evokes the mood you desire. Listen to music that relaxes and nourishes.

THIRTEEN

Rediscovering the Power of Kinship

In these manic times, many of us have a chronic need for some time alone, time to find our inner stillness far away from the din of the everyday. But for many people who are depressed, the problem is not enough time alone—but far too much.

This chapter explores how social isolation contributes to depression. Today, when the average family uproots and moves to a new location every five years, social ties and a sense of community become shattered—if they were ever there at all.

How is it with you? Do you have family and friends to fill that space with unconditional love and support? Do you feel like someone dear to you really knows you? If not, your spirit and body may be drained by lack of emotional sustenance, of communion with others.

"Human beings are highly social, communal animals. We are meant to live in families, tribes, and communities, and when we lack those connections we suffer," says Dr. Andrew Weil in *8 Weeks to Optimum Health*.

How can we possibly be lonely today? many wonder. My God, we are surrounded by people from dawn to dusk. We never have a moment alone. Our kids are always yelling for something, our boss is constantly in touch via e-mail or cell phone. And will someone please get the door?

We may indeed look heavily immersed in the world, but can still suffer from what Dr. Weil calls Disconnection Syndrome. "Because men are more likely than women to see themselves as self-contained and pride themselves on being independent, they are also more likely than women to suffer from the Disconnection Syndrome . . ."

Connection Banishes Depression

In our disconnected state, we often forget how to be just a little more vulnerable with others, trusting that they can offer us comfort, allowing our relationships to reach a new level of intimacy. Sometimes all we need in the way of comfort is someone just to be with us, says writer Parker Palmer. He remembers when he finally allowed his misery to be fully seen by his friends.

As he struggled with depression, many well-intentioned friends came to visit. They desperately wanted to rescue him and "fix" his depression with their practical advice and encouragement. And then came another friend.

"Every afternoon around five o'clock, he came to me, sat me in a chair, removed my shoe, and massaged my feet. He hardly said a word, but he was there, he was with me. He was a lifeline for me, a link to the human community and thus to my own humanity. He had no need to 'fix me.' He knew the meaning of compassion."

Connection is critical, even if you feel intimately connected with your work, as many of us do today. At the height of her research career at Harvard, Joan Borysenko remembers that kind of disconnection. "I was passionate about my science, but I got awfully isolated in the doing of it. I was scrambling for grants, seeing patients, and then going home and being with my children. I had almost no one who could discuss it with me who could really help me bring forth more of what was inside me. We need other people."

Affection Lengthens Your Life

We've lost track of how much we truly do need others, says Dr. Weil. In our Western industrialized society, we've substituted the nuclear family for the extended family, glorified frontier independence, and fostered a spirit of Every Man for Himself, he says. "This creates a deep, unsatisfied longing in people that may be at the root of much of our social malaise—the prevalence of addiction to drugs that numb feeling, for example, the growth of gangs among our youth, and rising violence everywhere."

And clearly depression. Studies show that people who spend time with others in meaningful relationships enjoy greater health. Isolation may be the greatest health risk today, says Dr. Dean Ornish who explores the power of human connections in his new book *Love & Survival: The Scientific Basis for the Healing Power of Intimacy*. With single-occupant households at an all-time high, loneliness is a cultural scourge, says Ornish. "The real epidemic today isn't physical heart disease. It's spiritual heart disease: loneliness and isolation."

Deep connections with other human beings may be the greatest source of strength and deterrent to depression today. Many researchers now believe that close ties to supportive family and friends are a more potent healing force than diet, exercise, or any other strategy. Affection clearly lengthens your life, says Dr. Ornish, who says he passes up professional opportunities to nurture his relationships.

Research Findings Show Power of Love

Mounting evidence of the power of intimacy is gaining new attention among physicians and health-care professionals. Some of the most riveting findings:

- A landmark series of studies by epidemiologist James House of twenty-two thousand men and women showed that people with few friends and supportive relationships had a death rate two to four times higher than those with substantial networks.
- Among eight thousand people studied by the University of California for more than seventeen years, women with the fewest social contacts were more than twice as likely to die of cancer than those with many social connections. Socially isolated women also were prone to hormone-related cancers, including breast cancer.
- Women who said they felt isolated were three and a half times as likely to die of breast, ovarian, or uterine cancer over a seventeen-year period.

- Men who said their wives didn't show them love suffered 50 percent more angina over a five-year period than those who said they did receive love.
- Women who sought care for menopausal and PMS symptoms had significantly less social support than comparison groups of symptom-free women.
- When the three-generation, churchgoing households in Rosetta, Pennsylvania, deteriorated in the 1970s, so did the health of its residents—even though their diet and other health habits remained the same.
- College students who report strained and cold relationships with their parents suffer extraordinary rates of hypertension and heart disease decades later.

Create Your Family of Choice

Some people are fortunate. They already enjoy deep and fulfilling relationships with their families. Many others need to create their own families of choice—especially in times of crisis and depression.

What does a Family of Choice look like? Its members function like a normal, healthy family, says Ellen McGrath. "They are a source of strength and encouragement and are available during times of emotional, physical, and financial crisis. They share our deepest vulnerabilities and provide support instead of criticism. They regularly share what's happening in their lives, even if doing so is only a brief phone call during an especially hectic day."

Stephanie had to create her own family when her biological family was too remote—both geographically and emotionally—to support her when she first discovered the meaning of despair. Her world shifted overnight when her daughter was diagnosed with a chronic, incurable illness.

The world she knew took on a distorted, surreal cast. The work she once gained great comfort and expression from had to be backburnered as she coped with her child's condition. Her friends tried to be supportive, but they were busy with their own lives or just admitted they couldn't relate.

The black hole of despair yawned wide. Drained by the lack of support and the fear of what the future held for her and her family, Stephanie sank deep into depression one winter. She realized she had been bursting into tears almost every day for longer than she could remember. Even the sight of a pile of unfolded laundry made her weep.

Much of her grief came from her feeling of isolation. "I missed my work, colleagues, and the support network I used to have. I also knew I needed to build a new support network of kindred spirits who also were coping with chronic health issues."

Stephanie began to talk with therapists. She deepened friendships with several new acquaintances who expressed their willingness to be part of her support system. She also hired more domestic help, began to exercise and take St. John's wort. She went to a women's conference and was restored by the high energy and affection she found there.

Stephanie found what many researchers are now confirming—the greatest healing force in the universe can come from the love and support of family and friends. When you are feeling awash in depression and floundering without a good support network, some days the only thing you want to do is crawl back into bed and have a good cry. That can be a necessary, nurturing part of your healing—but then you need to go outward for support.

But many people feel so lifeless, the prospect of being proactive and finding support is too exhausting and intimidating.

You Are Worthy of Unconditional Love

Dr. Alice Domar says if her clients lack the necessary energy and confidence to seek new connections, she often has to help them strengthen themselves first. "Often, we can develop strong social networks after we adopt other stress-management methods, including relaxation, cognitive restructuring, and self-nurturance."

A first critical step is to believe that you deserve good friends. You are worthy of unconditional love from others. Then start small. Dr. Andrew Weil suggests making a list of friends and acquaintances in whose company you feel more alive, happier, and more optimistic. "Resolve to spend some time with one of them this week," he advises.

Begin slowly. Talk with a neighbor over the fence or at the mailbox. Exchange a funny story with your child's teacher. Invite someone in for a cup of coffee or a sandwich. Attend a lecture in your community and try to meet one new person.

Visualize the type of friends and supporters you hope to attract to yourself. Mary Ellen Copeland, the author of *The Depression Workbook,* says we each need at least five good friends or supporters. Copeland says these people should be able to empathize with us, affirm our individuality and strengths, play with us, be open-minded, and accept our ups and downs without being judgmental.

They should be willing to work with and support us as we take new steps.

"Family members and partners are also candidates for your support network. Choose people whom you love and trust," Copeland says.

If you've habitually found it difficult to make friends, consider working with a counselor to develop appropriate social skills. Do volunteer work to meet others. Network more with those in your workplace.

Start a small weekly support group, even if with only three friends. Keep it simple. Each week go around the group and share the most exciting or fulfilling thing that happened to you that week. Then go back around and share one tough challenge you're facing. This is nothing new—there is a rich tradition in communal support.

Think of the early quilting circles, says Lucia Capacchione, whose story is shared in Chapter 7. One thing that helped Lucia heal her depression was to gather her group of friends for dinner in her big farmhouse kitchen in California.

"About that time the book *How to Make an American Quilt* came out, and I cried when I saw the quilt on its cover. As I envisioned these women sitting around making their quilts, I has this profound sense that these women had pioneered the idea of a women's support system. They didn't call it therapy, but that's what it had to be."

May you find the sweet comfort of your own circle. As you weave it, it helps to remember wonderful times you've shared with family and friends. What were they like—and could you re-create them where you are now?

Loretta LaRoche remembers how big, raucous family dinners eased the melancholy and tension in her large Italian family as she grew up. "I still remember lots of laughter in the midst of a lot of hard times. My grandfather would say, 'Tonight, we have lamb stew without the lamb,' but that would evaporate in the midst of lots of pasta and homemade wine.

"There were always a succession of characters coming in and out. They helped to create an opera which I revisit periodically in my mind. Now we watch other people's lives on TV. The love, the connection are missing. No wonder we feel alone.

"There are times I literally start crying when I reminisce about my grandmother in the kitchen. I can still see her gnarled hands chopping and chopping as wonderful odors wafted from the house."

Are there similar gatherings you miss and long for? If your family isn't close, who could you gather as your surrogate family to help ease your loneliness? Sometimes you must be willing to sacrifice a little privacy to recreate that sense of family. You must be willing to embrace a new family vision, as the writer Madeline L'Engle did. Some of her granddaughters lived with her during their college and postgraduate years, and sitting around the table "talking until the candles burned down" become one of Madeline's favorite pastimes.

Who's in your tribe? Who do you enjoy hanging out with? Who can help you ease your dark nights of the soul, hold you tight as you cry and witness your tears? Who can laugh with you as you relate a hysterical story from your day and help you celebrate the seasons? Just remember, your kindred spirits are out there, just longing to connect with you as much as you want to connect with them.

Main Messages

- Recognize that affection lengthens your life. Love for and from others banishes depression.
- Remember you are worthy of unconditional love.
- Get rid of toxic friends.
- Make new friends. Start small.
- Volunteer to meet others.
- Visualize the support you want.
- Work with a counselor to build your social confidence.
- Start a support group.
- Create your family of choice.
- Ask yourself, "Who's in my tribe now?"

FOURTEEN

Exploring the Tonic of Exercise

"If exercise could be packaged into a pill, it would be the single most prescribed and beneficial medicine in the nation," says Dr. Robert N. Butler of Mount Sinai Medical School in New York. Yet studies find that the majority of people who are depressed don't exercise.

Such was the case for Lynn. As her depression became bigger, so did her body. it was as if her outer self, her new heaviness, was a mirror of the inner weight pressing on her. She knew she should exercise. Her doctor kept asking her if she was getting enough physical activity. Her friends gently reminded her that it would lift her moods and asked her to join them during their workouts.

But the prospect of walking in her neighborhood, or worse yet, going to a health club, really intimidated Lynn. She knew people would be watching her, judging her harshly for being so heavy.

Among the millions of people who deal with depression, Lynn's story is not at all atypical. Depression and being overweight are often intertwined, for reasons researchers are still exploring. Many feel too overwhelmed and ashamed of their bodies. "I feel so awful already, I can't imagine that pounding my body on the pavement is going to make me feel better," Lynn thought.

Beginning an exercise program can be extremely tough. It may grate against your inner grain, which just wants to retreat to the nearest sedentary coffeehouse for a lift. Fitness may feel like yet another obligation on your already overstuffed "to do" list.

Begin Slowly

But if you can begin to exercise, even slowly at first, the effects are phenomenal. "Any kind of active physical exercise is incompatible with feeling depressed," writes Harriet Braiker in her book, *Getting Up When You're Feeling Down*.

"Exercise is a proven, immediate tonic for stress and depression—a surefire shortcut to simpler lives," says therapist Andrea Van Steenhouse, author of *A Woman's Guide to a Simpler Life*. She has conditioned herself to feel drawn, not driven, to her long walks outdoors along a canal that runs near her Denver home. Exercise, she says, "propels me physically away from the source of my stress and slows my pace sufficiently so that I can notice the new buds on the trees or the shade of yellow in the changing aspen leaves. In the midst of physical vigor, my problems pale; in the solitude of exercise, I hear my heartsongs."

Exercise as a Form of Self-Love

Shift your perspective to view exercise as one thing you do to be good to yourself. It removes barriers you might have about working out. You may find it extremely valuable to engage in some cognitive therapy to banish those negative body-image thoughts as you hit the track. No one finds pleasure in working out if they are constantly berating themselves for their less-than-perfect thighs.

Speaking of tracks, it is important that you choose forms of exercise or sports that are pleasurable to you. Don't allow well-meaning friends to railroad you into a form of movement that feels foreign to your body. We each have a unique feel for how our bodies most want to move and flow.

Consider skating, sailing, t'ai chi. Walk a dog. Take up ballroom dancing. Roughhouse with the neighborhood kids. Jump rope. Take a spinning class by the lake.

And as you move, so too will your physical and emotional chemistry. Exercise not only promotes the release of endorphins in your body, which lifts your moods, but like yoga, meditation, and service, it keeps your mind off your problems. "For faster, symptomatic treatment of depression I know no better method than aerobic exercise in the usual amount: thirty minutes of continuous activity at least five days a week," advises Dr. Andrew Weil in *Natural Health: Natural Medicine*.

Working Out Builds Confidence

Another benefit is the sense of empowerment and mastery you will feel, says Harriet Braiker. "Mastery—a sense of accomplishment and special skill attainment—and pleasure are psychological states that are incompatible with depression."

You might want to try in-line skating, skiing, racquetball, sailing, or tennis. The novelty of trying something new alone lifts your moods by shifting your energy as you attempt a new experience.

Start out small. Be patient with yourself. Break down your resistance to exercise, one step at a time, advises Ellen McGrath, author of *When Feeling Bad Is Good.* She also suggests you reward yourself when you do so.

One of the best ways to get motivated to exercise and eat healthier is to pamper yourself with a health spa getaway, McGrath says. "That's how I finally started exercising regularly after avoiding it most of my adult life. . . . It can dramatically change how you treat yourself, both physically and emotionally, when you come home."

A large and growing body of research supports your exercise program. Exercise is one of the most powerful antidepressants you can find. And the anecdotal evidence is all around you. It raises the levels of endorphins, chemicals in the body that shape our moods, making us feel happy, relaxed, and energetic. Holistic doctors also believe that exercise helps release toxins from the body.

Research on Exercise Convincing

The following research supports working out as you try to banish your depression:

- A series of studies led by psychiatrist John Griest at the University of Wisconsin showed that exercise can be as helpful as psychotherapy in the treatment of mild depression.

- A study in the January 1997 issue of the *Journal of Gerontology* showed that in a group of thirty-two depressed people, 60 to 84 years old, those who exercised the most and the hardest showed the most improvement in mood.
- A study at Tufts University found that subjects who were depressed improved their moods by strength training, and slept better, as well.

Exercise is also one of the best ways to lower your anxiety. In a study of ten thousand students at the University of Virginia in Charlottesville, researchers found that even moderate regular exercise reduced anxiety.

Tipper Gore discovered exercise's ability to loosen the grip of depression about ten years ago. Her son, Albert, then six, was hit by a car. His internal injuries were life-threatening, and it took two long years for him to get well.

In the wake of his recovery, Tipper found herself twenty-five pounds heavier—and weighed down with a sadness that she just couldn't shake.

Among other steps, she and the Gore family got psychological counseling, which she highly praises. Tipper also started exercising. Today, six days a week, she spends an hour running, biking, or in-line skating.

"Sometimes when I don't really feel like it, I do it because this is an investment in a bank, and I'll be able to withdraw it when I've seventy-five or eighty and I don't have osteoporosis."

Exercise simply helps put things in perspective, insists Helen Gurley Brown, former *Cosmopolitan* editor-in-chief. "I think exercise is the most important thing for a happier, healthier life. Exercise gets rid of cobwebs in the brain every morning.

"If you wake up slightly melancholy or depressed or worried or anxious, you don't have to be fabulous, an athlete, graceful or beautiful or young. Exercise belongs to you, and you should just do it!"

Brown is 75 and says she hasn't missed a day at the magazine for years.

Main Messages

- Are you getting enough exercise? Exercise is one of the surest ways to banish depression.
- Begin slowly. Examine what type of exercise is most enjoyable and comfortable.
- Remove any barriers you have to working out. View exercise as a form of self-care, a way to be good to yourself.
- Try alternative forms of exercise, from t'ai chi to kickboxing or spinning. Maybe roller-skating will rev you up.
- Bask in the confidence and pride you have after you work out.
- Reward yourself when you do work out. Maybe even try for a spa getaway.
- Mounting scientific evidence attests to the ability of exercise to lift your mood.

FIFTEEN

Herbs and Homeopathy

Some of the biggest buzz in depression treatment has centered on a colorful plant with a florid folk history: St. John's wort. In recent years this herb has been touted for its healing abilities in venues from talk shows to women's magazines. The media hype and rush to buy St. John's wort's may be new, but its healing prowess is anything but.

The long history of folk use of both herbs and homeopathy for depression lends great credence to their healing. Long before depression was identified as an illness by traditional Western doctors, we find evidence that St. John's wort—wort being the Middle English word for "plant"—was successfully treating the symptoms of depression, from extreme melancholy to "nerves" to insomnia.

"Its virtue cannot be described; how great it is and how great are its uses. And in all formulas there is no medicament that is so good and without detriment, without hazard as the healer St. Johnswort . . . its virtue shames all formulas and doctors, they may cry as they may," attested Paracelsus, a German-Swiss alchemist and physician who lived from 1493–1541.

An Ancient Herb

The plant was named for John the Baptist; by medieval times people believed that if you slept with a sprig of St. John's wort under your pillow on St. John's Eve—the night before St. John's Tide—"the Saint would appear in a dream, give his blessing, and prevent one from dying during the following year."

The petals and leaves of St. John's wort, covered with small black translucent dots, produce a deep red oil when they are rubbed. In the early days of Christianity, this crimson-colored oil was believed by many to symbolize the spilled blood of the first-century martyr St. John the Baptist, who was beheaded.

Many thought the distinctive yellow-colored flowers of St. John's wort may have signified healing spiritual light.

But it has taken hundreds of years for St. John's wort to be recognized by Western medicine as an effective antidepressant. European doctors have prescribed it for depression for about twenty years.

For thirty years, it has been the subject of intense scientific scrutiny, as confirmed by hundreds of major studies. Among those most cited is one done in 1996 by researchers at the Audie Murphy Veterans Hospital in San Antonio, Texas, and by colleagues in Germany.

The researchers, who published their findings in the *British Medical Journal*, combined twenty-three studies of St. John's wort involving 1,751 participants. Among those who took the placebo, 22 percent reported mood elevation. Among those who used St. John's wort, 55 percent said their moods were elevated, which was similar to that experienced from pharmaceutical antidepressants.

Effective for Mild–Moderate Depression

As St. John's wort, or hypericum, bounces off the grocery store shelves, researchers are stepping up the pace of research on the herb. So far its effectiveness has been documented in more than five thousand patients in more than twenty-five clinical trials. The results showed that hypericum is an effective antidepressant for mild to moderate depression.

Pharmacologists are still at a loss to explain how St. John's wort works. They assume that the herb slows the breakdown of the brain chemical serotonin. And in a few experiments the herb has shown broader activity, also altering the concentrations of other neurotransmitters like dopamine and norepinephrine, says Dr. Steven Bratman, author of *Beat Depression with St. John's Wort*.

Gingko is another herb gaining attention for its promise in treating depression. Gingko improves blood flow through the brain and also appears to normalize neurotransmitter levels. In one study, European researchers recruited forty elderly individuals who had both depression and poor cerebral blood flow. After these people took 80 milligrams of gingko extract three times a day for a few months, their depression lifted.

Never Mix Herbals with Antidepressants

If you plan to try herbal therapy, as with all the therapies shared in this book, do so only with a doctor's guidance. Do not mix St. John's wort with any kind of prescription antidepressant, particularly one of the selective serotonin reuptake inhibitors, such as Prozac. The results can be extremely dangerous. A potentially serious drug interaction called serotonin syndrome may occur if you do, says Dr. Alan Pressman, author with Nancy Burke of *St. John's Wort: The Miracle Medicine*.

Dr. Pressman also strongly advises not taking St. John's wort for bipolar disorder (manic depression) or severe depression that involves suicidal thoughts. At this time, hypericum is only indicated for mild to moderate depression and for seasonal affective disorder, he cautions.

"Although some recent research suggests that higher daily doses of hypericum (1,800 milligrams or more per day) may be effective in treating more severe depressions, significantly more research is needed to justify those claims."

Dr. Pressman also advises not using hypericum if you are pregnant or nursing or have a substance abuse problem.

The usual dose of St. John's wort in liquid extract is one-quarter teaspoon three times a day, for a total three-quarters teaspoon, in distilled water, with meals. Or in tablet or capsule form, 300 milligrams three times a day, with meals, for a total of 900 milligrams daily.

No Immediate Impacts

You also should be aware that herbal treatment won't have immediate effects, cautions Dr. Bratman. One of his patients, Laura, was a 43-year-old mother of three who was plagued by depression her whole life. "The cause was undoubtedly the shaming and verbal abuse that she experienced throughout her upbringing, but even after years of effective psychotherapy, her symptoms of depression lingered like a habit she couldn't break."

Laura had tried a series of antidepressants, but experienced symptoms ranging from headaches and anxiety to insomnia and nightmares when she did sleep. Dr. Bratman started Laura on a course of St. John's wort and told her she might interpret its gentleness as ineffectiveness. After about a week, Laura reported, "It's not doing anything. I'm back to my same old drudge of a self."

After two more weeks, she was ready to quit and go back to antidepressants. But Dr. Bratman, who noticed that Laura didn't appear so depressed, urged her to continue with St. John's wort.

It wasn't until the sixth week on St. John's wort that Laura noticed the change herself. "It suddenly dawned on me the other day that I don't feel so empty."

By the eight week, she reported, "I feel like a human being when I get up in the morning. I have enough energy to enjoy myself. I'm not just getting by; I feel like I'm starting to live."

Like many of the remedies in this book, St. John's wort, used by itself, is not an effective treatment for severe depression. But for adults with mild to moderate depression, the herb has great potential.

Try a Variety of Calming Herbs

If anxiety and irritability also accompany your depression, many calming herbs are available. Naturopathic

physician Mary Bove, a former director of the botanical
medicine department at Bastyr University in Seattle, recommends a calming tea made from a blend of lavender,
oats, linden flower, catnip, and lemon balm. During the
deep days of winter, you can enliven your tea with a little
cinnamon, a couple of cloves, and a pinch of coriander.

For an herbal bath, Bove suggests steeping four table-
spoons of dried herbs, choosing any blends of lavender,
catnip, oats, linden flower, and lemon balm in a quart of
hot water for twenty minutes. You then strain the liquid
and add the tea to your bathwater.

Wonders of Homeopathy

Homeopathy, too, is a powerful treatment for depression,
say homeopathic doctors. One thing that is different
about homeopathy is that it treats the patient, not the
disease. So there is no single homeopathic remedy used
to treat depression. Ten different people with depression
may need ten different homeopathic treatments.

For every imaginable state, from melancholy to intense terror, there is one homeopathic medicine that best
matches that state. Consider that for new mothers suffering from postpartum depression alone, there are at least
twenty-five possible homeopathic remedies, says Dr.
Gregory White, a Colorado homeopathic doctor and chiro-
practor. Homeopathic remedies come from natural substances from all over the world, from table salt to
tarantula.

A homeopathic doctor will prescribe a highly individual homeopathic remedy only after looking deeply at an
individual's life and history to determine the root of his
or her depression, says White. He analyzes factors rang-

ing from patients' childhood temperaments, phobias, and injuries, to their current relationships, dreams, food preferences, and skin tone.

"It's like taking human nature and putting it under a 10,000 power microscope to intimately become involved in the lives and affairs of your patients."

Sometimes White discovers that patients are depressed because they have let loss or trauma fester for decades. "After practicing homeopathy for twenty years, I am still in awe of the human body. I often, for the first time, tap into constrictions that people have stored within their flesh for years."

One patient broke into tears and cried deeply about how sad she was about her divorce. "The divorce took place twenty years ago," says White incredulously.

He has found homeopathy extremely effective in treating deep-seated depression. A business executive, Jack, came to White complaining of extreme fatigue and depression. "He was depressed because he didn't have enough energy to get his work done."

White first treated Jack with Sulfur and later Aurum Metallicum. The latter remedy is ideally suited to treat people who are very idealistic and have high standards. If they fail to achieve their goals, suffer bereavement, or are disappointed in love, they may react first with anger and then plunge into deep depression.

As White got to know Jack, he discovered he suffered deeply from a loss of self-esteem. When those and other feelings were uncovered and treated, Jack became angry and irritable. "When you disturb calmer water on top of the pool, other things rise back to the surface," says White, who then prescribed a remedy known as Anacardium. Jack's moods and low self-esteem rose significantly.

White also has much experience with a remedy known as Sepia. This remedy is very useful to those who have become indifferent to their family but dread being alone. They cry when talking about their illness, are easily offended, and are mentally and physically exhausted.

Again, as with herbal therapy, consult with an experienced homeopathic doctor if you want to try homeopathy. Your history will be carefully examined and only then can a definitive remedy be prescribed. Homeopathic remedies come in pellets, tablets, and liquid form.

Main Messages

- References to the effectiveness of St. John's wort go back to at least the fourteenth century.
- Over the last thirty years, hundreds of new studies confirm the effectiveness of St. John's wort as an antidepressant.
- Though researchers still don't know exactly how the herb works, they believe it slows the breakdown of the neurotransmitter serotonin.
- If you choose to try St. John's wort, do so only with a doctor's guidance.
- St. John's wort is advised only for mild to moderate depression.
- It should never be taken if you are already using traditional antidepressant medication. Mixing the two is extremely dangerous.
- It may take up to six weeks or longer to feel the effects of St. John's wort.

SIXTEEN

Let There Be Light

"Live in rooms full of light," advised A. Cornelius Celsus in the first century A.D. in his "Advice to Melancholics." With good reason. Without good quality light, either full-spectrum artificial lights or natural sunlight, we naturally become depressed. Our beings crave light. "The sky is the daily bread of the eyes," said Ralph Waldo Emerson.

Our need for light is that simple, but, for many, difficult to get. As we spend the majority of our time indoors, we are out of our evolutionary synch with the rhythms of nature. Dr. Thomas Wehr of the National Institute of Mental Health calls this "a massive uncontrolled experiment." One fallout of this experiment: Many of us aren't absorbing enough sunlight to keep our beings in balance.

About 10 million people may suffer from seasonal affective disorder, estimates the National Institute of Mental Health, especially those who live in geographic areas with fewer sunny days. Women appear to make up 75 percent of those with SAD.

SAD, which the medical community now recognizes as a real illness, disrupts personal relationships, causes people to overeat, gain weight, and to become indifferent toward their jobs, says Dr. Norman E. Rosenthal, a psychiatrist with the NIMH. "It is speculated that female reproductive hormones somehow sensitize the brain to the effects of light deprivation," says Rosenthal. He is the author of *Winter Blues*.

Other studies suggest that dimmed natural light plays havoc with the production of serotonin and a hormone called melatonin.

Do you become moodier, more depressed and lethargic in the winter? Do you crave carbohydrates and sweets more during winter months? Sleep much more—maybe even up to four hours more each night? You may suffer from seasonal affective disorder.

Try exposing yourself to more outdoor light, even for as much as fifteen minutes each day. That amount of light alone can help regulate the levels of melatonin and serotonin in your brain, which elevate your moods and curb insomnia. If you can't do so, resort to artificial light. Purchase a SAD light for indoor light therapy.

Artificial Lights Bring Relief

You can find tabletop units or visors that project light directly into your eyes. For a normal light-therapy treatment, you sit about two feet in front of a 10,000-lux SAD light for thirty minutes. Lux is the term used to measure the intensity of illumination; normal indoor light is 500 to 1,000 lux.

Researchers who have used the 10,000-lux protocol for thirty minutes say 60 to 80 percent of their patients show improvements in their SAD symptoms.

You can rest, read or watch TV, but it's best if the angle between your eyes and the light is as close to 90 degrees as possible.

But most doctors recommend you begin slowly with only twenty to forty minutes of no more than 5,000 lux until your eyes become accustomed to the light. Some of the SAD lights are extremely bright, so it's wise to shop for one with less glare.

If you have a hard time waking up in the morning, you may want a device that produces a gradual increase in the intensity of light, called a dawn simulator. "It can be used to wake you in the morning—a sort of light-alarm clock. It appears to offer all the benefits of real sunshine," says Dr. Jonathan Zuess.

Dawn simulators are rheostat timers that used with a bedside lamp. They gradually turn on the lamp before dawn to expose you to more light as you sleep.

Drs. Michael Norden and David Avery and colleagues at the University of Washington conducted the first controlled trials of dawn simulation and found it to be very effective in treating winter depression. In 1993, they published a study of dawn simulation in people who weren't depressed but complained about how they functioned in the winter.

Those studied improved after the first night. "On average, subjects reported cutting their energy and mood deficits by about half when using natural dawn simulation. The needed 'time to get out of bed' dropped from 25 minutes to 10 minutes, and the time to reach a reasonable level of alertness was cut by more than half."

Depending on the severity and form of your SAD, you

may need to use both a tabletop light or visor during the day, and a dawn simulator. Again, as with all the therapies in this book, work with a qualified health-care professional in choosing the right light protocol. It is possible to get too much artificial light exposure, which can cause irritability, agitation and fatigue. Your doctor can help you cut down on your exposure time if those symptoms appear.

Light visors, tabletop light units, and dawn simulators can be purchased from a growing number of companies around the world. A good light box can be anywhere from $250 to $500.

Two suppliers Dr. Zuess recommends are: Bio-Brite, Inc., a Bethesda, Maryland, company. Their number is 1-800-621-5483 or 1-301-961-8557; or The Sun Box Co., a Gaithersburg, Maryland, firm at 1-800-548-3968 or 301-869-5980.

Dr. Zuess says sitting in a sunroom in your work or home also may prove as effective.

Research Results

Since the early 1980s, many research studies have confirmed the benefit of light therapy. It is also effective for women with premenstrual syndrome (PMS). Using light therapy, women treated for PMS reported less depression, less moodiness, better sleep, improved concentration, and less craving for sweets and carbohydrates.

In a different twist, Dr. Joachim Fisch and his colleagues in Germany also wondered if light therapy would enhance the response of depressed patients to treatment with St. John's wort.

They divided forty depressed patients whose mood

changes weren't specifically related to the changing seasons into two groups of twenty each. Both groups received standard doses of hypericum—900 milligrams each day. For two hours each day, one group was exposed to bright environmental light, the other to dim environmental light.

The "bright light group" showed superior antidepressant effects after two and four weeks of treatment. After six weeks, however, both groups fared about the same. The researchers concluded that light therapy may speed up the antidepressant response to hypericum, which again lends credence to the idea of trying a spectrum of treatments to alleviate your depression.

Dr. Jacob Liberman, author of *Light: Medicine of the Future,* has pioneered some of the most sweeping research on the power of light. In trace amounts light is "a life-supporting nutrient," he says. Make sure that your life is supported by enough of this natural nutrient.

Main Messages

- About 10 million of us suffer from seasonal affective disorder, especially those who live in areas with less sunshine.
- Try getting more outdoor light, even as little as fifteen minutes a day.
- Experiment with some of the new artificial lighting. Work with a light therapist or trained practitioner to determine the proper protocol.
- Most doctors recommend you begin slowly with only twenty to forty minutes of no more than 5,000 lux until your eyes become adjusted to the light.
- In addition to overhead lights, SAD tabletop lights or visors are also available.

SEVENTEEN

Rediscovering the Power of Passion

Eleanor Roosevelt so loved people that she couldn't help reaching out to others, even complete strangers. Days after Eleanor died, a woman received a $10 check from her. It was one of the usual birthday checks Mrs. Roosevelt had been sending the child for years. The woman was the daughter of a hitchhiker Mrs. Roosevelt had once picked up.

Serving others was clearly a passion of Eleanor Roosevelt. What are you passionate about? What makes your heart sing, your spirit dance? Do you have a sense of your destiny on this earth? What particular gift did you come to earth to share?

Answering all these questions about your purpose for living are key to unlocking any blocks in your energy that may contribute to your depression.

Passion Is Key to Well-Being

The idea that we become ill if we suppress our life force, passions, and inner drive is an ancient one. As early as the Gnostic gospels, Thomas wrote, "If you bring forth what is within you, what you bring forth will save you. If you do not bring forth what is within you, what you do not bring forth will destroy you."

Later on, in Proverbs it is written: "Where there is no vision, we perish."

The dancer Martha Graham described this vision, this inner passion as "a vitality, a life force, a quickening that is translated through you into action, and because there is only one you in all time, this expression is unique. "

If we block or suppress our passions, Graham said, that passion will be lost to the world. "It is not your business to determine how good it is; nor how valuable it is; nor how it compares with other expressions. It is your business to keep it yours, clearly and directly, to keep the channel open."

How do we keep the channel open, the zest for life alive? How do we translate our inner motivations into outer actions? Finding the answer to this question is key for all of us. It is critical to our well-being.

"Our bodies are designed to function best when we're involved in activities and work that feel exactly right to us. Our health is enhanced when we engage in deeply creative work that is satisfying to us—not just because it pleases our boss, husband, or mother," says Dr. Chris Northrup.

"One reason why depression might be higher these days is many people are not focused on what they want to experience in the world—but on what those around them require and expect of them," says Dr. Mona Lisa

Schultz. "They have become detached or unbonded from the things they want to do in the world that feed their heart. So they become depressed, dispassionate."

Dispassionate: To be without passion. If we fail to express our inner power, energy and passion, we oppress our inner essence. "If this essential core of the person is denied or suppressed, he gets sick sometimes in obvious ways, sometimes in subtle ways, sometimes immediately, sometimes later," explained Abraham Maslow.

The key, says Schultz, is to do something in the world that makes you feel you are having an impact, something that "makes you feel you have potency and power."

But living your passion may require immense courage. It requires that you, and you alone, shape a life that fits you. You listen to your inner voice and create an outer life that fits your inner drive—despite the skeptics around you.

Don't expect a cheering section to manifest with well wishes. Be prepared that just the opposite may happen. When 21-year-old Mary Cassatt told her father she was going to Paris to become an artist, the Philadelphia businessman replied, "I would rather see you dead."

Examine Your Heart

Fortunately the now-renowned painter, who allayed herself with Impressionist Edgar Degas, followed her heart anyway. Search your own heart. What were you put on this earth to do? Are you doing it? If not, why not? What would your life be like if you weren't governed, dominated even, by the fear of what others think of you, or worse yet, your own fear?

What passions would you pursue if you truly broke

down the wall of self-doubts, family, and friends who say, "Who do you think you are? What are your chances for real success? How can you possibly do THAT when you can make so much more money elsewhere? Have you lost your mind?"

Dr. Elisabeth Kübler-Ross dealt with the derision of her colleagues when she broke new ground in her exploration of unconditional love for the terminally ill. Kübler-Ross had to proceed with her work despite her colleagues' ridicule when they judged her work a waste of time.

But Kübler-Ross persevered and is now an internationally acclaimed expert on living fully and on transition to the afterlife. "We've each picked our destiny before we were born. And if you can get in touch with that, it is an incredible feeling," Kübler-Ross told me for my book *Embracing Our Essence: Spiritual Conversations with Prominent Women.* "God put you here for a reason."

What Is Your Reason for Being Here?

What is your purpose? You've got to heed it and hew to your passions. That is exactly what Dr. Mona Lisa Schultz had to do when she was in medical school. People urged her to get her Ph.D. in biochemistry because that's where the money was. "But I wanted to study the brain and how emotions and behavior are interrelated. That is what I am here on earth to do."

So Schultz went to a neuroanatomy department with no money and the voices of dissension around her got shriller. "They said, 'This will be no good. You will never use this work.'

"But I said, 'If I go into biochemistry, one day I will get sad, depressed, and die. I just knew it. From my perspective, I was uncomfortable with the money, but I was in bliss with my study. I went with the bliss with some momentary monetary discomfort. How many people are doing that today? Their pain is associated with their wallet and their bliss. They are more likely to stay in a job that gives them money but no bliss."

Schultz remembers a client, Mary, who worked for an insurance company. She hated her job intensely, had chronic fatigue syndrome, and was seriously depressed. "But she wanted to stay in her job because it paid for her psychotherapy. It paid to treat the very illness she knew her job was creating."

One day, Mary walked out of her job and was hit by a car in the parking lot. She got fired and was left with no job—only her depression remained. "She should have left her job. Her depression was part of her intuitive warning system telling her this is not an area of growth for you. Even plants know to grow in the direction of the light and not into the darkness."

Finding Soulful Work

Unless we apply our energy, our life force toward creative, meaningful work, whether caring for children, creating art or a product, or restoring a natural habitat, we become impotent, stagnant, and depressed. Dr. Andrew Weil sees depression as a "state of high potential energy wound up and turned inward on itself." If that energy can be accessed and moved, it can be a catalyst for spontaneous healing.

A soulful, effective treatment for depression, then, is work. But it must be work you feel has an impact, work you feel you are meant to do, work that calls to something deep inside you. It might mean changing jobs, reinfusing your work with new meaning, or trying something new within the context of your present career.

That's what happened to Julia Cameron, the internationally acclaimed author of the best-selling *Artist's Way* and its sequel, *A Vein of Gold*. But even after helping millions of readers and workshop attendees discover their heart's desire and latent creativity, Cameron came to see something still tugged at her own.

"It was my buried dream to be musical." But Julia had always been told she had no musical ability. Meanwhile, her two brothers and sister were viewed as the musically talented ones. But one day Julia heard the message in her head, "Wouldn't it be fun to write a musical about Mervyn?"

Cameron's immediate thought was "Sure, if I was musical."

But despite her disbelief, something made her go to England. But the denial continued. She thought she was actually being guided there to date a man she knew. But when she arrived, she found he'd left the country.

Still thinking logically, she concluded, "In my persona as St. Julia of the Artist's Way, I'm here to spread the word. The *Artist's Way* has come to Britain. Isn't this good? Now we'll save them." But then the magic began. "The minute I landed in London, it was as if sheet music was in the air." Cameron stayed in England and wrote heartfelt, stirring, passionate music that later became the musical *Avalon*.

Stepping into the Unknown

As Cameron's story illustrates, following your passion means honing your ability to heed your inner voice, your intuition, your soul, whatever you wish to call your inner guidance system. Living with greater passion may mean change. It may require that you reinfuse your existing work with new meaning. And it may demand you leave your safe haven for unknown, even scary territory.

It may mean stepping away from everything you know now so passion can again well to the surface of your consciousness. This is precisely what Dr. Linda Peeno had to do.

Attracted by predictable hours and a great salary, Peeno became an HMO executive. In her new position, she got to approve or reject requests for care. She often found herself torn by the tension of having to choose between protecting her HMO's financial bottom line and compassionate care for patients.

"I'd begun to feel we were part of some psychology experiment designed to see how quickly we could abandon our humanity."

The turning point for Linda came when a patient, Elizabeth, requested HMO coverage for a computer voice program so she could communicate. The young woman had suffered a rare brain-stem stroke, which shut down the pipeline through which the nerve impulses controlling her voice travel.

Linda's colleagues, some of whom felt she wasn't tough enough, cautioned her not to approve the expense. One colleague warned, "Approve this and it will be your last!"

It was for Linda. She listened to her heart and intuition and left the HMO position—but not before she approved the computer program so Elizabeth could find her own voice again.

When the faxes are quiet, when the phones are still, when the dishes done and the kids in bed, what does your inner voice still call to you? What still whispers to your soul?

Main Messages

- We become ill if we suppress our life force. Examine whether you are following your true passion. If not, you set up conflict and space for depression in your being.

- You must translate your inner motivations and desires into outer actions. Our bodies function best when we are involved in activities and work that feel exactly right to us.

- Do something in your life that makes you feel you have an impact.

- Be prepared that you may get opposition, even derision, from those around you.

- Do you know your purpose for being here? Try to get in touch with your reason for being.

- Find soulful work that allows you to use your energy to the fullest. Suppressed energy lead to stagnancy and depression.

- Following your passion and purpose may be scary. It may mean stepping away from the life you've led so far.

- Above all, listen to your own heart. What still whispers to your soul?

EIGHTEEN

Seeking Spiritual Sustenance

The capacity of the human spirit to rise above adversity has been chronicled throughout history. But when you are depressed you often lose sight of this internal, sacred power. You may see absolutely no meaning or significance to your life and likely feel cut off from a divine force, a nurturing Creator, a loving God.

Seriously depressed, you might even feel beyond help from a sacred source. In such a spiritual void, alienation and depression begin to spiral. "I have myself an inner weight of woe that God himself can scarcely bear," said the poet Theodore Roethke.

French composer Hector Berlioz wrote that his depression created an unbearable longing and the "dreadful sense of being alone in an empty universe." Writer Victor Hugo said his soul "maintains its deathly sleep."

In these haunting words, you feel the palpable disconnection from spirit. Learning how to connect with and be supported by spiritual guidance, whether through prayer, meditation, visualization, or other means, is vital to creating new health.

Put Faith in Something More

Faith in a power of yourself, yet greater than yourself, provides deeper healing than many of the strategies you've read about in this book. "We live at the edge of the miraculous," the playwright Henry Miller once wrote. Being able to see the everyday miracles and being open to grace and awe can heal powerfully.

Seeking support from the Divine, and from your angels and spiritual guides, is as powerful as it gets. "When we invite the sacred into our lives by sincerely asking our inner wisdom, or higher power, or God for guidance in our lives, we're invoking great power. This can't be taken lightly," says Chris Northrup.

Immense power, indeed. The evidence of a connection between prayer and healing, for instance, is mounting. In *Healing Words,* Dr. Larry Dossey explores the healing power of prayer. He points out that research by the Spindrift organization in Salem, Oregon, shows that "nondirected prayer" is especially helpful.

In other words, instead of praying in a direct manner— "Get rid of this depression"—consider praying in a nondirect manner—"Thy will be done," or "May I realize the best outcome for the greatest good."

Jeffrey S. Levin, Ph.D., associate professor of family and community medicine at Eastern Virginia Medical School, found more than 250 published empirical studies in the medical literature since the nineteenth century that examine the link between spiritual practices and positive health outcomes.

More than two dozen studies show the health benefits of simply attending church or synagogue on a regular basis, Dossey says.

Spiritual faith clearly has proven to improve our mental health, say National Institutes of Health physician-researchers David B. Larson and Susan S. Larson. They looked at twelve years of the *American Journal of Psychiatry* and *Archives of General Psychiatry* and found that "when measuring participation in religious ceremony, social support, prayer, and relationship with God, 92 percent of the studies showed benefit for mental health," says Dr. Dossey.

Praying and meditating are just some forms of spiritual practice. Just being grateful each day for the cereal in your cupboard, the warmth from your furnace, or the Canadian geese flying overhead is another spiritual discipline. Many people say they most feel a transcendent connection with God when they are in nature.

The Spiritual Path Is Highly Individual

The forms of spiritual expression are as varied as people themselves, I found when I interviewed twenty-nine high-profile women such as Dr. Elisabeth Kübler-Ross, Naomi Judd, Jane Goodall, and Betty Ford about their spiritual beliefs and practices in my book *Embracing Our Essence: Spiritual Conversations with Prominent Women*. The ways in which these women received divine comfort and communion were extremely individual, I discovered. "This morning I woke up at 2 a.m. because we were having a blizzard and it was really beautiful. I spent two hours looking out the window, and that was my prayer," said author Alexandra Stoddard.

"Living a more spiritual life can be as simple—yet as rich—as joining together more often for good food, conversation and fun," observed author Madeline l'Engle.

Not surprisingly, Jane Goodall said, "Nature for me is the most powerful medium for experiencing spiritual power. Or when I go into an old cathedral where I can feel a sense of the past that will continue into the future."

It doesn't matter how you find your connection to the Source. If you've found it difficult, even painful, to seek connection with a traditional God, you may find it more comforting to think of embracing a loving, luminous light.

Working with the Light

"Through time, light is a concept that has infused religious, spiritual, philosophical, and even scientific beliefs, from ancient civilizations to advanced quantum physics," say Dr. Harold Bloomfield and Peter McWilliams, authors of *How to Heal Depression.*

If you regard light as "the invisible message of goodness from the Divine," you can close your eyes and visualize yourself surrounded, filled, and healed by divine light. Ask that the light be used "for the highest good of all concerned," advises Dr. Bloomfield.

"As depression is so often associated with darkness, asking those dark parts of your life—both inside and outside yourself—to be filled with light can be profoundly uplifting," writes Dr. Bloomfield.

If you do find solace in prayer, there are limitless prayers and affirmations to bolster your spirit as you heal from depression. Some powerful prayers for healing are found in Marianne Williamson's *Illuminata*. Williamson's Prayers for Healing include the following: "Dear God: My body is sick and I am so scared, so weak, so sad. Please heal me, Lord. . . . Please give me a miracle. Please give me hope. Please give me peace. Lift me up beyond the regions of my pain and despair. Prepare each cell to be born anew into health and happiness, peace and love."

Having faith in something greater than yourself also boosts your faith in yourself and your ability to weather tough times. Spiritual self-confidence gives you a hardiness, an inner knowing that you can deal with whatever life hands you. You can learn to stand firm even as the rug is pulled out from under you.

When you look at life through the window of your soul, you also begin to more fully see—and know deep to your marrow—your true preciousness. You begin to see your inner beauty and how important you are to the Creator.

Finding Meaning in Suffering

You may, hopefully, begin to see your depression not as a curse, but as part of a higher plan, a grander design for your growth here on earth. Maybe not immediately, but gradually. It's too much to expect that we make these huge leaps when we are often still stumbling through the raw pain of depression.

But if realized, these are all-powerful knowings that can banish the sense of worthlessness and loneliness that depression brings.

Strengthening your spiritual core will also bring profound insights into your depression, many people have said. If you look on yourself with the eyes of Spirit, you will come to see that everything happens for a reason.

If you have judged your depression as a personal weakness or problem to be quickly scoured away, like an unsightly stain, spiritual confidence allows you to view life with a sense of divine order. If everything unfolds as it's meant to for our learning, our depression takes on a new, deeper hue. It allows us to more fully see the meaning in our lives and the lessons to be learned.

That is what happened to Catherine Carrigan, who wrote about her struggle with depression in *Healing Depression.* "Although philosophers have debated for aeons why suffering exists in the world, I choose to believe that everything exists and everything happens for the total benefit of our spirits."

After years of suffering and treatment, which ranged from an intensive nutritional overhaul to a complete medical workup, Carrigan came to see her depression as a wise, spiritual teacher, a messenger to bring greater meaning to her life.

"I came to believe that all healing begins or ends with healing the spirit and that the real path of spiritual healing of depression in particular is indeed a journey."

Catherine came to believe that the more she understood the lessons her depression had to teach her, the less she would suffer. The more she accepted herself and saw the meaning of her depression, the more quickly she adapted and her pain diminished and even disappeared.

Her depression eventually helped Catherine develop greater confidence in herself, in her writing and in a world she once viewed as frightening and hostile. She also made a breakthrough epiphany when she saw that for thirty-six years she had been waiting for everyone else around her to change so she could finally be happy.

"I learned that by healing myself I could heal everyone around me. It's funny—as soon as I realized these lessons, my severe depression was ready to slip away."

We are all spiritual beings having a human experience. And when that experience includes despair and depression, spiritual support is critical. It doesn't matter whether you believe in the Goddess or God, the Source or the Creator, or "the Love that Loved us into Existence," as St. Augustine called the Divine. What matters is that you surrender your pain and ask for healing love and support from a greater power. What matters is that you ask the light to surround you, fill you, and banish your darkness. "Sadness flies on the wings of the morning and out of the heat of darkness comes the light," wrote Jean Giraudoux.

Main Messages

- Connecting with the Divine, Spirit, God, Creator, or whatever you wish to call it is key to your well-being.
- Seeking support from the spiritual realm is as powerful as it gets.
- Practice non-directed prayer, such as "May I realize the best outcome for the greatest good."
- Seek a direct connection with the Divine in nature and in moments of gratitude.
- Work with light, visualize yourself surrounded by light, to ease your depression.
- Develop greater inner faith so you will have more outer resilience in tough times.
- See the spiritual dimension of your illness. What meaning might be buried in your depression? What is your Spirit leading you to find?

NINETEEN

Embracing the Natural World

Most of us spend 90 percent of our lives in artificial settings, in our homes and offices. When was the last time your fingers caressed the bark of a tree, you watched clouds skitter across the sky, or the melody of a mountain stream cleansed your thoughts?

Nature is the great healer, but we have become sadly alienated from the natural world compared to our ancestors, many of whom lived on the land, bathed in clear, pure streams, gathered at the full moons, and celebrated the seasons. Until recent centuries, we knew, deep in our marrow, how potent the healing nature of the natural world could be.

"We find nature to be the circumstance which dwarfs every other circumstance. . . . These enchantments are medicinal, they sober and heal us," wrote Ralph Waldo Emerson.

Disconnection Leads to Despair

But now we are sadly and seriously disconnected from the earth, which can't help but upset our entire being. "We are bombarded by signals of distress—ecological destruction, social breakdown, and uncontrolled nuclear proliferation. Not surprisingly, we are feeling despair," says Joanna Macy, Buddhist scholar and author of *World as Lover, World as Self.*

"Our society at times severs us from the source of our own life forces," adds Dr. Jonathan Zuess, author of *The Wisdom of Depression.* "I believe that this sort of alienation from the natural world places us at risk emotionally; through the loss of a sense of groundedness and belonging in the world."

This idea that separation from the earth would cost us dearly is nothing new. Ancient mystics, such as Hildegard of Bingen, warned us not to disrespect the earth centuries ago.

In the 1950s, scientist and ecologist Rachel Carson lamented, "Whenever we destroy beauty, or whenever we substitute something man-made and artificial for a natural feature of the earth, we have retarded some part of man's spiritual growth." Now many wonder if we aren't impacting our physical and emotional growth, as well.

It's common sense that even if we have distanced ourselves from the natural world by spending more time online than in nature, our bodies and spirits still long for a deep spiritual and physical bond with the earth. Our being is distressed and depressed by the separation we've imposed.

So how much of our depression and despair comes from the fact that we have denied this bond—and destroyed much of our earthly womb? How much of our despair arises because we are haunted by the memory of and yearning to deeply live in the earth—not just on it like a disconnected interloper?

"As we've destroyed much of the natural world to create a so-called better standard of living we've lost sight of a very important truth," says Joan Borysenko. "We didn't realize how much diversity contributes to the standard of living."

Borysenko and her husband Kurt Kaltreider have studied the research of another environmental prophet, biologist Rene Dubos. Dubos wondered how much our changes to our own ecology, our own nest, have, in turn, caused chemical changes in our bodies, possibly leading to depression. Dubos maintained that human beings essentially evolved in the planet in response to the existing light, chemicals, and biostructure.

Earthly Mutants

"But now we have changed everything on the planet, from the amount of daylight to the amount of chemicals we are exposed to," observes Borysenko. "We are no longer native to this planet. We have become mutants, aliens, and if you think about it in that way, then maybe our brain chemicals won't work the way they did before. If we are alien to the way we evolved, that alone creates a sense of isolation and separation and despair."

As Dr. Michael Norden, author of *Beyond Prozac*, observes, "Our world is a stranger to the one from and for which we evolved. We are not quite fish out of water, perhaps, but certainly fish in a strange aquarium."

So if this is true, how do we rectify it? How do we

again immerse ourselves more in the healing waters of nature?

As in becoming more conscious about any sources of our inner pain, we must become fully aware of the pain we all share as the earth is abused and ignored. We are not separate from, we are of the earth. What we have lost, wrote Al Gore in his book *Earth in the Balance,* is a "direct experience of our connection to the vividness, vibrancy, and aliveness of the rest of the natural world. The froth and frenzy of industrial civilization masks our deep loneliness for communion . . . the price we pay is the loss of our spiritual lives."

Gore's prescription for healing is for us all to confront and fully understand our pattern of ecological destruction. The first step toward recovery is "mourning what we have lost . . . and coming to terms with the new story of what it means to be a steward of the earth."

Action Steps: Restoring Self and Nature

Part of our recovery, then, is restoration of the earth. Taking some action to heal the planet will also help heal our own angst, say ecopsychologists. "Each of us experiences, in some way, the earth's pain," believes Sarah Conn, a clinical psychologist at Harvard Medical School, one of the founders of the ecopsychology movement.

Reconnecting with nature and working to restore and strengthen the earth, no matter how little we do, will ease our own pain. Work to protect or create the natural world in your community. At your schools and workplace, urge leaders to become more environmentally active. Create a nature sanctuary for your community. Seek refuge in them—even ten minutes is powerful therapy.

It helps to remember that in ancient times, when people were depressed or out of sorts, they often journeyed to special places of healing power in nature.

If you actively spend time in nature each day, even if it's sitting under a maple tree in your own backyard for fifteen minutes, the solace and power of nature will help lift your depression.

If you're a city dweller, plant a flower box, keep flowers and plants on your desk, and hang pictures of your favorite natural settings in your home and office. Play tapes with natural sounds. Adding a miniature waterfall can be especially uplifting.

The impact of all of these measures can't be underestimated. Communion with nature "restores to us a level of our own human nature at which we are still sane, free from humbug, and untouched by anxieties about the meaning and purpose of our lives," wrote Alan Watts in *Nature, Man and Woman*.

If you are depressed, going into your garden, the forest, mountains, a park, the desert and asking that the earth help heal and strengthen you can have potent results. That desire to seek solace in the earth is instinctive and eternal. "When human connections fail us, we return to the source, to the font of health and sanity, to our Mother," writes Lorraine Anderson in *Sisters of the Earth*.

If we want to truly heal our depressions, we must come into greater communion with the earth, experts say.

There is now mounting scientific evidence of the power of nature to renew our spirits, points out Dr. Jonathan Zuess. For instance, a study done by W.C. Sullivan and F.E. Kuo shows that contact with nature, even as little as a walk among trees or seeing trees through a window, improves mental functioning and overall coping abilities if you are ill or under stress.

Inmates who participated in a horticultural therapy program at the San Francisco City Jail in 1994 showed lower rates of depression and less hostility. For many of the inmates, gardening was the first constructive work they had ever done. Four months after their release from prison, 6 percent of these gardeners committed offenses compared with 29 percent of other ex-inmates.

If your daily flow is so full, you don't have time to go to a natural setting, even sitting in your own backyard can be powerfully restorative.

Backyard Therapy

After especially draining days, sometimes the only energy I have left is to step outside, throw my head skyward, breathe in deeply, close my eyes, and whisper, "Oh, God, keep me on my path." Nature's a powerful listener.

Immersing herself in her garden restored Vanessa's equilibrium when she became depressed. Her depression began around Mother's Day, not long after she had suffered a miscarriage and then broke off a long-term relationship. A writer, Vanessa found her work too painful to even attempt.

Blindsided by the grief, she found that her garden became her refuge. "Everything made me cry. Everything made me hurt. Gardening was the only reprieve from that hurt."

For an entire month, Vanessa planted flowers, morning glories, purple coneflowers, daisies, sunflowers, and wildflowers. She cried as she worked and as she walked around her neighborhood. "Some days I worked fourteen hours outside. I even had so much dirt under my fingernails, I couldn't get them clean. All my clothes were grass stained."

When her depression led to insomnia, Vanessa would often go out to her garden in the middle of the night and just sit in the inky stillness, waiting for her pain to subside. After a month, she realized that she had done far more than create a beautiful flower garden.

She realized that as she dug into the loamy earth, she also unearthed fertile territory in her psyche, nurturing new growth and inner strength. She saw she had been easing into the earth—literally—to help ease the wounds of the loss of her child and of her relationship.

"Spending that month as I did made my pain manageable enough that I didn't feel it so intensely. It enabled me to get past the wound so it could heal on its own."

If you allow it, nature can help you heal. It can help you share your burdens so they don't feel so immense and overwhelming. Sinking your hands into dirt, sand, water can be a more potent tranquilizer than anything on the market.

A wonderful poem you can recite as you sink into the natural world is also found in *Sisters of the Earth*. It was written by Nancy Wood, a Santa Fe writer and photographer:

Earth cure me.
Earth receive my woe.
Rock strengthen me.
Rock receive my weakness.
Rain wash my sadness away.
Rain receive my doubt.
Sun make sweet my song.
Sun receive the anger from my heart.

"I find that my garden draws me into this other world. When I'm there, I transcend time and space and let go of cares and concerns," says Loretta LaRoche.

"There is nothing that puts things into perspective more than a squirrel that's trying for the hundredth time to get into a bird feeder with a cone-shaped top. Time after time it simply flips off and tumbles on the ground, yet without fail it tries again. It appears that the frustration is part of the game. For us, frustration is part of the struggle. I also realize there is a simpler, more majestic world where phones don't ring and no deadlines occur. Not one bird in my yard has voice mail or an e-mail address."

Sometimes merely sitting on the earth, not doing or thinking a thing, is enough. More than enough, found the late writer Edith Warner, who lived in New Mexico. "I cannot work. I go out into the sunshine to sit receptively for what there is in this stillness and calm. I am keenly aware that there is something. . . . Somehow I have no desire to name it or understand. It is enough that I should feel and be of it in moments such as this. And most of the hatred and ill will, the strained feeling is gone. I know not how."

Tending any portion of the earth, even if it's a small bed of nasturtiums, also allows you to see that the dark tempests of your life are part of the natural rhythm of life, just as weeds, hail, and winter freezes are natural cycles. In her book *The Garden,* Helen Bjornson says gardening allowed her to see her life "as a garden with seasons and cycles, occasionally pounded by storms, often infested by the pests and noxious plants of the human condition, full of surprises and always moving toward the harvest."

May reconnecting with the earth help keep you on

your path and bring you closer to the harvest you richly deserve.

Main Messages

- Nature is the great healer.
- Our disconnection from the earth and destruction of much of the natural world makes us all feel deep grief. It leads to a collective depression.
- If we disconnect from the earth, our bodies and spirits still long for a deep spiritual and physical bond with the earth.
- Taking steps to restore and heal the earth also heals our depressions.
- Spend at least fifteen minutes outdoors each day in the natural world. If you live in the city, always have flowers and plants in your office.
- Work to protect the natural world. Write letters, speak out for environmental protection.
- Spend time nurturing part of the earth. It teaches us that cycles of pain and stormy days are natural cycles of life.

TWENTY

Service, Gratitude, and Cultivating Joy

More and more medical practitioners are discovering service to be one of the most powerful antidotes to depression. Serving others allows you to step outside yourself and lift your own heaviness by alleviating someone else's.

Studies have found that a weekly habit of helping others can help you get out of a depressive rut, says Dr. Harold Bloomfield. "Service is key to helping you end your cycle of loneliness and depression. Loneliness is certainly an underpinning of depression because you get stuck in your own boundaries."

Altruism and caring are soothing to our entire being. They slow our heart rates and raise levels of the disease-fighting chemical immunoglobulin A (igA) for several hours. By forcing us to focus on others and step outside of ourselves, atruistic acts also help us gain greater clarity in our thinking, finds research.

This can be especially key when we're depressed and

sometimes painfully inner focused, overly aware of our own angst. In a 1994 study, University of Michigan psychologist Susan Nolen-Hoeksema studied 250 people who had just lost a loved one. Not surprisingly, those who said they ruminated or brooded the most were the most depressed. "Ruminative coping" is a tendency to focus inwardly and passively on one's emotions, she says.

In further research, when Nolen-Hoeksema distracted her subjects from their typical thought patterns, their ability to solve problems jumped.

Loving Others Heals

As this research points out, focusing on someone or something else is intensely therapeutic. Service can do that. It also can link you up with a bedrock sense of community and concern for humankind.

"If you are depressed and really locked into despair, the best cure as far as I am concerned for this kind of depression is to go out and help other people," says Dr. Bloomfield.

"It is in the service of other people that we pull out of ourselves and touch humanity at a very beautiful level. We know we are important and can make a difference in the world. The other things in our life may come and go. Nothing ever remains the same, but we know that whatever happens to us, we can remain important to people in the world."

Alex fell into despair after she broke up with a man she was engaged to and lost her job at the same time. She spent days not moving, just crying and mourning. Eventually, she was tired of being inactive. She decided to do volunteer work to forget about her own misery. As she did, she sparked into an animated, assertive, excited-about-life woman again.

Caroline Myss has seen the tremendous healing value of service in people who have become emotionally—and energetically—depleted after a crisis. "Often following a crisis, we are literally drained of all of our energy because, logically, we drew on that energy for survival. The state we are left in is one of lethargy, which requires healing because energetic depletion spins off into depression, and can even begin to activate chronic pain in the body."

After a crisis, you need to take a period of time to heal, Myss says. And then you must find a way to again become emotionally, psychologically, and physically "mobile."

"This means of movement doesn't require something dramatic, such as moving from your home, but it does require becoming exposed to some form of inspiration that allows even the subtlest connection to the future to begin."

Serving others can literally provide that inspiring movement of our minds, spirits, and energies, Myss says. It can give us the mobility to get on with our lives and go forward, which is the healthiest choice we can make.

Crisis Opens the Heart

Myss says one of the most inspiring people she ever met was a man whose wife had left him. Two years later, he was still so devastated by her leaving him that he could no longer go to his office on a daily basis, which caused him to be fired. Losing his job exacerbated his depression, so he began to drink, something he had never been in the habit of doing.

One day, he was at the hospital for an appointment,

and he saw two or three children in wheelchairs being moved down the hallway. He left the room he was in and followed the nurses pushing the wheelchairs.

Soon, the man found himself looking into a big room filled with children who were coping with life in a wheelchair. After watching the children for ten minutes, a nurse alerted him that he had an appointment to keep. "What stunned me," the man said, "was for that ten minutes I was watching these children, I wasn't thinking about myself. This was the first time in a long time that I wasn't dwelling on myself."

The man discovered that the feeling was so uplifting that he decided to volunteer at the hospital as often as they would let him. The courage he found in these children greatly surprised him. He expected to find great fear—fear of being handicapped, fear of being alone, fear of not being able to take financial care of themselves, fear of living a life filled with nothing but fear.

But they were not radiating this type of fear at all. In fact, ironically, they were the ones giving him courage to keep on going with his life.

"Today," he said, "when someone asks me how to get through a crisis, I tell them to go find someone who has experienced a crisis bigger than your own. If you are hungry, go find someone who is starving. I realize that we need some downtime after a painful situation. I took some. But I think I was making matters worse by taking too much downtime. It's important to get back into the motion of life because then life naturally will move you forward."

If you find yourself caught in depression, service may be one release. Even a weekly hour of volunteering can have a tremendous impact on your moods.

Service is a "great big deal," says Mona Lisa Schultz.

"You feel potency in the world and see your creativity make an impact. I say to my patients, 'What is the most potent antidepressant drug on the market? Remember, if you are my patient, you don't want me to withhold a very valuable treatment to you. That treatment is service.'"

When you are hollow with the pain of depression, service can replenish and restore you. Compassion for another human being soothes like nothing else, especially when you are making the transition from one stage of life to the next.

Joan Borysenko remembers one midlife woman, Sandy, who mourned the loss of her role as loving mother to her four grown children, once the center of her life. Convinced that her productive life was over, Sandy felt sad, worthless, fatigued, and self-critical. But her depression responded to a combination of psychotherapy—and outer-directed steps to support others.

Sandy realized that her love of helping others could be channeled in a new way. First, she began to direct her energy into volunteer work. Then she returned to school and earned a degree in social work, where she found new sense of direction—along with a new cadre of friends.

Find Ways to Be of Service

Dr. Richard O'Connor, head of a nonprofit community mental health clinic in Connecticut and author of *Undoing Depression: What Therapy Doesn't Teach You and Medication Can't Give You,* has said he can't count the number of times he has seen the potency of service. "You can't cure depression by giving all your money away; but if you can cultivate a true generosity of spirit, you can't be depressed."

In his groups, he sees someone in great pain tell their own story and others reach out in comfort, empathy, and support. "Often it's the tone as much as the words—somehow an emotional connection is established with someone who is feeling ashamed, alone, and afraid. . . . The sufferer is comforted, but the person who took a risk and reached out is enriched. She's learned that she herself, just by virtue of being herself, has something valuable to share."

Over and over, Dr. Andrew Weil has seen serving others do wondrous things to alleviate depression in his patients. One man, Richard, came to Dr. Weil complaining of low energy and chronic back pain. Dr. Weil also sensed an underlying sadness and desperation about him.

He found out that Richard, an accountant, was divorced, had no children, and few, if any, close friends. Among other things, Dr. Weil advised Richard to do some service work. Service helps us all realize our deep connection to one another, that we all suffer and need compassion, he says. "By devoting some of your time and energy to helping other individuals, you can make a difference in how you feel as well as how they feel, and that difference may translate into increased inner happiness and peace, and therefore into improved health."

Serving others, not fixing or judging, but serving others, is so powerfully healing because it ultimately brings us back into deep communion with the sacredness of all life, says Dr. Rachel Remen. "We serve life not because it is broken, but because it is holy. Service connects us to a larger reality that is unchanging, that draws us closer to it and strengthens us.

The best definition she's found for service has come from her friend, Marion, Dr. Remen says. "Years ago when I was preparing a talk on service for my medical students, I said, 'Marion, what is service?' And she said, 'One word—belonging.' Belonging. The lived experience that we are all connected to one another and life itself.

"The awareness that all suffering is like my suffering and all joy is like my joy and the instinctive kindness and sensitivity that comes from that awareness."

Do yourself a profound service and serve others. Ask that your talents and gifts be used by higher, divine forces for the greater good of others. Again, as in building friends, start small. Just look in your immediate neighborhood. Does your school, synagogue, medical clinic need volunteers? What burdens do you see others struggling to bear? Could you help shore them up with just a kind word, a cup of coffee, maybe even a pot of soup?

Stirring that soul in the kindness of service will stir many of the lifeless embers in your soul . . . and your journey along the path of healing is just a little farther along.

Main Messages

- Research confirms that regularly helping others gets you out of a depressive rut.
- Altruism raises your heart rate and immune system. It helps you think more clearly and put your life in perspective.
- Helping others gives you a greater love for yourself.
- Start small. What in your immediate neighborhood calls to you?
- Offer a cup of coffee or a pot of soup to someone in need.
- Ask that your talents and gifts be used by a Higher Power for the greater good of others.

TWENTY-ONE

Examining Food and Moods

Many of us turn to food for comfort and solace after a brutal day. But could the foods you are routinely eating— or not eating enough of—be contributing to your depression?

That's the resounding conclusion of many researchers and health professionals. They say that a simple and often overlooked cause of depression is a poor diet. Even in this land of seeming abundance, many people suffer from an impoverished diet.

It's only common sense that if we aren't getting the necessary vitamins and minerals, our bodies can become depressed, signaling that they want to be nourished better. But be aware—most doctors will never ask you about your diet. You likely will need to take responsibility for improving your nutrition.

Sugar Wreaks Havoc

That was certainly the experience of Dana Judy, whose story was shared in Chapter 7. Dana visited with numerous doctors about her depression, but none ever asked her about her diet. One day, her own intuitive inner voice raised the question: "What about all that sugar in your diet?"

Her inner voice served her well. For some sugar-sensitive people, eating large amounts of sugar can create emotional imbalance. Research conducted by Larry Christensen, Ph.D., chairman of the department of psychology at the University of South Alabama, shows that sugar and starches have different mood-altering effects. For some people, depression vanishes when sugar and caffeine are removed from their diet, finds Dr. Christensen.

"We see improvements in mood when sugar is eliminated, even in people who are not depressed; however, these sugar-sensitive people probably would have become depressed in the future," writes Elizabeth Somer in *Food and Mood: The Complete Guide to Eating Well and Feeling Your Best.*

Dana realized she consumed huge quantities of sugar every day—a habit from her childhood. Reducing her sugar intake helped her restore much emotional balance.

Could you be sugar-sensitive? Could that sensitivity be a major player in the cast contributing to your depression and mood swings? Do you crave sugary treats, hoard them, think no social function is complete without sugar? You may be addicted to sugar, as others are addicted to alcohol or drugs, says Kathleen DesMaisons in her illuminating book, *Potatoes Not Prozac.*

Candace Pert, the scientist who has pioneered research on the relationship between emotions and physiology, wrote the foreword to the book. She says she discovered "food as pharmacy" years ago. The daughter of an alcoholic, she knew she was a "sitting duck" for alcohol addiction. But her abstinence from alcohol instead pushed her toward her addiction to sugar, ice cream, pasta, bread, and soda, Pert says. "These seemingly harmless foods wrapped me in a cocoon so thick and numbing that I never missed the alcohol."

In her 30s, close to 240 pounds, and struggling with her feelings of inadequacy, Pert was asked to start a treatment center for alcoholics and drug addicts. As she guided her clients in surrendering to a higher power as part of their twelve-step program, Pert surrendered to something "deeper." Not long after, a friend told her about a food plan of protein and vegetables that was working for her. Pert began to do the same and not only lost weight, her emotional ups and downs evened out. "I wasn't confused or foggy at certain times in the day. I was able to think clearly. I got things done. I set goals and moved toward them without a constant struggle to stay focused."

Pert began to wonder if children of alcoholics and others inherit an alcoholic's body chemistry. Maybe alcoholics and compulsive eaters were hypersensitive to sugar, she speculated. So she began to add a food plan based on protein and complex carbohydrates, like whole wheat, potatoes, and rice, fruits and vegetables at her treatment center.

Hundreds of her clients responded remarkably, she found. Their moods mellowed and their cravings diminished. "People who had never been able to achieve sobriety, began getting and staying sober." Even the most difficult alcoholics had amazing recoveries. For instance, she worked for four months with one group of thirty "hopeless" alcoholics, like people whose licenses had been revoked. At the end of her outpatient treatment program 92 percent of that group had gotten sober and stayed sober.

Pert was so amazed at the results, she sold her house, and began to work on her Ph.D. so she could examine, among other things, the relationship between blood sugar and the production of brain chemicals like serotonin that control moods.

If you think Christmas is an abysmal failure without divinity fudge or gooey cookies, or if you have a stash of Hershey bars in your desk at work—and you suffer from mood swings and depression—you would be well advised to try the gentle, but powerful, nutrition plan in *Potatoes Not Prozac*. As you keep a food journal, the book helps you slowly replace sugars, including that found in alcohol, with proteins, complex carbohydrates, fruits and vegetables. It also helps you examine your relationship to food. For instance, it helps you do some self-examination about emotional blocks that may be leading you to use food as an emotional balm.

Foods That Boost Serotonin

Judith Wurtman, a researcher at the Massachusetts Institute of Technology, has studied the link between sugary foods and moods. Wurtman suspects that it may not be the sugar, but the fat in cookies, ice cream, and other sweet foods that poses a problem. "The fat in these foods slows down digestion and interferes with the serotonin effect," she says.

These and other dietary links to mood regulation are explored in *Food and Mood: The Complete Guide to Eating*

Well and Feeling Your Best. The book stresses that the neurotransmitters that help regulate mood are manufactured in the body directly from the food we eat. "The levels and activity of these neurotransmitters are sensitive to food intake, and changes in dietary patterns can have profound effects on behavior, eating patterns, sleep, and energy level," writes Elizabeth Somer, M.A., R.D., and a consulting nutritionist and contributing editor for *Shape Magazine.*

Somer points out that serotonin, for instance, is manufactured in the brain from an amino acid called tryptophan, which is found in protein-rich foods, with the aid of vitamins B6 and B12, folic acid, and other nutrients. That's why a high-carbohydrate snack like a wheat bagel may lift your moods—it is helping to release tryptophan and serotonin in your brain.

You may find that eating more complex carbohydrates, pasta, rice, whole grains, potatoes, even an English muffin with honey, not sugary jam, will greatly raise brain levels of tryptophan and serotonin, as they raise your moods and lower irritability.

Through questionnaires, the book helps you examine your own diet and its potential impact on your moods. It also includes diets, recipes, and snacks to keep brain chemistry optimal. Particularly helpful may be the "Feeling Good Diet," which combines the latest research and dietary advice into an eating plan.

Among other things, it advises that you eat more but smaller meals—at least five—and snacks. "Research has shown that people who divide their total daily food intake into mini-meals and snacks evenly distributed throughout the day maintain a more even temperament; are less prone to fatigue, insomnia and depression."

The diet also strongly advises eliminating sugar. The

book acknowledges that the relationship between food and depression is still controversial, but mounting research and anecdotal evidence is lending greater credence.

Creating a Food Plan

If you would like to build a food plan in your own life to see if your diet impacts your moods, DesMaisons's *Potatoes Not Prozac* contains some concrete, empowering guidelines. Her "Seven Steps to Feeling Great" include:

1) Create a journal that lists everything you eat.
2) Eat three meals a day.
3) Use vitamins B and C and zinc as supplements. (See specific recommendations in the book.)
4) Eat the recommended amount of protein at each meal. (The book recommends .4 and .6 grams per pound of body weight depending on your health needs.)
5) Add more complex carbohydrates to your daily diet.
6) Cut down on or eliminate sugars, including alcohol.
7) Develop a program to help you stay with the plan.

Step five may be most difficult for many people, but the book includes excellent ways to go from simple carbohydrates found in doughnuts, pastry, muffins, and cereal to more complex carbos in foods like whole grain cereals, whole wheat pastas, brown rice, black beans, and potatoes with skin.

The food plan in *Potatoes Not Prozac* "is designed to change your blood chemistry and improve your neurotransmitter function. Even though it may seem obvious and simple, the foods in this plan create profound physical and emotional change. Don't be deceived by the simplicity. This is powerful medicine."

The lack of nutrients is powerfully dangerous. One study of two thousand men and women between the ages of 18 and 90 found that dieting was the leading cause of depression in overweight people. Starving yourself can reduce your levels of serotonin and trigger depression.

Women taking birth control pills also can have deficiency of vitamins B6, B12, folic acid, and vitamin C, which alone can lead to depression, fatigue, and anxiety. Studies done at the Virginia Polytechnic Institute and State University and at the National Institute of Mental Health show that plasma levels of vitamin B6 were about 48 percent lower in depressed patients.

A deficiency of magnesium can also cause anxiety, irritability, and hypersensitivity to noise.

Psychonutrition, a growing field examining the link between nutrition and the mind, is examined in the book *Mood Foods* by Dr. William Vayda. Dr. Vayda has found that depression often goes hand in hand with a poor diet, food allergies, low blood pressure, low blood sugar, low thyroid functions, and low adrenal gland functions.

Among other strategies, Dr. Vayda has used foods high in the amino acid tyrosine or tyrosine itself to help ease depression. Many foods contain tyrosine—almonds, apples, cheese, eggs, chicken, peanuts, soy proteins, carrots, lettuce, and watermelon.

Tyrosine supplements alone, however, won't increase tyrosine levels in the brain, Dr. Vayda cautions. "The metabolism of tyrosine depends on a form of folic acid—biopterin—and a type of vitamin B3 as well as copper and vitamin C. Once tyrosin reaches the neurons, it is converted to dopamine and then norepinephrine, which helps lift depression."

Tryptophan-High Foods

Dr. Vayda also has reported good success lifting some forms of depression with tryptophan and foods containing tryptophan. Once tryptophan reaches the brain, it is changed into serotonin. Many people low in tryptophan often crave carbohydrates and sweets.

Kathleen DesMaisons, however, cautions that just eating tryptophan-high foods, such as chicken, ground beef, cheddar cheese, cottage cheese, tuna, and tempeh, won't automatically raise your serotonin levels. Tryptophan needs a lift to help it along. That's because there are many other amino acids scrambling to break the blood-brain barrier, and tryptophan is like the runt of the litter, DesMaisons says. It needs a hit of insulin to help it along.

So eating a tryptophan food—like baked chicken—along with a complex carbohydrate, such as a baked potato, an apple, a piece of toast or orange juice, provides that insulin boost to help your body metabolize the tryptophan.

If you want to explore the role of your diet in your depression, find a good holistic nutritionist. You may think your diet is basically OK, but in essence you may be malnourished in some key areas that impact your moods.

Deficiencies of vitamins B1, B6, C, and A, along with folic acid, niacin, magnesium, copper, and iron can all trigger depression when they alter your brain's synthesis of serotonin and norepinephrine.

In one study conducted at Harvard Medical School and USDA Human Nutrition Research Center at Tufts University in Boston, more than one out of four depressed patients was deficient in vitamins B6 and B12. "In fact, Vitamin B6 deficiency is reported in as many as 79 percent of patients with depression, compared to only 29 percent of other patients."

In many cases, giving these patients vitamin B6 supplements (in doses as low as 10 milligrams a day) raises vitamin B6 levels in the blood and improves or even alleviates the depression, providing convincing evidence that the deficiency might be the cause, rather than the effect, of the depression.

Author Jean Carper recently wrote about a new British study of 129 healthy young people who daily took nine B vitamins at ten times the recommended daily dose for a year. They reported feeling "more agreeable." In a group of thiamine-deficient women, mood improved after three months.

Foods rich in vitamin B6 include bananas, chicken, wheat germ, tomatoes, brown rice, broccoli, oranges, apples, green peas, nonfat milk, white bread, and peanut butter.

The Role of Omega-3 Fats

Carper also reports that omega-3 fat, such as that found in fish, manipulates brain chemicals to boost moods. In a new study, Harvard researcher Andrew Stoll found doses of omega-3 fatty acids improved the manic-depression symptoms in 64 percent of fourteen patients after four months. Stoll theorizes that omega-3 fat affects signaling among brain cells akin to lithium and valproate, drugs that treat manic depression.

Finally, in looking at the dietary link to depression, increasingly nutritionists and researchers are zeroing in on amino acids. For instance, if you are depressed and don't eat certain foods, like fish, you may be low in omega-3 fatty acids, like DHA. Along with other fatty acids, DHA is essential for brain development and mental function.

"Societies consuming large amounts of fish and omega-3 fatty acids appear to have lower rates of major depression," according to the *American Journal of Clinical Nutrition*. One study showed that North American and European populations have cumulative rates of depression ten times that of a Taiwanese population that consume a diet much richer in fresh fish.

Dr. C. Norman Shealy, founder of the Shealy Institute in Springfield, Missouri, found that nine out of ten depressed people had biochemical imbalances, including low levels of the hormone DHEA and a serotonin deficiency. But he also found they were almost always deficient in magnesium and in most of the essential amino acids.

Cold-water fish, such as sardines, salmon, or tuna, are great sources of DHA. If you don't eat fish or don't want to try DHA-rich seaweeds, like kombu, consider DHA supplements. To boost your fatty acid intake, you also can blend ground flaxseeds into a fruit smoothie. Recently, scientists have begun to investigate the amino acid SAMe, which stands for S-adenosyl-L-methionine. Numerous studies indicate that SAMe helps to stabilize mood.

Researchers wonder, among other roles, if SAMe stimulates the production or uptake of the neurotransmitters dopamine and norepinephrine. SAMe is not widely available, so it's best to supplement your diet with more B12 and folate, from milk, meat, eggs, and grains—or from vitamins. Studies indicate that people who are deficient in B12 and folate also have lower levels of SAMe.

However you wish to modify your nutritional plan, be sure to work closely with a qualified doctor or nutritionist. Find someone who not only is aware of the efficacy of the treatments explored in this chapter, but who has successfully used them to treat depression.

Main Messages

- Could you be sugar sensitive? For some people, sugar and starches can have different mood-altering effects.
- Examine whether you may be addicted to sugar. If you may be and have mood swings and depression, build a new food plan.
- Examine the books recommended in this chapter to build your own food plan and supplements.
- Work with a nutritionist to examine whether you may have some nutritional deficiencies.
- Try eating more foods high in omega-3 fats. Consider DHA supplements. Again, work with a qualified nutritionist.

TWENTY-TWO

Food and Chemical Sensitivities

Though still somewhat controversial, new investigations into the relationship between food allergies and chemical sensitivities and depression are helping many people and gaining momentum.

Dr. Morton Teich, an allergist and pediatrician in New York City, believes strongly that food allergies can be a powerful cause of depression.

"The body can only tolerate so much. If you are allergic to dust, mold, yeast, and pollen, and experience some psychological stress, the body's threshold is reached. In addition, our exposure to hormones and chemicals, both indoors and outdoors, has increased dramatically, adding to this load."

Specific foods, chemicals, additives, and allergens can either magnify or suppress key mood neurotransmitters in the brain, says Dr. Teich. That is what happened with one of Dr. Teich's patients, a nurse named Jeannette. She had both Crohn's disease and severe asthma. She became so severely depressed each spring that she had tried to commit suicide six times.

After gathering an extensive medical history from Jeannette, Dr. Teich exposed her to allergens gathered from trees. "She became hysterical and began to cry. She said she wanted to kill herself."

Dr. Teich also discovered Jeannette was highly reactive to grass and mold. He was able to neutralize her reaction to all these substances, and her health improved dramatically. She is no longer depressed or taking antidepressant medications.

Dr. Teich has found that some of his patients have suffered from emotional problems for years because their extreme sensitivity to an environmental or dietary allergen was overlooked.

"I am not anti-medication in treating depression and other illnesses. I work within the traditional medical system," explains Dr. Teich. "But if I can treat depression by not using medications, it's safer."

Tracing the Source of the Allergy

Above all, in investigating the role of allergens in depression, Dr. Teich stresses the importance of developing a thorough medical history on each patient, including both biological and psychological stressors. "I even get answers by going back to childhood. I had one patient with low thyroid and yeast problems, and it turned out she has been abused in childhood. These are all triggering factors for depression."

In fact, the combination of allergies, low thyroid functioning, and yeast infections can trigger severe depressions, Dr. Teich has found. Though it has been derided in the mainstream media, Dr. Teich has found that an overgrowth of yeast throughout the body can lead to depression, as was the case with Sylvia, whose doctors were ready to hospitalize her to treat her depression.

"She said she knew she had a yeast problem and that she had been on many antibiotics. I treated her, but after four months there was no change. I told her not to come back. I just didn't think I could help her."

Two months later, Sylvia—a new Sylvia—came back to visit Dr. Teich. She had stayed on her anti-yeast diet and medication and her moods had lifted. "Six years later, her sons came to my office. They wanted to thank me for saving their mother's life."

Chemical Sensitivities

Even low doses of the more than seventy thousand chemicals in use today can cause a wide variety of illnesses, including depression, says Dr. Adrienne Buffaloe, medical director of Healthcare for the 21st Century Environmental Medicine Center in New York City.

Dr. Buffaloe has advanced training in the diagnosis and treatment of physical and mental illnesses caused by environmental sensitivities. She was one of a select group of physicians who treated Gulf War veterans exposed to chemicals.

But, for many people, it doesn't take an extreme exposure to nerve gas to trigger emotional and psychological instability, says Dr. Buffaloe. "Closed buildings, inadequate ventilation systems, and toxic building materials have caused indoor air pollution that exceeds outdoor air pollution. Add the increase in colorings, additives, preservatives, and other chemicals in foods and beverages, and we have quite a chemical load to contend with."

Even common molds found in sick buildings and in food can wreak havoc with our immune and neurological systems, says Dr. Buffaloe, who redirected her career and went into environmental medicine after she became seriously ill and was treated for toxicity to specific chemicals.

The exact mechanism by which someone becomes environmentally sensitive, even to healthy organic foods, is not entirely clear, says Dr. Buffaloe. But she often finds her patients have immune system aberrations, like decreased white blood cells, increased levels of IgE, a marker for allergies, and abnormal gastrointestinal functioning. "Often several of these changes are present, and may be the result, rather than the cause, of environmental sensitivities."

Patients can become environmentally sensitive after severe infections, trauma, childbirth, chronic low-dose exposure to chemicals, and massive chemical exposures, says Dr. Buffaloe. She diagnoses chemical sensitivity and chemical toxicity by taking a thorough patient history, measuring blood levels of toxic chemicals, and by chemical challenge tests in which patients are exposed to specific chemicals and monitored for their symptoms. She also relies on brain scans to record abnormalities in brain function and blood flow.

"There are compounds, especially chemicals, that cross the blood-brain barrier and cause significant changes in mood and clarity of thinking. Chronic exposure to chemicals can cause depression."

The Most Common Chemicals Can Be Toxic

Even commonly used chemicals can cause brain disruptions by decreasing blood flow to areas of the brain, says Dr. Buffaloe. Exposure to normal household chemicals, like that emitted by new carpeting, the flame retardants on stuffed animals, or chemicals in perfumes and cosmetics, can be toxic to some people, she adds. "But this is reversible with detoxification to chemicals. We see depression lift when chemicals are lifted from the body."

A critical part of Dr. Buffaloe's investigation is to gather a detailed medical history since birth. Insightful links between chemical exposures and mental illness often emerge. Patients complain of headaches, mental confusion, extreme fatigue, skin rashes, muscle pains, obesity, abdominal bloating, and many other symptoms.

When Bill came to see Dr. Buffaloe his anxiety and depression were so great he'd dropped out of his graduate school program. Over ten years, he had been treated intermittently with medication, but nothing eased his symptoms.

As Dr. Buffaloe looked at Bob's history, one significant event stood out. Bob mentioned that he once did some spray painting at a construction site. "But the pieces he sprayed were not done in the open air. He worked on them in a closed garage, where gasoline also had been spilled on the floor."

When Bob's blood was measured for solvents, Dr. Buffaloe found elevated levels of methylpentaine, toluene, and DDE. After Bob was detoxified, he reclaimed his life.

Detoxification involves removing stored quantities of chemicals from the body. "A major thrust of detox is to allow the liver to transform and excrete any stored chemical compounds."

Patients are given a combination of co-factors, including magnesium, vitamin C, glutathione, zinc, copper, selenium, and other nutrients, which boost the liver's ability to clear out the chemicals. Exercise, heat treatments, and massage are also used to help the body release chemicals stored in the body's fat.

If you want to explore your chemical sensitivity, find a qualified and experienced environmental medicine practitioner. Be persistent. Many doctors aren't familiar with this specific area of medicine and want to dismiss your concerns.

If it's determined that you have some chemical sensitivities, managing them is a lifelong challenge. Once people become chemically sensitive, they will always be, says Dr. Buffaloe. They must always manage their environment for future exposure to unwanted chemicals. "I protect myself in two ways. My home is chemical-free, and I work in a chemical-free work environment. Most of the time I'm not around chemicals, and that's by design. I live an active life apart from my work. I ski and play tennis in competition. I've learned how to deal with this."

Main Messages

- Though often overlooked, food allergies can cause depression.
- Work with a qualified allergist to see if there is a link between your depression and possible allergens.
- Chemical sensitivities can also lead to mental disorders, including depression.
- Again, find an experienced environmental medicine practitioner to work with.
- If you are found to be chemically sensitive, you will always need to manage your environment to avoid offensive chemicals.

CONCLUSION

We hope this book has given you inspiration, renewed strength, and strategies you can actively use for your own healing and growth. Keep remembering: Your depression is not a source of shame or a failure. It can be an illuminating messenger full of fertile insights. It can lead you to a higher level of consciousness where life is richer, deeper, and suffused with wonder again.

Be tender with yourself. Be an advocate for your own health. Reach out to others for sustenance and strength. Pray that you will receive comfort, healing, and guidance. Know you are not alone and never have been.

With depression, like any suffering, can come a grace greater than anything we could have imagined. Maybe this awareness is what inspired Rainer Maria Rilke when he said: "So you must not be frightened . . . if a sadness rises up before you larger than any you have ever seen; if a restiveness, like light and cloud-shadows, passes over your hands and over all you do. You must think that . . . life has not forgotten you, that it holds you in its hand; it will not let you fall."

We hope this book has comforted you as you seek answers. Keep remembering you have abundant company. Depression appears to be something millions in our culture are going through in this phase of our evolution.

The passage from darkness to light is something we are doing together, something we will be remembered for. For as millions of us peer into our depression and transform the darkness that envelops us, we awaken. And as we do so, we suffuse the world with light. Illumination is something the world desperately needs.

As difficult as it can be, try to keep in mind that your depression can be your gateway, your wellspring to greater inner strength and health. In the middle of your suffering, keep remembering your preciousness and your power.

Sometimes we have to literally fall apart into despair so we can construct a stronger, more viable and authentic self. I hope this book has taken you well along the way toward creating that stronger self. In the spirit of that hope, I leave you with these words from Rashani, cofounder of Earthsong, a woman's sanctuary in Hawaii:

There is a brokenness out of which comes the unbroken, a shatteredness out of which blooms the unshatterable. There is a cry deeper than all sound whose serrated edges cut the heart as we break open to the place inside which is unbreakable and whole, while learning to sing.

May the spirit of this book help you sing again with joy, resilience, and passion.

SOURCES

Articles

Alfvin, Carolyn, "Reach out and touch someone: benefits of a hands-on approach make real sense," *Chicago Tribune*, Nov. 2, 1997.

Burbach, Frank R., "The efficacy of physical activity interventions within mental health services: anxiety and depressive disorders," *Journal of Mental Health*, December 1997.

Callahan, Jean, "High anxiety?," *New Age Journal*, November/December 1994.

Campbell, Don, "The riddle of the Mozart effect," *Natural Health*, January/February 1998.

Carey, Benedict, "The sunshine supplement," *Health*, January 1998.

Carper, Jean, "5 good-mood foods," *USA Weekend*, January 1–3, 1999.

——, "The latest on St. John's Wort, and more," *USA Weekend*, January 2–4, 1998.

Colt, George Howe, "The magic of touch," *Life*, August 1997.

Conway, Claire, "Treating the blues," *Parenting*, March 1998.

"Cyberspace a sad, lonely place, researchers discover," *The Rocky Mountain News*, August 30, 1998.

Das, Lama Surya, "Enlighten up," *New Age Journal*, March/April 1998.

DeWolf, Rose, "Get a howl of yourself," *Washington Post*, May 7, 1998.

Dirkse, Lynda, "Tilling the soul," *Rocky Mountain News*, December 20, 1998.

Elias, Marilyn, "Aiming acupuncture at depression," *USA Today*, September 4, 1997.

Fain, Jean, "The pen has healing power," *Boston Globe*, March 23, 1998.

Fenyvesi, Charles, "Herbal tonic," *U.S. News and World Report*, January 19, 1998.

Firshein, Richard, "Lifting spirits," *Psychology Today*, September 1998.

Fremerman, Sarah, "DHA," *Natural Health*, January/February 1998.

Fugh-Berman, Adriane, M.D., "Woman to woman: The best supplements for treating depression," *Natural Health*, January/February 1998.

Gerber, Suzanne, "Dark days/light relief," *Country Living's Healthy Living*, February/March 1998.

Howe, Maggy, "Acupuncture," *Country Living's Healthy Living*, Summer 1996.

Iovine, Julie, "Solving and preventing 'sick building' illnesses," *New York Times*, January 8, 1998.

Kelly, Dennis, "Life got you stressed out? Laugh it off, expert says," *USA Today*, August 16, 1996.

Klein, Alice, "Marion Woodman: Jungian high priestess pumps feminity's political potential," *M.E.N. Magazine*, November 1995.

"Laughing Matters," *Good Housekeeping*, September 1998.

Light, Luise, "Beyond St. John's Wort," *New Age Journal*, November/December 1998.

Mays, Patricia, "Suicide prevention plan unveiled," *Associated Press News Service*, October 21, 1998.

McNichol, Tom, "The power of touch," *USA Weekend*, Febuary 6–8, 1998.

Nelson, Miriam, "Lifting weights lifts your moods and more," *Prevention*, October 1998.

Peeno, Linda, "A voice for Elizabeth," *Reader's Digest*, August 1998.

Pettus, Elise, "Help the earth, heal your mind," *Country Living's Healthy Living*, May 1998.

Rechtschaffen, Stephan, M.D., "The rhythm method: how the power of ritual can transform your relationship to time," *Utne Reader*, March/April 1997.

Schrader, Ann, "Postpartum psychosis called rare and preventable," *Denver Post*, April 11, 1998.

Shea, Christopher, "Why depression strikes more women than men:

'Ruminative coping' may provide answers," *Chronicle of Higher Education,* January 30, 1996.

Steiner, Zannah, "Reversing autism and depression with bodywork," *Alternative Medicine,* Issue 24, July 1998.

Talen, Jamie, "Can trauma be relieved by the wave of a hand? The controversy over eye-movement therapy," *Washington Post,* April 21, 1998.

Thornton, Jim, "Getting inside your head," *USA Weekend,* January 1–3, 1999.

Underwood, Anne, "The magic of touch," *Newsweek,* April 6, 1998.

"Walk away from depression," *Better Homes and Gardens,* October 1997.

Werblin, Jan Marie, "Sing the body electric," *Changes,* June 1995.

Winner, Karen, "Eyeing a new trauma therapy," *New Age Journal,* July/August 1998.

Young, Leslie A. "The baby blues," *Rocky Mountain News,* November 8, 1998.

Books

Anderson, Lorraine. *Sisters of the Earth,* New York: Vintage Books, 1991.

Ballentine, Rudolph. *Radical Healing.* New York: Harmony Books, 1999.

Ban Breathnach, Sarah. *Something More: Excavating Your Authentic Self.* New York: Warner Books, 1998.

Banks, Heide. *It Works for Me!* Boston: Journey Editions, 1996.

Baumel, Syd. *Dealing with Depression Naturally.* New Canaan, CT: Keats Publishing, 1995.

Belitz, Charlene, and Meg Lundstrom. *The Power of Flow: Practical Ways to Transform Your Life with Meaningful Coincidence.* New York: Harmony Books, 1997.

Benson, Herbert, M.D. *The Relaxation Response.* New York: Avon Books, 1976.

Bjornson, Helen. *The Garden.* Fargo, ND: Seventh Elm, 1993.

Bloomfield, Harold H., M.D. *Healing Anxiety with Herbs.* New York: HarperCollins Publishers, 1998.

——. *Hypericum and Depression*. Los Angeles: Prelude Press, 1996.

——, and Peter McWilliams. *How to Heal Depression*. Los Angeles: Prelude Press, 1994.

Blumenfeld, Larry, ed. *The Big Book of Relaxation*. New York: The Relaxation Company, 1994.

Borysenko, Joan. *Minding the Body, Mending the Mind*. New York: Addison-Wesley Publishing Company, 1987.

——. *Fire in the Soul: A New Psychology of Spiritual Optimism*. New York: Warner Books, 1993.

——. *A Woman's Book of Life: The Biology, Psychology, and Spirituality of the Feminine Life Cycle*. New York: Riverhead Books, 1996.

Braiker, Harriet. *Getting Up When You're Feeling Down: A Woman's Guide to Overcoming and Preventing Depression*. New York: G.P. Putnam's Sons, 1988.

Bratman, Steven, M.D. *Beat Depression with St. John's Wort*. Rocklin, CA: Prima Publishing, 1997.

Burns, David, M.D. *Feeling Good: The New Mood Therapy*. New York: Avon Books, 1999.

Cameron, Julia. *The Artist's Way*. Los Angeles: Tarcher Putnam, 1992.

Capacchione, Lucia. *The Well-Being Journal: Drawing Upon Your Inner Power to Heal Yourself*. North Hollywood, CA: Newcastle Publishing Co., Inc., 1989.

——. *The Picture of Health: Healing Your Life with Art*. North Hollywood, CA: Newcastle Publishing Co., Inc., 1996.

Carlson, Richard, and Benjamin Shield. *Handbook for the Soul*. Boston: Little, Brown and Company, 1995.

Carrigan, Catherine, *Healing Depression: A Guide to Making Intelligent Choices about Treating Depression*. Santa Fe, NM: Heartsfire Books, 1997.

Claire, Thomas. *Bodywork: What Type of Massage to Get and How to Make the Most of It*. New York: William Morrow, 1995.

Cleve, Jay. *Out of the Blues: Strategies That Work to Get You Through the Down Times*. New York: Berkley Books, 1996.

Copeland, Mary Ellen, and Matthew McKay. *The Depression Workbook: A Guide for Living with Depression and Manic Depression*. Oakland, CA: New Harbinger Publications, Inc., 1992.

Cronkite, Kathy. *On the Edge of Darkness*. New York: Doubleday, 1994.

Dayton, Tian, Ph.D. *Heartwounds: The Impact of Unresolved Trauma and Grief on Relationships.* Deerfield Beach, FL: Health Communications, Inc., 1997.

DesMaisons, Kathleen, Ph.D. *Potatoes Not Prozac.* New York: Simon and Schuster, 1998.

Domar, Alice, M.D., and Henry Dreher. *Healing Mind/Healthy Woman.* New York: Henry Holt, 1996.

Dominguez, Joe, and Vicki Robin. *Your Money or Your Life: Transforming Your Relationship with Money and Achieving Financial Independence.* New York: Penguin Books, 1993.

Dossey, Larry, M.D. *Healing Words: The Power of Prayer and the Practice of Medicine.* New York: Harper, 1997.

Duerk, Judith. *A Circle of Stones.* San Diego, CA: LuraMedia, 1989.

Dusek, Dorothy E., George S. Everly, Jr., and Daniel A. Girdano. *Controlling Stress and Tension.* Boston: Allyn & Bacon, 1996.

Dyer, Wayne W. *Your Sacred Self.* New York: HarperCollins Publishers, 1995.

Elkins, Rita. *Depression and Natural Medicine: A Nutritional Approach to Depression and Mood Swings.* Pleasant Grove, UT: Woodland Publishing, Inc., 1995.

Ford, Gillian. *Listening to Your Hormones.* Rocklin, CA: Prima Publishing, 1996.

Forrest, Margot Silk, and Francine Shapiro. *EMDR: The Breakthrough "Eye Movement" Therapy for Overcoming Anxiety, Stress and Trauma.* New York: Basic Books, 1997.

Foster, Richard. *Freedom of Simplicity.* New York: Harper, 1998.

Gach, Michael Reed. *Acupressure's Potent Points.* New York: Bantam Doubleday Dell, 1990.

Gold, Mark, M.D., and Lois B. Morris. *The Good News About Depression.* New York: Bantam Books, 1995.

Goldberg, Burton, M.D. *Alternative Medicine Guide to Women's Health,* Volumes 1 and 2. Tiburon, CA: Future Medicine Publishing, 1998.

Goldberg, Natalie. *Writing Down the Bones.* Boston: Shambhala, 1986.

Goldstein, Nikki. *Essential Energy: A Guide to Aromatherapy and Essential Oils.* New York: Time Warner, 1997.

Gottlieb, Bill, ed. *New Choices in Natural Healing.* New York: Bantam Books, 1997.

Hendricks, Gay and Kathlyn. *At the Speed of Life: A New Approach to*

Personal Change Through Body-Centered Therapy. New York: Bantam Books, 1994.

Huber, Cheri. *Being Present in the Darkness: Depression as an Opportunity for Self-Discovery*. New York: Berkley Publishing Group, 1991.

Jamison, Kay Redfield. *An Unquiet Mind: A Memoir of Moods and Madness*. New York: Random House, 1997.

Jeffers, Susan. *End the Struggle and Dance with Life: How to Build Yourself Up When the World Gets You Down*. New York: St. Martin's Griffin, 1996.

Keen, Sam. *Fire in the Belly: On Being a Man*. Bantam Doubleday Dell, 1992.

Keene, Julie, and Ione Jenson. *Emerging Women: The Widening Stream*. Santa Monica, CA: Hay House, 1997.

Krieger, Dolores. *Therapeutic Touch*. New York: Prentice-Hall, 1979.

Kübler-Ross, Elisabeth, M.D. *The Wheel of Life: A Memoir of Living and Dying*. New York: Scribner, 1997.

LaRoche, Loretta. *Relax: You May Only Have a Few Minutes Left*. New York: Villard Books, 1998.

Leider, Richard J., and David Shapiro. *Repacking Your Bags: Lighten Your Load for the Rest of Your Life*. San Francisco: Berrett-Koehler Publishers, 1995.

Levine, Stephen. *Guided Meditations, Explorations, and Healings*. New York: Doubleday, 1991.

Liberman, Jacob. *Light: Medicine of the Future*. Santa Fe, NM: Bear & Company Publishing, 1992.

Lindbergh, Anne Morrow. *Gift from the Sea*. New York: Vintage Books, 1991.

Lockie, Andrew, M.D. *The Family Guide to Homeopathy: Symptoms and Natural Solutions*. New York: Fireside, 1993.

Macy, Joanna. *World as Lover, World as Self*. Berkeley, CA: Parallax Press, 1991.

Mayell, Mark. *52 Simple Steps to Natural Health: A Week-by Week Guide to More Healthful Living*. New York: Pocket Books, 1995.

McGrath, Ellen, Ph.D. *When Feeling Bad Is Good*. New York: Henry Holt, 1992.

McWilliams, Peter. *You Can't Afford the Luxury of a Negative Thought*. Berkeley, CA: Prelude Press, 1995.

Miller, Alice. *For Your Own Good.* New York: Farrar, Straus and Giroux, 1990.

Mitchell, Jann. *Home Sweeter Home: Creating a Haven of Simplicity and Spirit.* Hillsboro, OR: Beyond Words Publishing Inc., 1996.

Moore, Thomas. *Care of the Soul.* New York: HarperPerennial, 1994.

Murdock, Maureen. *The Heroine's Journey.* Boston & London: Shambhala, 1990.

Myss, Caroline. *Anatomy of the Spirit: The Seven Stages of Power and Healing.* New York: Harmony Books, 1996.

——. *Why People Don't Heal and How They Can.* New York: Harmony Books, 1997.

Norden, Michael J., M.D. *Beyond Prozac: Brain-Toxic Lifestyles, Natural Antidotes & New Generation Antidepressants.* New York: Regan Books, 1995.

Northrup, Christiane, M.D. *Women's Bodies, Women's Wisdom.* New York: Bantam Books, 1994.

O'Connor, Richard, Ph.D. *Undoing Depression: What Therapy Doesn't Teach You and Medication Can't Give You.* New York: Berkley Publishing Group, 1999.

Ornish, Dean, M.D. *Love and Survival: The Scientific Basis for the Healing Power of Intimacy.* New York: HarperCollins, 1999.

Pennebaker, James. *Opening Up: The Healing Power of Expressing Emotions.* New York: Guilford Press, 1997.

Pert, Candace, M.D. *Molecules of Emotion: Why You Feel the Way You Feel.* New York: Scribner, 1998.

Peter, Laurence J., M.D., and Bill Dana. *The Laughter Prescription: How to Achieve Health, Happiness, and Peace of Mind Through Humor.* New York: Ballantine, 1982.

Pressman, Alan H., and Nancy Burke. *St. John's Wort: The Miracle Medicine.* New York: Dell Publishing Group, 1998.

Radetsky, Peter. *Allergic to the Twentieth Century.* New York: Little, Brown and Company, 1997.

Real, Terrence. *I Don't Want to Talk About It: Overcoming the Secret Legacy of Male Depression.* New York: Fireside, 1998.

Reilly, Patricia Lynn. *A God Who Looks Like Me: Discovering a Woman-Affirming Spirituality.* New York: Ballantine, 1995.

Remen, Rachel Naomi, M.D. *Kitchen Table Wisdom: Stories That Heal.* New York: Riverhead Books, 1996.

Rosenthal, Norman, M.D. *Winter Blues*. New York: Guilford Press, 1993.

——. *St. John's Wort: The Herbal Way to Feeling Good*. New York: HarperCollins, 1998.

Rountree, Robert; Rachel Walton; and Janet Zand. *Smart Medicine for a Healthier Child*. New York: Avery Publishing Group, 1994.

Sachs, Judith. *Nature's Prozac*. New York: Prentice Hall, 1997.

Samuels, Michael, M.D., and Mary Rockwood Lane. *Creative Healing: How to Heal Yourself by Tapping Your Hidden Creativity*. New York: HarperSan Francisco, 1998.

Schultz, Mona Lisa, M.D. *Awakening Intuition: Using Your Mind-Body Network for Insight and Healing*. New York: Harmony Books, 1998.

Shimberg, Elaine Fantle. *Depression: What Families Should Know*. New York: Ballantine Books, 1996.

Skog, Susan. *Embracing Our Essence: Spiritual Conversations with Prominent Women*. Deerfield Beach, FL: Health Communications, 1995.

Somer, Elizabeth. *Food and Mood: The Complete Guide to Eating Well and Feeling Your Best*. New York: Henry Holt, 1995.

Souter, Keith. *Homeopathy: Heart & Soul: Treatments for Emotional Problems*. Woodstock, NY: Beekman Publishing, 1994.

St. James, Elaine. *Living the Simple Life*. New York: Hyperion, 1998.

Steinem, Gloria. *Revolution from Within: A Book of Self-Esteem*. Boston: Little, Brown and Company, 1992.

Stoddard, Alexandra. *Making Choices: Discover the Joy in Living the Life You Want to Lead*. New York: Avon Books, 1995.

Van Steenhouse, Andrea, Ph.D., and Doris A. Fuller. *A Woman's Guide to a Simpler Life*. New York: Random House, 1999.

Vayda, William. *Mood Foods*. Berkeley, CA: Ulysses Press, 1995.

Watts, Alan. *Nature, Man and Woman*. New York: Vintage Books, 1991.

Wegscheider Hyman, Jane. *The Light Book: How Natural and Artificial Light and Affect Our Health, Mood, and Behavior*. Los Angeles: Jeremy P. Tarcher, 1990.

Weil, Andrew. *8 Weeks to Optimum Health*. New York: Fawcett, 1998.

——. *Natural Health, Natural Medicine: A Comprehensive Manual for Wellness and Self-Care*. Boston: Houghton Mifflin Company, 1990.

——. *Spontaneous Healing*. New York: Alfred A. Knopf, 1995.

Welwood, John. *Journey of the Heart: The Path of Conscious Love.* New York: Harper Perennial, 1996.

Williams, Terry Tempest. *Refuge: An Unnatural History of Family and Place.* New York: Vintage Books, 1992.

——. *An Unspoken Hunger: Stories from the Field.* New York: Vintage Books, 1995.

Williamson, Marianne. *Illuminata: Thoughts, Prayers, Rites of Passage.* New York: Random House, 1994.

Zuess, Jonathan, M.D. *The Wisdom of Depression.* New York: Harmony Books, 1998.

Zweig, Connie. *Sacred Sorrows: Embracing and Transforming Depression.* New York: Jeremy P. Tarcher, 1996.

Web Sites

Overview of the tomatis method

http://www.tomatis.com/overview.html

Sound therapy: high frequencies for learning disabilities, vitality, creativity, IQ

http://superlearning.com/pr_sound_therapy.htm

Stress, energy, and sound therapy

http://www.intouchmag.com/soundtherapy4.html

Depressive tendencies

http://www.tomatis.com/depression.html

The hypericum home page

http://www.hypericum.com/nuts.htm

Non-drug therapies: herbal medicine.

htp://www.depression.com/anti/anti_26_herbal.htm

Hypericum and depression

http://www.all-natural.com/hyp35.htm

Non-drug therapies: Acupuncture

http://www.depression.com/anti/anti_28_acupuncture.htm

Chemical Injury Information Network

http://biz-comm.com/CIIN/what.htm

Multiple chemical sensitivities
http://www.thehealthconnection.com/Disease%20 Center/diseases/
    MCS.asp

Personal Interviews

Harold Bloomfield, M.D.

Joan Borysenko

Helen Gurley Brown

Adrienne Buffaloe, M.D.

Lucia Capacchione

Tian Dayton

Alice Domar, M.D.

Jean Houston

Susan Jeffers

Naomi Judd

Dana Judy

Loretta LaRoche

Ron Minson, M.D.

Caroline Myss

Christiane Northrup, M.D.

James Pennebaker

Diane Roberts

Jessica Saperstone

Mona Lisa Schultz, M.D.

Gregory White

ORGANIZATIONS AND RESOURCES

For More Information on Depression

Depression, Awareness, Recognition and Treatment
D/ART Program
National Institute of Mental Health
5600 Fishers Lane
Room 15C-05
Rockville, MD 20857
(800) 421-4211

National Foundation for Depressive Illness
2 Pennsylvania Plaza
New York, NY 10121
(800) 248-4344

National Depressive and Manic Depressive Association
730 N. Franklin St., Suite 501
Chicago, IL 60610
(800) 826-3632

Mind-Body Medicine

Dr. Alice Domar
Division of Behavioral Medicine
Deaconess Hospital
1 Deaconess Road
Boston, MA 02215
(617) 632-9530

Dr. Herbert Benson
Mind/Body Medical Institute
Deaconess Hospital
1 Deaconess Road
Boston, MA 02215

Dr. Christiane Northrup
Women to Women
One Pleasant St.
Yarmouth, ME 04096
(207) 846-6163

Joan Borysenko
Mind-Body Health Sciences
393 Dixon Road
Boulder, CO 80302
(303) 440-8460

Dr. Andrew Weil
P.O. Box 457
Vail, AZ 85641

Jon Kabat-Zinn
Stress Reduction Clinic
University of Massachusetts Medical Center
Worcester, MA 01655
(508) 856-1616

Institute for Noetic Sciences
475 Gate Five Road
Suite 300
Sausalito, CA 94965
(415) 331-5650

The Center for Cognitive Therapy
The Science Center
Room 754
3600 Market Street
Philadelphia, PA 19104

American Holistic Medical Association
4101 Lake Boone Trail
Suite 201
Raleigh, NC 27607
(919) 787-5181

American Association of Naturopathic Physicians
2366 Eastlake Ave. East, Suite 322
Seattle, WA 98102
(206) 323-7610

Acupuncture

Council of Colleges of Acupuncture and Oriental Medicine
8403 Colesville Rd., Suite 370
Silver Spring, MD 20910
(301) 608-9175

American Association of Acupuncture and Oriental Medicine
433 Front St.
Catasauqua, PA 18032
(610) 266-1433

American Foundation of Traditional Chinese Medicine
505 Beach St.
San Francisco, CA 94133
(415) 776-0502

Aromatherapy

National Association for Holistic Aromatherapy
3072 Edison Ct.
Boulder, CO 80301
(303) 444-0533

Chemical Sensitivity

Healthcare for the 21st Century
964 Third Ave.
New York, NY 10155
(212) 355-2315

EMDR

EMDR Institute
P.O. Box 51010
Pacific Grove, CA 93950
(408) 372-3900

Herbalism

American Herbalists Guild
P.O. Box 1683
Soquel, CA 95073
(408) 469-4372

American Botanical Council
P.O. Box 201660
Austin, TX 78720
(512) 331-8868

Homeopathy

International Foundation for Homeopathy
2366 East Lake E., No. 301
Seattle, WA 98192
(206) 324-8230

National Center for Homeopathy
801 Fairfax St., Suite 306
Alexandria, VA 22314
(703) 548-7790

Humor

Loretta LaRoche, M.D. (Mirth Doctor)
15 Peter Road
Plymouth, MA 02360
(508) 224-2280

Massage/Bodywork

American Massage Therapy Association
820 Davis St., Suite 100
Evanston, IL 60201
(708) 864-0123

Associated Bodywork and Massage Professionals
28677 Buffalo Park Rd.
Evergreen, CO 80439-7347
(303) 674-8478

The Reiki Alliance
P.O. Box 41
Cataldo, ID 83810
(208) 682-3535

Rolf Institute
205 Canyon Blvd.
Boulder, CO 80302
(303) 449-5903

Yoga Therapy
International Association of Yoga Therapists
109 Hillside Ave.
Mill Valley, CA 94941
(415) 383-4587

Seasonal Affective Disorder and Light Therapy

National Organization for SAD
P.O. Box 40133
Washington, D.C. 20016

Depression and Related Affective Disorders Association
Johns Hopkins University School of Medicine
Meyer 3-181
600 N. Wolfe St.
Baltimore, MD 21287-7381

Center for Environmental Therapeutics
Box 532
Georgetown, CO 80444
(303) 569-0910

Jacob Liberman
P.O. Box 4058
Aspen, CO 81612

Sound Therapy

The Center for Inner Change
55 Madison St., Suite 400
Denver, CO 80206
(303) 320-4411

The Spectrum Center
Valerie DeJean, Patricia Dixon
4715 Cordell Ave., 3rd Floor West
Bethesda, MD 20814
(301) 657-0988

Tomatis Listening and Learning Center
Pierre Sollier
3700 Mt. Diablo Blvd., Suite 300
Lafayette, CA 94549
(510) 284-8431

The Listening Center—Dallas
Jim and Harl Asaff
12800 Hillcrest Road, Suite 101
Dallas, TX 75230
(214) 404-8152

INDEX

PLUNKITT *of*
Tammany Hall

EX-SENATOR GEORGE WASHINGTON PLUNKITT, ON HIS ROSTRUM, THE
NEW YORK COUNTY COURT-HOUSE BOOTBLACK STAND.

[From a halftone in the first edition, 1905]

PLUNKITT of Tammany Hall

A Series of Very Plain Talks on
Very Practical Politics, Delivered by
Ex-Senator George Washington Plunkitt,
the Tammany Philosopher,
from His Rostrum—the New York
County Court-House Bootblack Stand—
and Recorded by

WILLIAM L. RIORDON

Introduction by ROY V. PEEL

1 9 4 8

ALFRED A. KNOPF · New York

This is a Borzoi Book
Published by Alfred A. Knopf, Inc.

FIRST BORZOI EDITION

INTRODUCTION

Plunkitt of Tammany Hall is a historical document. It breathes the nostalgic air of the turn of the century, redolent with the fumes of beer, the smell of good food which had never been disgracefully confined in a can, the odors of livery stables, bootblack stands, commission houses, brick dust and iron filings, newspaper ink, and polished wood. It is a commentary on the kind of urban civilization we had developed by 1900, and even more faithfully on the way of life achieved in New York City at the turn of the century. Its basic assumptions with respect to the party system, reforms and reformers, progress, business enterprise, and social obligations are the same as those to be found in Tammany Hall souvenirs, the speeches of great orators, and the actions of political conventions.

I

George Washington Plunkitt was tall and rather slim in youth. In his early days as leader he sported a scraggly beard, but when he grew older he shaved off the beard and gave the edges of his mustache a little twist. In middle life he was a handsome man, his features more delicately sharp than those of any of his colleagues. When these discourses were recorded, he had added some weight and the contours of his face were rounded, but he never developed a paunch or an "aldermanic tic." He ate moderately and did not drink, at any rate not publicly, and he frequently asserted that none of the Tammany bosses who amounted to anything would touch a drop of liquor.

While it is true that Plunkitt held several offices in 1870, four simultaneously, this has no great significance. He was undoubtedly a close associate of Charles F. Murphy, but probably no more influential than his fellow Sachems, John Whalen, Dan MacMahon, Randolph Guggenheimer, and Asa B. Gardiner. Several of his fellow Tammanyites came to be much better known; Henry A. Gildersleeve, J. A. O'Gorman, O. H. P. Belmont, George Gordon Battle, and Nathan Straus were all "ornaments of Tammany Hall." Once, during a summer absence of Richard Croker, Plunkitt sat on the "Steering Committee" of the Hall, with James J. Martin, Lawrence Delmour, and Augustus Peters. Somehow the great reformers of the time—Thomas Nast, Reverend Parkhurst, Seth Low, R. F. Cutting, George W. Curtis, and others—never troubled to dig into the affairs of Plunkitt. The state legislative investigations, the Fasset, Lexow, and Mazet committees, passed him by; they were preoccupied with Croker and with official wrongdoers.[1] As Croker faded out of the picture with his millions, Murphy took his place and Plunkitt remained close to Murphy.

Superficially, there was nothing striking about Plunkitt the man. Physically, mentally, morally, he was average. We have only Riordon's and Murphy's word that he was unusually frank. What, then, of his techniques of dominance and control? How did he rise to be a Sachem of Tammany Hall and for a short time one of the leaders of the general committee?

Many men have written about leaders, their traits, and techniques. In his introduction to Sir Henry Taylor's *The Statesman*,[2] Harold Laski points out that Taylor warned the ambitious leader "against too nice a conscience and too much imagination." He cannot be startlingly original or sensitive. "The chief moral characteristic must be the ability to listen to the cheers of their own side and the power to discount the derision

---

[1] The press attacked Plunkitt as commander of the Black Horse Cavalry but did not waste much time on him.
[2] Heffer and Sons, Cambridge, 1927.

of their opponents." This is substantially what many others have said. If we piece together what we know of the average run of ward leaders with what Plunkitt did and said we arrive at nearly the same catalogue of techniques for political success.

On the whole, George W. Plunkitt was a typical New York ward boss. The majority of the local bosses of Plunkitt's youth were Anglo-Saxon. Germans and Irishmen began to appear around 1876 and from then up to 1925 the Irish increased in numbers and power. Plunkitt rose to a position of influence when the Irish were becoming conscious of their power and as long as he lived he regarded the Irish as the cream of New York political society. Meantime, as immigration from Germany, Russia, and Italy swelled the Jewish and Italian population, leaders representing these nationality groups appeared. Although patterns vary, the dominant political leader of a community usually has the same nationality and religion as the most numerous and aggressive group among his constituents. Plunkitt observed that bosses generally reflected the educational and cultural levels of their constituencies, a fact which Lipkin and Salter found to be true in Philadelphia and other cities. Since the most populous communities do not have high cultural standards, neither do bosses of their wards. In Plunkitt's time they were frequently, though not invariably, physically strong men who were expected to take part in the fighting which accompanied every primary contest. When Jimmie Hines fought for the leadership of the Nineteenth in 1911, his opponent,

Ahearn, won a dubious battle at the cost of a broken arm. In 1912, under an "honest" election law, Jimmie triumphed. Here is how Dick Butler won an interparty fight in 1902:

> Ballots were easy to get, and we took plenty. Each candidate could get all he wanted. Why, kids even played with them. I got huge stacks of ballots and carried them home to Mary.

> "Your sweet little husband has never been defeated in all his life, although Tammany thinks I'm a big sap," I said to Mary.

> "They're using repeaters all over the district, and I'm going to show them some real repeating.

> "Mary, put your irons on the fire," I told her. She put three or four irons on the coal stove, and when they were nice and hot, we went to work on the ballots. We folded the ballots in sets of ten, dampened them with water like the Chinamen do in the laundries, and then Mary pressed the bundles of ten until they were thin enough to slip through the slit in the ballot boxes.

> I distributed these ballots to my longshoremen and iron workers and they slipped in ten at a time while Murphy's mob thought they were doing a smart thing by piling in two at a time. The ballots were all the same color, and the poll clerks didn't get wise. One of my repeaters went to the polls twenty times and dropped in ten ballots every time.

> It was wonderful to see how my men slugged the opposition to preserve the sanctity of the ballot and stop the corruption of Tammany Hall. They

not only slugged our opponents but threw them in basements and rolled ash cans on them.[3]

II

What manner of men were the rest of the old ward bosses? Here and there in the United States you might still find one at this late date. But if you do he will probably prove to be some ancient relic living in the past. They are all gone now, gone with their vices and their virtues. Ten or fifteen years ago there were still a few left around New York. I can remember reading Breen's description of Sheehan, one of Plunkitt's colleagues,[4] and comparing the men I knew with this gay old buccaneer. I saw many who looked and behaved the way Breen said Sheehan looked and behaved. But the species was already becoming extinct.

The average boss of Plunkitt's time was greedy and generous, nearly always tolerant and humorous. He ate well, sometimes he drank openly, and he managed his affairs with women so discreetly that only a few hundred people knew about them. Actually, although the majority of bosses were abstemious as to food and drink and, when they had families, lived lives of spotless purity, no one cared particularly what a man did with his private life. It was more important that he be available

---

[3] Richard J. Butler and Joseph Driscoll, *Dock Walloper—The Story of "Big Dick" Butler* (New York: G. P. Putnam's Sons, 1933), pp. 67-8.
[4] *Thirty Years of New York Politics* (New York: Published by the author, 1899).

at home or at the club when petitioners came a-calling. Hanging around a saloon or restaurant never hurt as much as absence in Florida—or at the race track. There are no race tracks in Manhattan.

What the old bosses like Plunkitt valued most were a reputation for success, a reputation for personal integrity ("a man's word is his bond"), love of country, and loyalty to the organization. Harmony within the party was something they desired when they were in power. But a goodly number of them preferred opposition and contests. I think they would have been bored to distraction by peace and quiet in the district. Manipulation was their trade and they liked to work at it.

It would not be easy to convince any living New York City journalist that George Washington Plunkitt was a more noteworthy character than the bosses of the Thirties. He was certainly less respected than Marty McCue, the ex-pugilist who controlled a piece of the gas-house district on the East Side in the Twenties. At a time when most bosses were waxing fat and rich by questionable means, McCue was functioning as an almost ideal boss, striving to maintain a high moral level in his district, dispensing favors as fairly as he knew how, and holding dissension down to an irreducible minimum. Another boss, whose bailiwick was not far from McCue's, was a pleasant but rather stodgy type of person who could never understand why Judge Seabury was so curious about his financial transactions. One evening, after the Judge had been particularly persistent in the hearings before the Hofstadter Committee, this boss sat in a

Third Avenue restaurant and cried in his beer because in his opinion the Judge was depriving him of the prestige and position he had been forty years building. Maybe even Plunkitt would have quaked and become incoherent under the merciless grilling which Judge Seabury inflicted on "Tin-Box" Farley and other luminaries of the tempestuous Twenties and Thirties.

Yet when I strive to recall what bosses were like in New York a decade or so ago, I can think of only one whom future generations will regard as colorful as Plunkitt. Surely not lumbering John Theofel of Flushing; nor the taciturn Thomas Jefferson Cox of Brooklyn's sprawling Second District. Not the dull and unimaginative Heffernan brothers, nor Pete Hammil, overshadowed by his district's great man, Alfred E. Smith. Not even the silent and sinister Eddie Ahearn who inherited his post from his father. Not McCormick, or Curry, or McKeever, or frail old Mara. Not any of Flynn's men in the Bronx. I do not count Republican leaders since they were shut off from all but a small share of city, county, and state patronage, even though they were sustained by federal and private business patronage during the mayoralties of Hylan, Walker, McKee, and O'Brien. But one man does stand out, and he is Pete McGuinness, the irrepressible, exuberant Sage of Greenpoint. He was, I am inclined to believe, a sport in the biological sense of the term, tolerated because he struck a responsive chord in the breasts of men who grew to manhood in the era of gaslights, saloons, Rector's, and Clarence Day, Senior.

Even when a boss grew older, he could not always decline physical combat or hire some thug or plug-ugly to do his fighting for him. By 1930 physical power had ceased to be essential, but even in that year a Tammany boss hit a judge so hard that a few days later he died of apoplexy. During the Twenties, both in Chicago and New York, many decisions were enforced by gangsters and thugs. Many times I have seen the henchmen of Larry Fay, Ciro Terranova, Jack "Legs" Diamond, and "Lucky" Luciano in intimate conversation with political bosses. Men who got "out of line" were beaten and murdered. Still I believe that despite prohibition and its evils the dry decade was not so boisterous or cruel as Plunkitt's era. In his day, as Herbert Asbury has pointed out in *The Gangs of New York,* mayhem and murder were established business, serving political bosses. But I can find nothing to show that Plunkitt was ever publicly involved in these tactics. It is my opinion that he never allowed himself to become responsible for the grosser kinds of wrongdoing.

III

Plunkitt's prescription for rising in politics seems reasonably sound, at least for the stage of political development we had reached at the turn of the century. He began working around the district club at the age of twelve, running errands, gathering Republican ballots for bonfires, and performing other chores. His amanuensis tells us that he started life as driver of a cart,

then became a butcher's boy, and finally went into the
business for himself. There is nothing in all this to distinguish his record, nor in the next step, which was to
form a group of persons loyal to him. Scores of others
were doing the same thing at the same time, and some of
them were to become more powerful than Plunkitt. Perhaps the vital factor in his early success was that he
built the George Washington Plunkitt Association
around himself. As an impartial observer, I once attended a meeting to organize a Young Democratic Club
in Brooklyn. It never had another session. It failed because three Jewish boys, who had invited some youths of
Italian, Irish, and Polish parentage to help them create
a club, tried to secure their assent to a constitution which
placed all power in the hands of the three who called the
meeting. Plunkitt understood that in forming a new
political group there must be only a small number of
adherents, willing to give unquestioning obedience to
their leader; and he understood that such a group must
grow slowly, never bringing in more new members than
were already enrolled in the organization. A club can be
initiated in other ways. If a man has money he can buy
followers; if he controls patronage, either public or
private, he can use it to command the loyalty of those
upon whom it is conferred.

At any rate, once established, the road to power is not
too difficult. Plunkitt is very vague about the next step—
consolidating one's position—but we know that he asked
for a job immediately, and got it. As Assemblyman,
Alderman, or Police Magistrate, he took care of his own

interests and those of his constituents. Apparently he was always careful to follow the organization line, but it is not clear from the record how he managed to do this. He seems to have kept himself out of the Tweed Scandal, and to have moved quietly from Tweed's side to Kelly's. When Kelly was losing his grip on the Hall, Plunkitt was moving over to Croker. By the time Croker had reached the point where he gave only casual attention to politics, Plunkitt was one of those who saw that Murphy had the reins of power clutched tightly in his muscular fists and he established himself as one of Murphy's lieutenants. This was the pattern for successful ward bosses of the late 1900's. Plunkitt not only "seen his opportunities" and took them, he also knew his limitations.

Soon after he "entered" politics, Plunkitt gave up his butcher shop and went into the contracting and real estate business, a common enough procedure on the part of ward bosses.[5] Before long he became wealthy. How did he become so rich that he was accounted a millionaire in 1905? In the same way that all the other bosses in Croker's, Kelly's, and Murphy's machines became rich. He used his official position and his political contacts to buy land which he knew he could sell at a large profit, to buy surplus public property for a song, and—although Plunkitt was silent on this point—to accept gifts and other tokens of gratitude from recipients of his favors. Now it is true that Plunkitt avoided the "penal code,"

---

[5] See H. F. Gosnell, *Machine Politics: Chicago Model* (Chicago: University of Chicago Press, 1937), p. 49.

i.e., illegal graft. He did not steal outright, which is probably something in the nature of a virtue, considering his environment. "A politician who steals," he said, "is worse than a thief. He is a fool." Plunkitt usually deferred to the powers that be in Tammany. There is nothing to show that he was any judge of character, good or bad. So long as his districts turned out on election day, the higher bosses were generous with him and he let them worry about the caliber of the men he recommended for jobs.

Since Plunkitt believed in party control over public employment, he also believed in private patronage and the whole spoils system. Committed to this system of favoritism, the average ward boss personally, or through his deputies, fights every attempt to break it up. He may even support and benefit by the candidacies of popular leaders like Tilden, Cleveland, Al Smith, or Franklin D. Roosevelt. It was La Guardia's belief that Ed Flynn never once won a contest in the Bronx; every Democratic victory there, he said, was produced by Smith or Roosevelt.[6] If the big name, on whose coat-tails the county and ward bosses ride to victory, is far enough removed from the local government so that he cannot interfere with local spoils, the little bosses will labor manfully to turn out a heavy vote whether they like him or not. But if the hero is a governor who strives to limit local patronage, the local bosses resist. Since there are numerous patterns of resistance, we need not go into them all; two examples

[6] "Bosses are Bunk," *Atlantic Monthly,* July 1947, pp. 21-4.

should suffice. When Tammany's own Mayor Grace ignored the Hall, the bosses indulged in a communal passive resistance. When Governor Franklin D. Roosevelt took steps to clean up city politics in 1932, the bosses forced Mayor Walker to resign, and purged their ranks of the more notorious grafters. In Plunkitt's time the ward bosses who lasted the longest took their cue from the leader of the Hall, and they made sure that they never exceeded him in graft or public attention.

Plunkitt's conception of "human nature" was very simple: Every man has his price, never too high if you study him carefully. And yet many men who were active in politics during Plunkitt's day could not be bought, and they demonstrated that there were occasions when honest and upright men had more influence than the grafters and payers of bribes. To summarize Plunkitt's techniques for success as ward leader, they were: First, secure a few followers who will vote as you direct; then go to the regular leader and exchange these votes for influence, specifically jobs and favors. Second, see that your success is advertised so that you gain more loyal adherents. Third, repeat this process until you are the strongest man in the district. When this point is reached, a decision respecting the nominal boss is necessary. How you answer this question depends on the latter. You either bide your time until he falters and dies, or you evict him, peaceably or forcibly (in the primaries) depending on your estimate of which method is better. Once in the saddle, you carry on precisely like other bosses. You are selfish, cold, calculating, and corrupt, but you maintain constantly the illusion that you are generous, warm, informal, and honest. You deftly present one picture of yourself to your equals and still another to your superiors. You remain in power until times change and another younger man drives you into obscurity.

Plunkitt pretended to live in a static world. He must have known that the days of the machine were numbered. I doubt whether he believed half of what he said. Naturally verbose, he could not help marking how the great masters of the metropolis from Tweed to Croker to Murphy became more and more taciturn and reticent. In his fulminations against the merit system there is a half-hearted confession of defeat. And here is a lesson. It is not oratory which permanently affects the balance and structure of political power. It is constitutional and administrative changes which accomplish that—regional planning, new charters, integrated governments, the merit system, accounting and fiscal control, centralized purchasing, and a standardized excess condemnation procedure.[7] These new techniques of governance inexorably impoverish the boss. Modern scientific analysis even more effectively strips the boss of his accouterments and blows away the aura of romance which envelops him.

[7] This is the "practice of taking by public authority under the right of eminent domain more land than is actually needed for a contemplated public improvement, with a view to selling the excess when the improvement is finished." It is a procedure for enabling the government to buy land at a fair price and to reserve the profits arising out of public expenditures enhancing real estate values.

IV

Although the recorded sayings of George W. Plunkitt have some general significance, he is one of that small, exclusive class of men who were Tammany leaders. He cannot be understood properly unless he is placed in this context.

Tammany Hall is a name which has been associated with the dominant faction of the Democratic-Republican County Committee of New York County, or Manhattan. In common parlance it is extended to cover the county organizations of Bronx County as well. Frequently it is used as though it signified all five of the county organizations of New York City. Shortly after the Revolutionary War, a number of social and "quasi-political" societies grew up in New York. The one which became identified with the Democratic party was the "Tammany Society" or "Columbian Order." Although there have been times when the leaders of the Democratic party were not members of the Tammany Society, or were not admitted to its historic headquarters on Fourteenth Street, or when they even set up rival organizations, such as Mozart Hall, Irving Hall, or the "County Democracy," usually the society and the party organization were regarded as identical. This was particularly true from 1900 to about 1940.

Modern Tammany began about 1868 when Tweed took complete control of the Hall. Kelly was boss from 1872 to 1886; Croker ran the Hall from 1886 to 1902; Murphy built it up to its peak of power from

1902 to 1924. Under Olvany and Curry, the momentum developed under Murphy carried it to even greater heights. But a new headquarters, newer techniques of management, and lowered morale, all of which were incidents of Judge Olvany's rule, marked the beginnings of Tammany's decline.

Plunkitt lived during the regimes of Tweed, Kelly, Croker, and Murphy. It was a time of great authority in the Hall, but it was also a time which tried the souls of the regulars, who were being attacked from within the party by such powerful figures as Tilden, Cleveland, and Grace and by rival local organizations. From without the party they were being attacked by Republicans like Theodore Roosevelt and by the reformers.

On the positive side, the machine did much that was good. But it tended also, as in other cities, to foster a destructive philosophy of government. It condoned in others and itself employed favoritism, force, and corruption. In good times, with population growing, wealth increasing, and opportunities abundant, the machine has ample sustenance for development and entrenchment. But in time of depression the spoils system is self-destructive. Greater individual distress, more mouths to feed, a depressed economy, and a corrupt, incompetent, and indolent administration pave the way for reorganization and reform. In this situation the characteristics and techniques of a particular ward leader are of relatively little importance.

Plunkitt's analysis of successful ward leadership

makes him seem typical of the ward boss in any dominant municipal machine. Actually he is a less-publicized type—the minor leader, the regimental commander who kept his place in the Tammany organization regardless of external pressures and internal upheavals. Sometimes machine authority has been concentrated in City Hall, or closely distributed among a small clique of bosses. But in Plunkitt's time, and for many years afterward, another pattern prevailed in New York. Those were the days when the ward boss, the Assembly District leader, was the most important single element in a complex organization. As Plunkitt himself observed, there were significant differences among ward bosses; and even Murphy nominated him for distinction when he emphasized his frankness. I do not quite accept this judgment. I think that in many respects George W. Plunkitt was fairly representative of the type of boss who served the wards in New York City from 1890 to 1930. His discourses are valuable because they throw light on many of the ward bosses, rather than revealing only Plunkitt himself.

I think of an old Irish woman, widow of one of Charley Murphy's lieutenants, on whom I called with a friend early one evening in 1930. There she sat at the dinner table, with her daughters-in-law and four sons. Grown men, one was a detective, one a bartender, one a horse-player, and one a lawyer. Although my friend and I had just finished dinner, we were ordered to sit down and consume generous helpings of corned beef and cabbage, washed down with beer. The conversation, directed with great gusto and good humor by the old lady, bore on the same subjects that engross a district boss. Gossip about friends, advice to one son to call on a sick old woman in the hospital, an admonition to another to intercede officially on behalf of a boy arrested for petty thievery. Smooth the way for someone's naturalization; see that Mrs. O'Brien's boy gets a job in the Department of Sanitation. "And you, Joe, did you go to Mass Sunday? Did you go to confession? Oh, you rascal you, what a lot of sins you have to confess!" She went on and on like this, never saying anything sinister or evil. No criticism of anyone associated with the Hall passed her lips, or at least none for their public offenses. But she expressed her contempt for captains and district leaders who were unkind to their wives, and her sympathy for those whose children were not a credit to them. This is the way bosses talk when they are with their families.

In the district clubs it is another story. Here one observes the anomalous situation of cynicism and benevolence inextricably interwoven. I have spent an evening at one of Jimmie Hines' levees. Early in the evening a few secretaries and regular hangers-on were present, some working, others talking. Then the petitioners began to appear. Little people mostly, some shabby, others flashily dressed. Elderly Jewish merchants, Irish laborers, Anglo-Saxon housewives, here a befuddled taxpayer, there a shifty gangster. All kinds, all degrees of citizens, all wanting something—

few of them hopeful. Suddenly Hines comes out from a corner. No one had seen him enter; probably he had been there all along.

He moves to the middle of the floor and people approach him one at a time. No line-up, no queuing, but a rough kind of order. Tugging at his left ear, Hines inclines his head first to this one, then to that one. He says very little, and speaks softly in low tones. The petitioners do most of the talking. It is not easy to hear what they say, only a word or a phrase is audible. But there is no obvious effort at concealment. "I'll try it," Hines says. "I'll do what I can." Suddenly five huge policemen enter, lieutenants and sergeants. They march to the rear and Hines joins them. It is a quiet but convivial meeting. There is an exchange of confidences. Everyone is apparently pleased; whatever it was they discussed, all issues were amiably settled.

When do district bosses cook up their crooked deals? Sometimes right there, in the club-house. Actually, most of the district bosses do not set out in advance to accomplish a specific corrupt objective. The corruption is part of a pattern which they do not recognize when it is born or even when it is emerging. It is also part of the pattern to articulate certain standards. Plunkitt's was to eschew illegal graft. Some bosses I have known would do nothing to rescue a pickpocket from the clutches of the law. Others would refuse to intercede on behalf of men accused of sex crimes. These were personal variations. The average boss adjusts his tolerances and avoidances to the mores and moral standards of his constituents—as he understands them.

V

Even as *Plunkitt of Tammany Hall* reflects the political ideals, attitudes, and mores of the average American political leader of the time, it also reflects the attitudes and customs which are peculiar to New York City. Practically all the books about bosses which are worth reading concern politicians of the New York area. Budd Schulberg's *What Makes Sammy Run?* is little more than Samuel Ornitz's *Haunch, Paunch and Jowl* in a different environment and with a new twist. The municipal boss in America is a metropolitan phenomenon. There have been bosses in Chicago, Detroit, San Francisco, and New Orleans who merit study, but in most of the smaller cities today the bosses who struggle to profit by political corruption are usually contemptible crooks—mouldy imitations of the great scoundrels who once played with the destiny of New York City.

Plunkitt, like Riordon, was a dyed-in-the-wool New Yorker. His little world was bounded by the East River, the Bronx, the North River, and Staten Island —a vague geographic expression of Manhattan Island. It was peopled by the Irish, who were the true Fourth-of-July Americans, and miscellaneous other breeds without the law—Republicans, reformers, businessmen, and immigrants from Brooklyn and other outlandish places. Plunkitt loved New York with a feeling so pas-

Introduction

sionate that we are sorely tempted to forgive him. Time and again I myself have encountered his whole-souled devotion among New York's minor politicians, whether Republicans or Democrats or Socialists. It does not keep some of them from shaming their city any more than filial love keeps men from disgracing their mothers. As an incorrigible Manhattanite, Plunkitt had only a very hazy knowledge of the rest of the United States. He had no real sentiment for New York State, and he looked upon Brooklyn with acute revulsion.

These days you do not hear much about the provincialism of Brooklyn. What you do hear, I think, is artificially created to bolster the morale and profits of the Dodgers. Manhattanites are still prejudiced against Brooklynites. When Plunkitt excoriated them as "natural-born hayseeds," he merely repeated what others were saying. The greater city had been formed just a few years earlier and the citizens of New York County were not yet used to their newly incorporated brethren. In the years since then progress toward unification has been slow. Brooklyn has had more than its share of mayors, with Hylan and O'Dwyer, but the Bronx has never been more than an appendage to Manhattan. Queens, now the largest borough in size, still lacks cohesion; it is a sprawling federation of many different types of urban and suburban agglomerations. We can all share Plunkitt's sad repugnance to the passing of Manhattan's insular hegemony. But it is not yet time for tears of despair. The old New York still lives and its center is still the New York county of Manhattan, that is, the Borough of Manhattan.

Plunkitt's irate denunciation of the state legislature, which always regarded the city as "pie for the hayseeds," has been a constant element in Tammany ideology and an important factor in its success. Many Republican bosses have felt the same way about Albany's appropriation of New York City's taxes. Since Republicans seldom won power in the city—not once in the past fifty years—they had to look to Albany for favors beyond those which their Tammany neighbors doled out. Every Republican ward leader I ever talked with was disturbed by his vain efforts to reconcile his party interests with his devotion to his city. La Guardia never labored under this handicap. He could lambaste the state legislature as hard as any Democratic mayor, and that is one of the reasons why he remained in power so long. La Guardia never ignored the annexed boroughs—Bronx, Queens, or Brooklyn. By his time it was both possible and expedient to recognize the Greater City as a whole. But this was not true in Plunkitt's day. At the turn of the century a Manhattan ward boss could win the affection of his constituents by speaking scornfully of those who lived on the other side of the East River and north to the Bronx.

Although life in America has now become monotonous and standardized, there is still much to set New York off from the rest of the country. It is not merely larger, richer, more populous, and more colorful than any other city. It is also unique in its devotion to inconsistent and irreconcilable ideals—not just one or two, but scores of ideals. *Plunkitt of Tammany Hall* is a book of, by, and for New Yorkers. New Yorkers will read it again if they have read it before, and it will make them smile a little, to pause and consider the progress of their city in the past fifty years.

VI

What one finds after diligent search in the way of a political philosophy in Plunkitt is typical of the average machine politician. His views on the party system are interesting. Fred Bays, formerly state chairman of the Democratic party in Indiana, once told me that he did not care what party a man voted for, so long as he voted. George W. Plunkitt would never have uttered such nonsense. He was pleased to see any Democrat vote, except for some rival in the primary. He tolerated Republicans only because the law commanded it. Most ward bosses know little and care less about issues, unless the issue is a new bridge, or a new technique of administration. Plunkitt distrusted all thinkers and all orators. He believed in patronage. This was the central issue, even if it actually was not an issue but a technique.

To the observant reader it is immediately apparent that Plunkitt accepted the two-party system as proper and inevitable for Americans. He had some opinions about great public issues, but these are interesting rather than important. Tammany Hall, which Abram S. Hewitt once characterized as a "machine . . . offensive to the self-respect of intelligent Democrats," and "an anomaly which should not be perpetuated or tolerated," nevertheless nominated and elected Hewitt for mayor in 1886. Ten years later, Tammany opposed Bryan for president, although it went on record as endorsing him. "The prevalent Democracy has wandered into error," said Henry D. Purroy, a Tammany Sachem, "but it is far better . . . entitled to my support than can ever be its irreconcilable enemy, the Republican party, that organization of monopolies and trusts." [8] Plunkitt knew little and cared less about such issues. Like most of his fellow-bosses, he made a successful pretense of always supporting the party. The party was the local party, the Democratic County Committee.

When we come to the subject of loyalty, which is one of our most baffling political problems, we get precious little help from Plunkitt. Murphy attested to his belief in political organizations, "all-the-year-around work," and giving preference to party workers in making appointments. Loyalty, which is spelled "party loyalty" but means loyalty of a personal sort to men who have helped you in the past and will support you in the future, was the first article of Plunkitt's creed. Having passed through a period when Tammany had been split several ways on a number of occasions and when the Republicans, too, were torn by the internal dissension between Platt and Odell, and when even the

[8] Euphemia Vale Blake, *History of the Tammany Society* (New York: Souvenir Publishing Company, 1891), p. 163.

reformers were knifing each other, Plunkitt was disturbed by the operation of this principle. If a politician "hustles around" and gets jobs for his constituents he is entitled to gratitude, but if he is selfish or "shows no talent" or lacks nerve to demand a fair share of the good things, "his followers may be absolved from their allegiance." [9]

While Plunkitt was growing up in the machine, learning his trade and acquiring his beliefs from the older bosses, many New Yorkers, some of them dwelling only a short distance from Plunkitt's house, were attending a different school. They actually dwelt in a different milieu; they were learning from the reformers. Throughout Plunkitt's youth and early manhood the reformers were active. A few were interested only in theories of governance; many thought only in national terms; still others specialized in various local reforms, such as civil service, the relief of the poor, public education, the monetary system, or raising the standard of public morality. One man, the philosopher of the Single Tax, Henry George, scorned no occasion as too far from his central interests. He even ran for mayor twice. Periodically, the confluence of reformist efforts produced a tangible result. Although Plunkitt was no reformer, he was influenced by them, perhaps more than he knew.

In 1883 the National Civil Service Act was passed, and in 1884 Cleveland was elected president over

[9] Cf. J. T. Salter, *The Pattern of Politics* (New York: The Macmillan Company, 1940), p. 51.

Blaine. New York State adopted its civil service law in 1883; New York City followed suit in 1898. "Before then," said Plunkitt, "when a party won, its workers got everything in sight. That was somethin' to make a man patriotic." Since 1898, despite bitter opposition by the machine, the merit system has steadily advanced. There are still men who inveigh against it exactly as Plunkitt did, but each year their voices grow fainter and more querulous. Honest and efficient administration in state and city began in Albany with Grover Cleveland and Theodore Roosevelt, and in New York City with Seth Low and his friends in the Citizens' Union. In the state this principle has been faithfully promoted by both Republican and Democratic governors; but, notwithstanding great strides forward under Fusion mayors or as a result of Fusion educational and legislative activity, it was not until La Guardia began his twelve-year tenure in 1934 that the city administration was able to keep in step with the state.

During the same period scores of other reforms were launched and were translated into action. Among them were welfare legislation, endorsed by Tammany, school reforms, hospital and health reforms, recreation and slum clearance, planning and zoning, and rapid transit. Most of the political reforms came after Plunkitt's time. It was younger men who promoted the direct primary, the short ballot, honest elections, and "Home Rule." Of these, only the latter would have won Plunkitt's endorsement.

Plunkitt's aversion to the merit system actually has

no point today. To most students of government it is incomprehensible. They think of the tremendous strides forward we have made in civil service since 1883. But an attitude of hostility to the merit system based on exactly the same grounds as those given by Plunkitt still persists in many quarters. In the more progressive states politicians have given up direct attacks on the system, but they continue to sabotage the efforts of competent and honest officials to enforce it. Although the Republican party has been most vocal in attacking civil service abuses in Washington and New York City, during the war when the regulatory machinery broke down it was not the Democratic party, or even the party system itself, which profited by irregularities. Many bureau chiefs who circumvented the law did so under the pressure of necessity—or of personal ambition. However, when men ridicule the merit law, they use Plunkitt's stale generalities. What Plunkitt said about the civil service is amusing, but it does not reveal any serious thinking about this important political problem.

Since he believed in human corruptibility and in the materialistic philosophy of "every man looking out for himself," Plunkitt naturally detested the reformers. He felt for Republicans the same gentle scorn which the professional feels for the amateur. But he could never fathom why reformers persisted in their efforts to create a better society, and since he did not understand them he feared them. Because he feared them, he hated them.

Plunkitt listed four counts in his indictment of reformers: (1) They are "mornin' glories" and do not
last; (2) they are ridiculous; (3) they are not con-
versant with the real job to be done; (4) they are
selfish. In modern times ridicule is not used so frequently. Today it is only in the smaller towns and
rural areas that cartoonists and editors use sneers re-
sembling Plunkitt's "I remember one name—Ollie Teall
—dear, pretty Ollie and his big dog." And yet, as late
as 1945, demoralized Tammanyites in the lower brack-
ets were consoling each other by ridiculing "Butch"
La Guardia, his radio comics, and his big black hat.
But the strong men of the machine did not resort to
ridicule; they were fearful and respectful of the Little
Flower. Plunkitt was guffawing in 1905, "Could a
search party find R. W. G. Welling?" Yet it was this
great and good man who more than any other in the past
fifty years successfully contributed to the cause of good
government and the demolition of the machine.[10] When
Plunkitt hinted that reformers were not willing to assume the true burdens of municipal politics, he was
right. Amos Pinchot said the same thing:

> In the midst of great and real issues, we have
> chosen little, false issues . . . we have made the
> fatal mistake of standing for men instead of meas-
> ures. . . . The average man in New York has an
> annual income of less than seven hundred dollars.

---

[10] Welling founded and maintained the National Self-Government
Committee, which, until his death in 1947, had done more than any
other agency to make the teaching of government in the schools
realistic and inspiring.

. . . He is, in fact, a poor man. What he and his wife and children care about is neither that "political uplift" . . . nor yet is it respectability in the city hall, with the added concealment and suavity in graft and corruption which reform administrations have been able to ensure. What men want is economic rather than political improvement. Give them an increased purchasing power for their wage or salary, a lower charge for some of the necessities of life, such as rent, fuel, light, and transportation. Give them (these) . . . and half the battle of political reform and good citizenship has been won.[11]

But Pinchot was wiser than Plunkitt, since what enabled Tammany to survive from 1917 to 1933 was not the "district relief" advocated by Plunkitt as a cure-all, but Tammany's social and economic program, articulated and applied by Smith, Wagner, Hylan, Walker, and their associates. When Tammany collapsed in 1933, it was because La Guardia convincingly represented a liberal point of view as well as administrative integrity and efficiency.

William Allen, one of New York's first municipal research workers, put his finger on the real cause of the retardation and occasional defeat of reform. Plunkitt thought reform administrations failed because they did not copy Tammany's ways. Allen maintained that the opposite was true:

---

[11] "A Letter to the County Chairman," in C. C. Maxey, *Readings in Municipal Government* (New York: Doubleday & Co., 1924), pp. 154 ff.

Mass psychology puts Tammany and anti-Tammany in entirely different categories: Tammany is always playing the game of politics where anything is fair that works; anti-Tammany is expected not to play at all, but to be in deadly earnest working for ideals. Tammany is credited for good deeds because they are not expected of it; anti-Tammany is blamed for failures to deliver good deeds and for bad deeds done, however few, because they are not expected. Tammany is judged cynically, practically; anti-Tammany is judged ideally. Publics feel about anti-Tammany as Rockefeller said he felt about being cheated: he would rather lose one thousand dollars than be cheated out of five cents.[12]

It is not correct to say that Fusion failed under La Guardia, not when O'Dwyer, his Democratic successor has tried to conserve the gains made under the Little Flower. But it is true that La Guardia became increasingly unpopular with the Fusion rank-and-file when he made more and more concessions to the rich and powerful, in both business and politics. Most of the bosses I have known had very little respect for the people who surrounded La Guardia. Once, shortly after I was elected Chairman of the Fusion party, a Tammany district leader invited me to dinner and as we sat over our cognac and coffee he said, "Professor, I've been thinking over this business and I think I can

---

[12] William H. Allen, *Why Tammanies Revive: La Guardia's Mis-Guard* (New York: Institute for Public Service, 1937), p. 2.

give you some suggestions about taking care of yourself downtown." "Oh, no," I hastily interposed, "I'm afraid you don't understand, even after knowing me all these years. I don't want anything for myself. I've tried time and again to tell you we're working for the good of the city." He looked pained, then continued in a level, earnest voice. "You, yes, you are. But the rest of that gang down there! They'll ask you and every idealist in the city to work your heads off for them. They'll put their juicy salary checks in the bank, they'll find a dozen ways to pick up fees and gifts and graft on the side. And what will you get out of it? I'll be surprised if any one of them ever so much as buys you a beer." He was genuinely sorry when I declined his well-meant advice.

As a matter of fact, none of the authentic Fusionists who accepted responsible positions under La Guardia ever took a penny he did not earn. There were deadheads on the payroll, to be sure, and there were tightwads. Only a small handful of them ever made any notable contributions to the Fusion cause. If they had done so the party would be in power today. My friend —whom I shall not name since he occupies a prominent position in New York public life today—was wrong. Reformers are not crooks, nor do they as a rule use the information and influence they obtain in public office to advance their own interests. But Plunkitt was right on one count. In his day the reformers had not learned the necessity of making pecuniary sacrifices for the good of the organization. Even now, in New

York City and in many smaller cities, it is difficult to get those who directly profit from political reform to make contributions to reform movements.

What Plunkitt said about graft and corruption related to the technique of machine control and personal aggrandizement. As Brooks remarked, it is "not a matter of either ethics or economics but of caution." Plunkitt gave the impression that he never accepted bribes. He did, of course. "Big Dick" Butler lived in the same general neighborhood and he has told how it was managed:

Grafting used to be open and above board, like it should be if it's fairly honest. In the olden days, you paid the ward man in his saloon or right out on the street corner or on the church steps, wherever you happened to meet him. And the collector put the money in his sock or in his bank and thought no more about it.

Most of the graft nowadays passes through the hands of lawyers, disguised as legal fees. If you want to get a favor from Tammany, just hire one of their leading lawyers and pay him fifty thousand dollars fee, part of which he keeps for himself and part of which he passes on to the boys who actually do the favor. You're safe then, because the courts are run by lawyers and lawyers stick together like the Forty Thieves. Lawyers can do no wrong.[13]

---

[13] Butler and Driscoll, *op. cit.*, pp. 129–30. Cf. also Roy V. Peel, *The Political Clubs of New York City* (New York: G. P. Putnam's Sons, 1935).

Introduction

The various investigations which preceded, accompanied, and followed the Fusion victory of 1933, exposed and discouraged "legal graft" but probably did not destroy it altogether. Plunkitt did not use these indirect methods: what he says has therefore only historical significance.

Plunkitt's political interests and prejudices colored his attitudes on great municipal questions. He favored the removal of gas-houses from his district to Astoria for public reasons and because he had money invested in land which he expected to appreciate in value. Governor Odell "crossed him up" on this deal, and the reform press criticized him on the Spuyten Duyvil proposition. These were good measures. Where Plunkitt went wrong was in thinking the public would always agree to his "making a little on the side." His magnificent dream of a self-governing city of New York has been echoed by serious students of politics. Merriam has urged and predicted a similar development. Scores of city planners feel that it will come all in good time. I like the idea myself, though neither I nor any serious student desires that the independent city-state should be ruled by Tammany organization or Tammany methods. But it is worth noting that Plunkitt and his spiritual forefather, Fernando Wood, who created Central Park, are among the few machine leaders who ever had such a vision.

I find myself intrigued by Plunkitt's suggestion that the greater city "make some sort of appropriation for them (the up-staters) for a few years, but . . . under the distinct understanding that they must get busy right away and support themselves." A little more imposed industry and self-reliance would not hurt the smaller towns and rural areas of the country. On the other hand, what Plunkitt and all the little Plunkitts can never comprehend is that metropolitan prosperity is derived from strategic advantages entirely unrelated to the knowledge, training, and deserts of the people who live in large cities. Each region is an entity and all regions are integral parts of the greater entity, the nation. The balancing of political benefits and obligations cannot be solved by simple Plunkitt formulas, however appealing they may be.

At a time when relief was a personal and neighborhood concern, Plunkitt could conceive of no other relief agency but the political club. I do not know what he thought of Jacob Riis; I doubt if he ever knew that Riis and his fellow welfare-workers even existed. The bosses of the following generation knew them but were still prone to seize credit for all the relief work ever done. Time and again I have had them tell me that their overhead was zero, whereas the "Russell Sage" people spent 85 per cent on administration and only 15 per cent on direct relief. As administrators, the bosses did a poor job; their relief was unsystematic, unfair, and uncertain.

In 1931 the secretary of the 23rd A. D. Democratic Club had in his possession some of the official cards used in assigning unemployed men to relief jobs in Central Park. I told him he could not do that, that it was improper and illegal. "Illegal, hell," he said, "Tammany has always taken care of relief." But the next week he was forced to return them to the office of the Emergency Relief Administration. The bosses did not give up without a struggle, but it has now come to be generally accepted that public funds and activities will be administered impartially by public officials. The bosses, however, rendered an invaluable service in keeping alive the idea of welfare as an essential public function.

There is much to be said for Plunkitt's thesis, implicit in his discourses, that a growing city needs ward bosses, or some kind of responsible community leader. When Steffens asked Croker, "Why must there be a boss, when we've got a mayor and—a council—and—" Croker broke in, "That's why. It's because there's a mayor *and* a council *and* judges—*and*—a hundred other men to deal with." [14] I have had scores of bosses tell me the same thing. But La Guardia demonstrated, at least during his first term, that a really responsible and energetic mayor can perform the uniting and integrating function of municipal leadership without becoming a dictator, like Hague or Crump.

As to the "Little Father" of the neighborhood, we still need such a man. As a matter of fact, such a person is needed today even more than in Plunkitt's time. We need a "district leader" who is competent, who is responsible, and who is honest. Probably, he should be given official status and a salary.

---

[14] Lincoln Steffens, *Autobiography* (New York: Harcourt, Brace & Co.), pp. 236-7.

VII

Scores of political scientists have quoted Plunkitt's famous words on honest and dishonest graft, none of them, I am happy to say, with approval. But privately I have heard too many respectable people condone legal graft. The bosses may have possibly influenced this attitude. "Police graft is dirty graft," said Croker. "We have to stand for it. If we get big graft, and the cops and small fry politicians know it, we can't decently kick at their petty stuff." Croker thought he exculpated himself by refraining from taking "dirty" graft. Plunkitt was consoled by abstaining from outrageously illegal acts like stealing the courthouse dome. Notorious New York grafters whom I have interviewed salved their consciences by observing that there was more graft in Queens or Albany or Washington. A young man I know, who was brought up in New York, bribed a Congressman—and both he and the Congressman went to jail. As these two sit in jail they can meditate on the irony of fate which leaves outside scores of others who have more flagrantly violated the canons of good citizenship.

We cannot expect a reform administration to change people's habits overnight. I remember one Christmas Eve in New York when I was in a luggage shop, a policeman came in and forced the proprietor to give him an expensive piece of luggage. After the marauding cop had left, I asked the proprietor if he didn't know that Chief Valentine had strictly forbidden such levies by officers in the police force. "Sure I know that," he said.

"But what good does it do? I refuse to give this guy a suitcase for his daughter. Then what happens? Even if this cop gets transferred to Canarsie, the next one bears down on me. He won't let delivery trucks park out front long enough to deliver a package here. Inspectors will be around here every hour. Violation, violation! Pfui!"

It is a long, hard road. Unyielding pressure on officials by the reformers outside the administration—this helps. And in the schools, the churches, the clubs, the press, the radio—continuous assertion of high standards of morality also helps. Political success is more effective than preaching. But let reform win and it need not rely exclusively on preaching. It must, as Amos Pinchot said, adopt a socially progressive economic program. And it must institutionalize the welfare program —most of it, but not necessarily all of it.

VIII

What makes *Plunkitt of Tammany Hall* unique? It is not the reputation of Riordon, who has left only this monument to his fame. A free-lancer, as so many newsmen were in his day, Riordon contributed articles to several New York papers and to the *Boston Transcript*. There is no record that Riordon ever gave any aid and comfort to R. Fulton Cutting, the Citizens' Union leader whose work on the Union had just been printed. Alfred Henry Lewis, a crony of the West Side bosses, had only a few years earlier published two books on practical politics, a life of Croker and *The Boss*. I believe that the success of these works was what inspired Riordon. Riordon undoubtedly admired Plunkitt for his "absolute frankness and vigorous unconventionality of thought and expression." I think that he greatly overestimated Plunkitt's influence. He was not "one of the great powers in Tammany Hall." I once amused myself asking old-time leaders about him; they responded vaguely but graciously, and I am sure that very few of them had any clear recollection of Plunkitt. The meticulous care with which Riordon wrote down what Plunkitt said suggests that he felt an honest distaste for the ethics both of Plunkitt and Charles F. Murphy. But I think he was "taken in" by Plunkitt's personal charm.

When Riordon's book was in press, Al Smith had just gone to Albany to begin, with Robert F. Wagner and James W. Wadsworth, the career that was to lead him to the Democratic presidential nomination. Smith, a product of Tom Foley's Seymour Club, could never bring himself to disapprove of the creatures of his early environment.[15] Neither could his supporters in 1928—able and conscientious men devoted to the public service. As a matter of fact, Riordon and Al Smith were precursors of a period of growing tolerance toward municipal corruption and bossism. Public indifference was jarred by the victory of John Purroy Mitchell in 1913, only to be nourished again during the

---

[15] See Alfred E. Smith, *The Citizen and His Government* (New York: Harper & Bros., 1935), Chapter I. Cf. also the biographies of Smith by Henry F. Pringle, Norman Hapgood, and Henry Moscowitz.

eight hectic years when the bumbling, erratic John F. Hylan was mayor. The machine was tolerated, even respected, during most of this period because Charles F. Murphy was a quiet, efficient, sober man, and even more because he gave free rein to men like Smith, Wagner, and James Foley who stood high in public esteem. After Smith was replaced by Roosevelt in public favor, the machine began to crumble and the public once again responded to an awakened conscience.

In some respects, *Plunkitt of Tammany Hall* is a treatise on practical politics.[16] Bryce is credited with introducing realistic interpretation into American political science, an accolade which seems to be deserved when one compares *The American Commonwealth*, published in 1888, with Jesse Macy's *Party Organization and Political Machinery*, a native American textbook written in 1904 by an Iowa college professor. Of

---

[16] By overzealous and misguided scholars it has even been placed in the same category as Machiavelli's *The Prince*. It does bear a remote resemblance to Balzac's *Le Prince* (1631) and Sir Thomas Elyot's *Boke of the Governour* (1531). For a long time, scholars immersed in studies of the law refreshed themselves by reading Bacon's *De Augmentis,* especially the eighth book. In America, budding statesmen learned lessons in practical politics from watching the men who wrote the letters, made speeches, debated constitutional questions, and controlled nominations. Sometimes a leader such as John or Samuel Adams would make a tart observation, reinforcing the impressions thoughtful men had received as a precipitate from their considering "both sides" in the lively, often acrimonious political controversies of the day. Later, by searching diligently in de Tocqueville's *Démocratie en Amérique* (Paris, 1835) or in Ostrogorski's *Democracy and the Organization of Political Parties* (New York, 1902) they would recognize truth in the objective observations of these foreign commentators.

course, the muckrakers were almost alone instrumental in getting into print something less perishable than newspaper articles. In our own time the men who have done the most to describe and analyze the art of politics are Charles E. Merriam and Robert E. Brooks. Merriam, who was also an active participant, inspired more analytical and suggestive works in the field of political power and influence than anyone else. Independently, many other writers brought their intelligence to bear on the same subject. Although none has had great influence, collectively they have made us all acutely aware of the nature of political power and influence.[17]

Political thought about party organization and leadership has evolved the way a branching tree grows. Periodically, someone attempts to bind together the errant boughs and twigs and give the whole some coherence and meaning, but we seem now to be in the middle of one of those phases where everyone follows his own bent. Altogether too many of the writers in

---

[17] Of the muckrakers, Lincoln Steffens achieved undying fame with his *The Shame of the Cities* (New York, 1904), a reprint of his magazine articles. Late in life he stimulated recollection in his *Autobiography*. See also John Wanamaker, *Speeches on Quayism* (Philadelphia, 1898), Henry Champernowme's *The Boss* (New York, 1894)—Champernowme was a pseudonym for Professor D. M. Means—and Jane Addams' "Why the Ward Boss Rules" (*Outlook*, April 2, 1898). Defenses of "the system" ranged from scathing denunciations of reformers by such master scoundrels as Roscoe Conkling in his *Life and Letters* (New York, 1889, p. 538), to the mellowed recantations of aging journalists, best represented by Fremont Older's *My Own Story* (New York, 1919). Cf. also D. G. Thompson, *Politics in a Democracy* (New York, 1893).

the field of practical politics have been satisfied merely to describe political phenomena, although a few, such as Gosnell and Lasswell, have successfully applied statistical and psychological instruments of analysis. The combined efforts of scholars, journalists, and reformers have given us a fairly satisfactory picture of the political boss. Now that we have it we are not quite sure what we will do with it. And yet we need not be unduly concerned. Other forces, released and abetted by these studies, have nearly destroyed machines and bosses.

Now to return to the journalist as political commentator. The muckrakers were all on the side of honesty and reform, notwithstanding a queasy reluctance on the part of a few of them to prosecute their campaigns to the limit of utterly ruining a minor politician. The majority of the reporters were cynical —morally much better than their employers but still not disposed to extend themselves in attacks on vice and corruption. Those who could not contain themselves, radicals such as Samuel Ornitz and Michael Gold (*Jews Without Money*), made slashing attacks on the machine through the transparent medium of fiction.[18]

---

[18] At a somewhat later date, Samuel G. Blythe, Charles Francis Coe, and Clarence Buddington Kelland in thinly disguised fiction allowed virtue to triumph over vice in the pages of the *Saturday Evening Post*. In a more serious vein, journalistic scholars of the rank of Walter Lippmann, William Allen White, Walter Davenport, Denis T. Lynch, Frank Kent, George Creel, Henry Pringle, and Burton Heath made numerous efforts to learn how men became and remained bosses. In this same class belong the books

IX

When I first learned that William Riordon's *Plunkitt of Tammany Hall* was to be reissued, I confess that I had some misgivings. Although I have myself long been active in reform politics, I have a wide acquaintance among political leaders of the "boss" type and count several of them friends. District leaders or ward bosses, particularly those in large cities—I might even say *only* those in large cities—are frequently warmly human persons quite outspoken on some subjects, and capable of evoking sincere admiration. But they are also purveyors of unethical principles and sometimes downright malefactors.

Many of the students who have sat in my classes in the past twenty years had grown up in neighborhoods where machine influence was strong. They had early in life been indoctrinated by men who believed in the machine, and had come to accept its standards and evaluations. They regarded my classes in political parties as an opportunity to develop whatever talents they possessed for rising in politics and for acquiring the rewards of political influence and power. There was a time when I wondered whether I did well by society to

written by John Salter, who has the reportorial skill of the journalist although he was trained as a professor. One of the earliest and best journalistic exposures of bosses was written and published by a reforming lawyer, Matthew P. Breen (*Thirty Years of New York Politics*, 1899). Breen was unsparing of his contempt for the bosses, but even he was fond of the more picturesque characters, as his pen picture of Sheehan reveals.

make known to my students how men entered "politics" and clawed and smirked and blustered and connived to reach positions of power; and how, once entrenched, they became cogs in a machine which inexorably rode down the opposition offered by the reformers. Later I found no reason to regret that I gave them every opportunity to observe the political process at first hand and to study the primary written sources of American political history. The average student, even more than his elders, is aware of changing patterns in public morality. He knows, too, that bossism is dying out and that new standards of political ethics, administrative efficiency, and scientific competence are beginning to prevail in municipal government.

In evaluating the moral character of ward bosses, we have to define our terms carefully. Every objective observer from M. Ostrogorski down to John Salter agrees that ward bosses do not have a fine sense of honor. When Plunkitt was at the height of his powers, business was reputedly at loggerheads with Tammany. But Croker did not make his millions from petty graft. In Murphy's time business and politics grew closer together. It became difficult to distinguish one area of activity from the other. It was hard to find some ward bosses in their club-houses in the late Twenties and early Thirties. They were negotiating deals with their business friends in the elegant social clubs of Manhattan or in private dining rooms of restaurants. After the crash of 1929 the pretty bubble burst. Simultaneously with the increase of Tammany's need to care for the poor, came the decline in machine revenues from big business and the virtual extinction of Tammany's capacity to grant favors to the rich and powerful. This also meant the destruction of Tammany prosperity. It did not mean the demise of dishonesty.

Plunkitt's utterances were published at a time when the machine was groggy from numerous blows, and just before its last great period of power which came to an end in 1932. The onslaught against the machine was led by reformers, but it was probably successful because of deep social and economic forces. Today the prevailing attitude toward bosses and machines is scientific. We want to know as much as we can about institutions, in what environments they were nurtured, how they were led, how they grew, and how they declined. To the political scientist, *Plunkitt of Tammany Hall* is scientific material. It is data for observation, analysis, and interpretation. If we were ambitious to understand Plunkitt, we should have to soak ourselves in the lore of the city at the turn of the century. There is no shortcut; it does not exist in any one book. But, assuming that the curious reader knows a lot about New York City and at least something about how political machines operate, he can obtain in this little volume a satisfactory view of the ward boss as he was before he was routed by the new political forces characteristic of the twentieth century.

As a historical document, *Plunkitt of Tammany Hall* is a delightful work. It should prove a delectable dish to the avid and undiscriminating reader of biographies. The serious student of politics can learn from it that a kind heart, a sense of humor, and a modest set of prejudices are indispensable elements in the enjoyment of life. The reformer will possibly learn from Plunkitt that reforms which blunt the impulses to forthrightness, generosity, and fun may produce a civilization not worth the effort of saving.

ROY V. PEEL

CONTENTS

Contents

PREFACE

THIS VOLUME DISCLOSES THE
mental operations of perhaps the most thoroughly
practical politician of the day—George Washington
Plunkitt, Tammany leader of the Fifteenth Assembly
District, Sachem of the Tammany Society and Chairman of the Elections Committee of Tammany Hall, who
has held the offices of State Senator, Assemblyman,
Police Magistrate, County Supervisor and Alderman
and who boasts of his record in filling four public offices
in one year and drawing salaries from three of them at
the same time.

liii

Preface

The discourses that follow were delivered by him from his rostrum, the bootblack stand in the County Court-house, at various times in the last half-dozen years. Their absolute frankness and vigorous unconventionality of thought and expression charmed me. Plunkitt said right out what all practical politicians think but are afraid to say. Some of the discourses I published as interviews in the *New York Evening Post*, the *New York Sun*, the *New York World*, and the *Boston Transcript*. They were reproduced in newspapers throughout the country and several of them, notably the talks on "The Curse of Civil Service Reform" and "Honest Graft and Dishonest Graft," became subjects of discussion in the United States Senate and in college lectures. There seemed to be a general recognition of Plunkitt as a striking type of the practical politician, a politician, moreover, who dared to say publicly what others in his class whisper among themselves in the City Hall corridors and the hotel lobbies.

I thought it a pity to let Plunkitt's revelations of himself—as frank in their way as Rousseau's "Confessions"—perish in the files of the newspapers; so I collected the talks I had published, added several new ones, and now give to the world in this volume a system of political philosophy which is as unique as it is refreshing.

No New Yorker needs to be informed who George Washington Plunkitt is. For the information of others, the following sketch of his career is given. He was born, as he proudly tells, in Central Park; that is, in the territory now included in the park. He began life as a driver of a cart, then became a butcher's boy, and later went into the butcher business for himself. How he entered politics he explains in one of his discourses. His advancement was rapid. He was in the Assembly soon after he cast his first vote and has held office most of the time for forty years.

In 1870, through a strange combination of circumstances, he held the places of Assemblyman, Alderman, Police Magistrate and County Supervisor and drew three salaries at once—a record unexampled in New York politics.

Plunkitt is now a millionaire. He owes his fortune mainly to his political pull, as he confesses in "Honest Graft and Dishonest Graft." He is in the contracting, transportation, real estate, and every other business out of which he can make money. He has no office. His headquarters is the County Court-house bootblack stand. There he receives his constituents, transacts his general business and pours forth his philosophy.

Plunkitt has been one of the great powers in Tammany Hall for a quarter of a century. While he was in the Assembly and the State Senate he was one of the most influential members and introduced the bills that provided for the outlying parks of New York City, the Harlem River Speedway, the Washington Bridge, the 155th Street Viaduct, the grading of Eighth Avenue north of Fifty-seventh Street, additions to the Museum of Natural History, the West Side Court, and many other important public improvements. He is one of the closest friends and most valued advisers of Charles F. Murphy, leader of Tammany Hall.

WILLIAM L. RIORDON

A TRIBUTE TO PLUNKITT
BY THE LEADER OF
TAMMANY HALL

SENATOR PLUNKITT IS A STRAIGHT organization man. He believes in party government; he does not indulge in cant and hypocrisy and he is never afraid to say exactly what he thinks. He is a believer in thorough political organization and all-the-year-around work and he holds to the doctrine that, in making appointments to office, party workers should be preferred if they are fitted to perform the duties of the office. Plunkitt is one of the veteran leaders of the organization, he has always been faithful and reliable and he has performed valuable services for Tammany Hall.

CHARLES F. MURPHY

PLUNKITT *of*
Tammany Hall

ONEST GRAFT AND DISHONEST GRAFT.

.
.
.
.
.
.
.
.
.
.

👉

EVERYBODY IS TALKIN' THESE days about Tammany men growin' rich on graft, but nobody thinks of drawin' the distinction between honest graft and dishonest graft. There's all the difference in the world between the two. Yes, many of our men have grown rich in politics. I have myself. I've made a big fortune out of the game, and I'm gettin' richer every day, but I've not gone in for dishonest graft—blackmailin' gamblers, saloon-keepers, disorderly peo-

3

ple, etc.—and neither has any of the men who have made big fortunes in politics.

There's an honest graft, and I'm an example of how it works. I might sum up the whole thing by sayin': "I seen my opportunities and I took 'em."

Just let me explain by examples. My party's in power in the city, and it's goin' to undertake a lot of public improvements. Well, I'm tipped off, say, that they're going to lay out a new park at a certain place.

I see my opportunity and I take it. I go to that place and I buy up all the land I can in the neighborhood. Then the board of this or that makes its plan public, and there is a rush to get my land, which nobody cared particular for before.

Ain't it perfectly honest to charge a good price and make a profit on my investment and foresight? Of course, it is. Well, that's honest graft.

Or, supposin' it's a new bridge they're goin' to build. I get tipped off and I buy as much property as I can that has to be taken for approaches. I sell at my own price later on and drop some more money in the bank.

Wouldn't you? It's just like lookin' ahead in Wall Street or in the coffee or cotton market. It's honest graft, and I'm lookin' for it every day in the year. I will tell you frankly that I've got a good lot of it, too.

I'll tell you of one case. They were goin' to fix up a big park, no matter where. I got on to it, and went lookin' about for land in that neighborhood.

4

I could get nothin' at a bargain but a big piece of swamp, but I took it fast enough and held on to it. What turned out was just what I counted on. They couldn't make the park complete without Plunkitt's swamp, and they had to pay a good price for it. Anything dishonest in that?

Up in the watershed I made some money, too. I bought up several bits of land there some years ago and made a pretty good guess that they would be bought up for water purposes later by the city.

Somehow, I always guessed about right, and shouldn'+ I enjoy the profit of my foresight? It was rather amusin' when the condemnation commissioners came along and found piece after piece of the land in the name of George Plunkitt of the Fifteenth Assembly District, New York City. They wondered how I knew just what to buy. The answer is—I seen my opportunity and I took it. I haven't confined myself to land; anything that pays is in my line.

For instance, the city is repavin' a street and has several hundred thousand old granite blocks to sell. I am on hand to buy, and I know just what they are worth.

How? Never mind that. I had a sort of monopoly of this business for a while, but once a newspaper tried to do me. It got some outside men to come over from Brooklyn and New Jersey to bid against me.

5

Was I done? Not much. I went to each of the men and said: "How many of these 250,000 stones do you want?" One said 20,000, and another wanted 15,000, and another wanted 10,000. I said: "All right, let me bid for the lot, and I'll give each of you all you want for nothin'.

They agreed, of course. Then the auctioneer yelled: "How much am I bid for these 250,000 fine pavin' stones?"

"Two dollars and fifty cents," says I.

"Two dollars and fifty cents!" screamed the auctioneer. "Oh, that's a joke! Give me a real bid."

He found the bid was real enough. My rivals stood silent. I got the lot for $2.50 and gave them their share. That's how the attempt to do Plunkitt ended, and that's how all such attempts end.

I've told you how I got rich by honest graft. Now, let me tell you that most politicians who are accused of robbin' the city get rich the same way.

They didn't steal a dollar from the city treasury. They just seen their opportunities and took them. That is why, when a reform administration comes in and spends a half million dollars in tryin' to find the public robberies they talked about in the campaign, they don't find them.

The books are always all right. The money in the city treasury is all right. Everything is all right. All they can show is that the Tammany heads of depart-

6

ments looked after their friends, within the law, and gave them what opportunities they could to make honest graft. Now, let me tell you that's never goin' to hurt Tammany with the people. Every good man looks after his friends, and any man who doesn't isn't likely to be popular. If I have a good thing to hand out in private life, I give it to a friend. Why shouldn't I do the same in public life?

Another kind of honest graft. Tammany has raised a good many salaries. There was an awful howl by the reformers, but don't you know that Tammany gains ten votes for every one it lost by salary raisin'?

The Wall Street banker thinks it shameful to raise a department clerk's salary from $1500 to $1800 a year, but every man who draws a salary himself says: "That's all right. I wish it was me." And he feels very much like votin' the Tammany ticket on election day, just out of sympathy.

Tammany was beat in 1901 because the people were deceived into believin' that it worked dishonest graft. They didn't draw a distinction between dishonest and honest graft, but they saw that some Tammany men grew rich, and supposed they had been robbin' the city treasury or levyin' blackmail on disorderly houses, or workin' in with the gamblers and lawbreakers.

As a matter of policy, if nothing else, why should

7

the Tammany leaders go into such dirty business, when there is so much honest graft lyin' around when they are in power? Did you ever consider that?

Now, in conclusion, I want to say that I don't own a dishonest dollar. If my worst enemy was given the job of writin' my epitaph when I'm gone, he couldn't do more than write:

"George W. Plunkitt. He Seen His Opportunities, and He Took 'Em."

HOW TO BECOME A STATESMAN

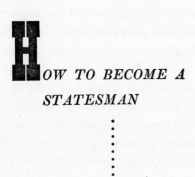

THERE'S THOUSANDS OF YOUNG men in this city who will go to the polls for the first time next November. Among them will be many who have watched the careers of successful men in politics, and who are longin' to make names and fortunes for themselves at the same game. It is to these youths that I want to give advice. First, let me say that I am in a position to give what the courts call expert testimony on the subject. I don't think you can easily find a better example than I am of success in politics.

9

After forty years' experience at the game I am—well, I'm George Washington Plunkitt. Everybody knows what figure I cut in the greatest organization on earth, and if you hear people say that I've laid away a million or so since I was a butcher's boy in Washington Market, don't come to me for an indignant denial. I'm pretty comfortable, thank you.

Now, havin' qualified as an expert, as the lawyers say, I am goin' to give advice free to the young men who are goin' to cast their first votes, and who are lookin' forward to political glory and lots of cash. Some young men think they can learn how to be successful in politics from books, and they cram their heads with all sorts of college rot. They couldn't make a bigger mistake. Now, understand me, I ain't sayin' nothin' against colleges. I guess they'll have to exist as long as there's bookworms, and I suppose they do some good in a certain way, but they don't count in politics. In fact, a young man who has gone through the college course is handicapped at the outset. He may succeed in politics, but the chances are 100 to 1 against him.

Another mistake: some young men think that the best way to prepare for the political game is to practise speakin' and becomin' orators. That's all wrong. We've got some orators in Tammany Hall, but they're chiefly ornamental. You never heard of Charlie Murphy delivering a speech, did you? Or

Richard Croker, or John Kelly, or any other man
who has been a real power in the organization? Look
at the thirty-six district leaders of Tammany Hall
to-day. How many of them travel on their tongues?
Maybe one or two, and they don't count when business is doin' at Tammany Hall. The men who rule
have practised keepin' their tongues still, not exer-
cisin' them. So you want to drop the orator idea
unless you mean to go into politics just to perform
the sky-rocket act.

Now, I've told you what not to do; I guess I can
explain best what to do to succeed in politics by
tellin' you what I did. After goin' through the ap-
prenticeship of the business while I was a boy by
workin' around the district headquarters and hustlin'
about the polls on election day, I set out when I cast
my first vote to win fame and money in New York
city politics. Did I offer my services to the district
leader as a stump-speaker? Not much. The woods
are always full of speakers. Did I get up a book on
municipal government and show it to the leader?
I wasn't such a fool. What I did was to get some
marketable goods before goin' to the leaders. What
do I mean by marketable goods? Let me tell you:
I had a cousin, a young man who didn't take any
particular interest in politics. I went to him and
said: "Tommy, I'm goin' to be a politician, and I
want to get a followin'; can I count on you?" He

11

said: "Sure, George." That's how I started in business. I got a marketable commodity—one vote. Then I went to the district leader and told him I could command two votes on election day, Tommy's and my own. He smiled on me and told me to go ahead. If I had offered him a speech or a bookful of learnin', he would have said, "Oh, forget it!"

That was beginnin' business in a small way, wasn't it? But that is the only way to become a real lastin' statesman. I soon branched out. Two young men in the flat next to mine were school friends. I went to them, just as I went to Tommy, and they agreed to stand by me. Then I had a followin' of three voters and I began to get a bit chesty. Whenever I dropped into district headquarters, everybody shook hands with me, and the leader one day honored me by lightin' a match for my cigar. And so it went on like a snowball rollin' down a hill. I worked the flat-house that I lived in from the basement to the top floor, and I got about a dozen young men to follow me. Then I tackled the next house and so on down the block and around the corner. Before long I had sixty men back of me, and formed the George Washington Plunkitt Association.

What did the district leader say then when I called at headquarters? I didn't have to call at headquarters. He came after me and said: "George, what do you want? If you don't see what you want, ask for it. Wouldn't you like to have a job or two in the departments for your friends?" I said: "I'll think it over; I haven't yet decided what the George Washington Plunkitt Association will do in the next campaign." You ought to have seen how I was courted and petted then by the leaders of the rival organizations. I had marketable goods and there was bids for them from all sides, and I was a risin' man in politics. As time went on, and my association grew, I thought I would like to go to the Assembly. I just had to hint at what I wanted, and three different organizations offered me the nomination. Afterwards, I went to the Board of Aldermen, then to the State Senate, then became leader of the district, and so on up and up till I became a statesman.

That is the way and the only way to make a lastin' success in politics. If you are goin' to cast your first vote next November and want to go into politics, do as I did. Get a followin', if it's only one man, and then go to the district leader and say: "I want to join the organization. I've got one man who'll follow me through thick and thin." The leader won't laugh at your one-man followin'. He'll shake your hand warmly, offer to propose you for membership in his club, take you down to the corner for a drink and ask you to call again. But go to him and say: "I took first prize at college in Aristotle; I can recite all Shakspere forwards and backwards; there ain't nothin' in science that ain't as familiar to me as blockades on the elevated roads and I'm the real thing in the way of silver-tongued orators." What will he answer? He'll probably say: "I guess you are not to blame for your misfortunes, but we have no use for you here."

THE CURSE OF CIVIL SERVICE REFORM

THIS CIVIL SERVICE LAW IS THE biggest fraud of the age. It is the curse of the nation. There can't be no real patriotism while it lasts. How are you goin' to interest our young men in their country if you have no offices to give them when they work for their party? Just look at things in this city to-day. There are ten thousand good offices, but we can't get at more than a few hundred of them. How are we goin' to provide for the thousands of men who worked for the Tammany ticket? It can't be done. These men were full of patriotism a short time ago. They expected to be servin' their city, but when we tell them that we can't place them,

15

do you think their patriotism is goin' to last? Not much. They say: "What's the use of workin' for your country anyhow? There's nothin' in the game." And what can they do? I don't know, but I'll tell you what I do know. I know more than one young man in past years who worked for the ticket and was just overflowin' with patriotism, but when he was knocked out by the civil service humbug he got to hate his country and became an Anarchist.

This ain't no exaggeration. I have good reason for sayin' that most of the Anarchists in this city to-day are men who ran up against civil service examinations. Isn't it enough to make a man sour on his country when he wants to serve it and won't be allowed unless he answers a lot of fool questions about the number of cubic inches of water in the Atlantic and the quality of sand in the Sahara desert? There was once a bright young man in my district who tackled one of these examinations. The next I heard of him he had settled down in Herr Most's saloon smokin' and drinkin' beer and talkin' socialism all day. Before that time he had never drank anything but whisky. I knew what was comin' when a young Irishman drops whisky and takes to beer and long pipes in a German saloon. That young man is to-day one of the wildest Anarchists in town. And just to think! He might be a patriot but for that cussed civil service.

16

The Curse of Civil Service Reform

Say, did you hear about that Civil Service Reform Association kickin' because the tax commissioners want to put their fifty-five deputies on the exempt list, and fire the outfit left to them by Low? That's civil service for you. Just think! Fifty-five Republicans and mugwumps holdin' $3000 and $4000 and $5000 jobs in the tax department when 1555 good Tammany men are ready and willin' to take their places! It's an outrage! What did the people mean when they voted for Tammany. What is representative government, anyhow? Is it all a fake that this is a government of the people, by the people and for the people? If it isn't a fake, then why isn't the people's voice obeyed and Tammany men put in all the offices?

When the people elected Tammany, they knew just what they were doin'. We didn't put up any false pretenses. We didn't go in for humbug civil service and all that rot. We stood as we have always stood, for rewardin' the men that won the victory. They call that the spoils system. All right; Tammany is for the spoils system, and when we go in we fire every anti-Tammany man from office that can be fired under the law. It's an elastic sort of law and you can bet it will be stretched to the limit. Of course the Republican State Civil Service Board will stand in the way of our local Civil Service Commission all it can; but say!—suppose we carry the State

17

some time won't we fire the up-State Board all right? Or we'll make it work in harmony with the local board, and that means that Tammany will get everything in sight. I know that the civil service humbug is stuck into the constitution, too, but, as Tim Campbell said: "What's the constitution among friends?"

Say, the people's voice is smothered by the cursed civil service law; it is the root of all evil in our government. You hear of this thing or that thing goin' wrong in the nation, the State or the city. Look down beneath the surface and you can trace everything wrong to civil service. I have studied the subject and I know. The civil service humbug is underminin' our institutions and if a halt ain't called soon this great republic will tumble down like a Park-avenue house when they were buildin' the subway, and on its ruins will rise another Russian government.

This is an awful serious proposition. Free silver and the tariff and imperialism and the Panama Canal are triflin' issues when compared to it. We could worry along without any of these things, but civil service is sappin' the foundation of the whole shootin' match. Let me argue it out for you. I ain't up on sillygisms, but I can give you some arguments that nobody can answer.

First this great and glorious country was built up by political parties; second, parties can't hold to-

gether if their workers don't get the offices when they
win; third, if the parties go to pieces, the government they built up must go to pieces, too; fourth,
then there'll be h—— to pay.

Could anything be clearer than that? Say, honest
now; can you answer that argument? Of course you
won't deny that the government was built up by the
great parties. That's history, and you can't go back
of the returns. As to my second proposition, you
can't deny that either. When parties can't get offices,
they'll bust. They ain't far from the bustin' point
now, with all this civil service business keepin' most
of the good things from them. How are you goin'
to keep up patriotism if this thing goes on? You
can't do it. Let me tell you that patriotism has been
dying out fast for the last twenty years. Before then
when a party won, its workers got everything in
sight. That was somethin' to make a man patriotic.
Now, when a party wins and its men come forward
and ask for their reward, the reply is, "Nothin' doin',
unless you can answer a list of questions about
Egyptian mummies and how many years it will take
for a bird to wear out a mass of iron as big as the
earth by steppin' on it once in a century?"

I have studied politics and men for forty-five
years, and I see how things are driftin'. Sad indeed
is the change that has come over the young men, even
in my district, where I try to keep up the fire of

19

patriotism by gettin' a lot of jobs for my constituents, whether Tammany is in or out. The boys and men don't get excited any more when they see a United States flag or hear the "Star Spangled Banner." They don't care no more for firecrackers on the Fourth of July. And why should they? What is there in it for them? They know that no matter how hard they work for their country in a campaign, the jobs will go to fellows who can tell about the mummies and the bird steppin' on the iron. Are you surprised then that the young men of the country are beginnin' to look coldly on the flag and don't care to put up a nickel for fire-crackers?

Say, let me tell of one case. After the battle of San Juan Hill, the Americans found a dead man with a light complexion, red hair and blue eyes. They could see he wasn't a Spaniard, although he had on a Spanish uniform. Several officers looked him over, and then a private of the Seventy-first Regiment saw him and yelled, "Good Lord, that's Flaherty." That man grew up in my district, and he was once the most patriotic American boy on the West Side. He couldn't see a flag without yellin' himself hoarse.

Now, how did he come to be lying dead with a Spanish uniform on? I found out all about it, and I'll vouch for the story. Well, in the municipal campaign of 1897, that young man, chockful of patriotism, worked day and night for the Tammany ticket.

Tammany won, and the young man determined to devote his life to the service of the city. He picked out a place that would suit him, and sent in his application to the head of department. He got a reply that he must take a civil service examination to get the place. He didn't know what these examinations were, so he went, all light-hearted, to the Civil Service Board. He read the questions about the mummies, the bird on the iron, and all the other fool questions—and he left that office an enemy of the country that he had loved so well. The mummies and the bird blasted his patriotism. He went to Cuba, enlisted in the Spanish army at the breakin' out of the war, and died fightin' his country.

That is but one victim of the infamous civil service. If that young man had not run up against the civil examination, but had been allowed to serve his country as he wished, he would be in a good office today, drawin' a good salary. Ah, how many young men have had their patriotism blasted in the same way!

Now, what is goin' to happen when civil service crushes out patriotism? Only one thing can happen: the republic will go to pieces. Then a czar or a sultan will turn up, which brings me to the fourthly of my argument; that is, there will be h—— to pay. And that ain't no lie.

REFORMERS ONLY MORNIN' GLORIES

. . . .

☞

COLLEGE PROFESSORS AND PHI-
losophers who go up in a balloon to think are always
discussin' the question: "Why Reform Administrations Never Succeed Themselves!" The reason is
plain to anybody who has learned the a, b, c of politics.

I can't tell just how many of these movements I've
seen started in New York during my forty years in
politics, but I can tell you how many have lasted
more than a few years—none. There have been re-

form committees of fifty, of sixty, of seventy, of one
hundred and all sorts of numbers that started out to
do up the regular political organizations. They were
mornin' glories—looked lovely in the mornin' and
withered up in a short time, while the regular machines went on flourishin' forever, like fine old oaks.
Say, that's the first poetry I ever worked off. Ain't
it great?

Just look back a few years. You remember the
People's Municipal League that nominated Frank
Scott for mayor in 1890? Do you remember the reformers that got up that league? Have you ever
heard of them since? I haven't. Scott himself sur-
vived because he had always been a first-rate politician, but you'd have to look in the newspaper
almanacs of 1891 to find out who made up the
People's Municipal League. Oh, yes! I remember one
name: Ollie Teall; dear, pretty Ollie and his big dog.
They're about all that's left of the League.

Now take the reform movement of 1894. A lot
of good politicians joined in that—the Republicans, the State Democrats, the Stecklerites and the
O'Brienites, and they gave us a lickin', but the real
reform part of the affair, the Committee of Seventy
that started the thing goin', what's become of those
reformers? What's become of Charles Stewart Smith?
Where's Bangs? Do you ever hear of Cornell, the
iron man, in politics now? Could a search party find

23

R. W. G. Welling? Have you seen the name of Fulton McMahon or McMahon Fulton—I ain't sure which—in the papers lately? Or Preble Tucker? Or —but it's no use to go through the list of the reformers who said they sounded in the death knell of Tammany in 1894. They're gone for good, and Tammany's pretty well, thank you. They did the talkin' and posin', and the politicians in the movement got all the plums. It's always the case.

The Citizens' Union has lasted a little bit longer than the reform crowd that went before them, but that's because they learned a thing or two from us. They learned how to put up a pretty good bluff— and bluff counts a lot in politics. With only a few thousand members, they had the nerve to run the whole Fusion movement, make the Republicans and other organizations come to their headquarters to select a ticket and dictate what every candidate must do or not do. I love nerve, and I've had a sort of respect for the Citizens' Union lately, but the Union can't last. Its people haven't been trained to politics, and whenever Tammany calls their bluff they lay right down. You'll never hear of the Union again after a year or two.

And, by the way, what's become of the good government clubs, the political nurseries of a few years ago? Do you ever hear of Good Government Club D and P and Q and Z any more? What's become of the infants who were to grow up and show us how to govern the city? I know what's become of the nursery that was started in my district. You can find pretty much the whole outfit over in my headquarters, Washington Hall.

The fact is that a reformer can't last in politics. He can make a show for a while, but he always comes down like a rocket. Politics is as much a regular business as the grocery or the dry-goods or the drug business. You've got to be trained up to it or you're sure to fall. Suppose a man who knew nothing about the grocery trade suddenly went into the business and tried to conduct it according to his own ideas. Wouldn't he make a mess of it? He might make a splurge for a while, as long as his money lasted, but his store would soon be empty. It's just the same with a reformer. He hasn't been brought up in the difficult business of politics and he makes a mess of it every time.

I've been studyin' the political game for forty-five years, and I don't know it all yet. I'm learnin' somethin' all the time. How, then, can you expect what they call "business men" to turn into politics all at once and make a success of it? It is just as if I went up to Columbia University and started to teach Greek. They usually last about as long in politics as I would last at Columbia.

You can't begin too early in politics if you want to

succeed at the game. I began several years before I
could vote, and so did every successful leader in Tammany Hall. When I was twelve years old I made myself useful around the district headquarters and did
work at all the polls on election day. Later on, I
hustled about gettin' out voters who had jags on or
who were too lazy to come to the polls. There's a
hundred ways that boys can help, and they get an
experience that's the first real step in statesmanship.
Show me a boy that hustles for the organization on
election day, and I'll show you a comin' statesman.

That's the a, b, c of politics. It ain't easy work to
get up to y and z. You have to give nearly all your
time and attention to it. Of course, you may have
some business or occupation on the side, but the great
business of your life must be politics if you want to
succeed in it. A few years ago Tammany tried to mix
politics and business in equal quantities, by havin'
two leaders for each district, a politician and a business man. They wouldn't mix. They were like oil and
water. The politician looked after the politics of his
district; the business man looked after his grocery
store or his milk route, and whenever he appeared at
an executive meeting, it was only to make trouble.
The whole scheme turned out to be a farce and was
abandoned mighty quick.

Do you understand now, why it is that a reformer
goes down and out in the first or second round, while

a politician answers to the gong every time? It is because the one has gone into the fight without trainin', while the other trains all the time and knows every fine point of the game.

NEW YORK CITY IS PIE
FOR THE HAYSEEDS

. . . .

THIS CITY IS RULED ENTIRELY by the hayseed legislators at Albany. I've never known an up-State Republican who didn't want to run things here, and I've met many thousands of them in my long service in the Legislature. The hayseeds think we are like the Indians to the National Government—that is, sort of wards of the State, who don't know how to look after ourselves and have to be taken care of by the Republicans of St. Lawrence, Ontario, and other backwoods counties. Why should anybody be surprised because ex-Governor Odell comes down here to direct the Republican machine? Newburg ain't big enough for

28

him. He, like all the other up-State Republicans, wants to get hold of New York City. New York is their pie.

Say, you hear a lot about the downtrodden people of Ireland and the Russian peasants and the sufferin' Boers. Now, let me tell you that they have more real freedom and home rule than the people of this grand and imperial city. In England, for example, they make a pretense of givin' the Irish some self-government. In this State the Republican government makes no pretense at all. It says right out in the open: "New York City is a nice big fat Goose. Come along with your carvin' knives and have a slice." They don't pretend to ask the Goose's consent.

We don't own our streets or our docks or our water front or anything else. The Republican Legislature and Governor run the whole shootin' match. We've got to eat and drink what they tell us to eat and drink, and have got to choose our time for eatin' and drinkin' to suit them. If they don't feel like takin' a glass of beer on Sunday, we must abstain. If they have not got any amusements up in their backwoods, we mustn't have none. We've got to regulate our whole lives to suit them. And then we have to pay their taxes to boot.

Did you ever go up to Albany from this city with a delegation that wanted anything from the Legislature? No? Well, don't. The hayseeds who run all

29

the committees will look at you as if you were a child that didn't know what it wanted, and will tell you in so many words to go home and be good and the Legislature will give you whatever it thinks is good for you. They put on a sort of patronizing air, as much as to say, "These children are an awful lot of trouble. They're wantin' candy all the time, and they know that it will make them sick. They ought to thank goodness that they have us to take care of them." And if you try to argue with them, they'll smile in a pityin' sort of way as if they were humorin' a spoiled child.

But just let a Republican farmer from Chemung or Wayne or Tioga turn up at the Capital. The Republican Legislature will make a rush for him and ask him what he wants and tell him if he doesn't see what he wants to ask for it. If he says his taxes are too high, they reply to him: "All right, old man, don't let that worry you. How much do you want us to take off?"

"I guess about fifty per cent will about do for the present," says the man. "Can you fix me up?"

"Sure," the Legislature agrees. "Give us somethin' harder, don't be bashful. We'll take off sixty per cent if you wish. That's what we're here for."

Then the Legislature goes and passes a law increasin' the liquor tax or some other tax in New York City, takes a half of the proceeds for the State

Treasury and cuts down the farmers' taxes to suit. It's as easy as rollin' off a log—when you've got a good workin' majority and no conscience to speak of.

Let me give you another example. It makes me hot under the collar to tell about this. Last year some hayseeds along the Hudson River, mostly in Odell's neighborhood, got dissatisfied with the docks where they landed their vegetables, brickbats, and other things they produce in the river counties. They got together and said: "Let's take a trip down to New York and pick out the finest dock we can find. Odell and the Legislature will do the rest." They did come down here, and what do you think they hit on? The finest dock in my district. Invaded George W. Plunkitt's district without sayin' as much as "by your leave." Then they called on Odell to put through a bill givin' them this dock, and he did.

When the bill came before Mayor Low I made the greatest speech of my life. I pointed out how the Legislature could give the whole water front to the hayseeds over the head of the Dock Commissioner in the same way, and warned the Mayor that nations had rebelled against their governments for less. But it was no go. Odell and Low were pards and—well, my dock was stolen.

You heard a lot in the State campaign about Odell's great work in reducin' the State tax to almost nothin', and you'll hear a lot more about it in the

31

campaign next year. How did he do it? By cuttin' down the expenses of the State Government? Oh, no! The expenses went up. He simply performed the old Republican act of milkin' New York City. The only difference was that he nearly milked the city dry. He not only ran up the liquor tax, but put all sorts of taxes on corporations, banks, insurance companies, and everything in sight that could be made to give up. Of course, nearly the whole tax fell on the city. Then Odell went through the country districts and said: "See what I have done for you. You ain't got any more taxes to pay the State. Ain't I a fine feller?"

Once a farmer in Orange County asked him: "How did you do it, Ben?"

"Dead easy," he answered. "Whenever I want any money for the State Treasury, I know where to get it," and he pointed toward New York City.

And then all the Republican tinkerin' with New York City's charter. Nobody can keep up with it. When a Republican mayor is in, they give him all sorts of power. If a Tammany mayor is elected next fall I wouldn't be surprised if they changed the whole business and arranged it so that every city department should have four heads, two of them Republicans. If we make a kick, they would say: "You don't know what's good for you. Leave it to us. It's our business."

32

To HOLD YOUR DISTRICT—
STUDY HUMAN NATURE
AND ACT ACCORDIN'

THERE'S ONLY ONE WAY TO hold a district; you must study human nature and act accordin'. You can't study human nature in books. Books is a hindrance more than anything else. If you have been to college, so much the worse for you. You'll have to unlearn all you learned before you can get right down to human nature, and unlearnin' takes a lot of time. Some men can never forget what they learned at college. Such men may get to be district leaders by a fluke, but they never last.

To learn real human nature you have to go among the people, see them and be seen. I know every man, woman, and child in the Fifteenth District, except them that's been born this summer—and I know some of them, too. I know what they like and what they don't like, what they are strong at and what they are weak in, and I reach them by approachin' at the right side.

For instance, here's how I gather in the young men. I hear of a young feller that's proud of his voice, thinks that he can sing fine. I ask him to come around to Washington Hall and join our Glee Club. He comes and sings, and he's a follower of Plunkitt for life. Another young feller gains a reputation as a baseball player in a vacant lot. I bring him into our baseball club. That fixes him. You'll find him workin' for my ticket at the polls next election day. Then there's the feller that likes rowin' on the river, the young feller that makes a name as a waltzer on his block, the young feller that's handy with his dukes—I rope them all in by givin' them opportunities to show themselves off. I don't trouble them with political arguments. I just study human nature and act accordin'.

But you may say this game won't work with the high-toned fellers, the fellers that go through college and then join the Citizens' Union. Of course it wouldn't work. I have a special treatment for them. I ain't like the patent medicine man that gives the same medicine for all diseases. The Citizens' Union kind of a young man! I love him! He's the daintiest morsel of the lot, and he don't often escape me.

Before telling you how I catch him, let me mention that before the election last year, the Citizens' Union said they had four hundred or five hundred enrolled voters in my district. They had a lovely headquarters, too, beautiful roll-top desks and the cutest rugs in the world. If I was accused of havin' contributed to fix up the nest for them, I wouldn't deny it under oath. What do I mean by that? Never mind. You can guess from the sequel, if you're sharp.

Well, election day came. The Citizens' Union's candidate for Senator, who ran against me, just polled five votes in the district, while I polled something more than 14,000 votes. What became of the 400 or 500 Citizens' Union enrolled voters in my district? Some people guessed that many of them were good Plunkitt men all along and worked with the Cits just to bring them into the Plunkitt camp by election day. You can guess that way, too, if you want to. I never contradict stories about me, especially in hot weather. I just call your attention to the fact that on last election day 395 Citizens' Union enrolled voters in my district were missin' and unaccounted for.

I tell you frankly, though, how I have captured

some of the Citizens' Union's young men. I have a plan that never fails. I watch the City Record to see when there's civil service examinations for good things. Then I take my young Cit in hand, tell him all about the good thing and get him worked up till he goes and takes an examination. I don't bother about him any more. It's a cinch that he comes back to me in a few days and asks to join Tammany Hall. Come over to Washington Hall some night and I'll show you a list of names on our rolls marked "C.S." which means, "bucked up against civil service."

As to the older voters, I reach them, too. No, I don't send them campaign literature. That's rot. People can get all the political stuff they want to read—and a good deal more, too—in the papers. Who reads speeches, nowadays, anyhow? It's bad enough to listen to them. You ain't goin' to gain any votes by stuffin' the letter-boxes with campaign documents. Like as not you'll lose votes, for there's nothin' a man hates more than to hear the letter-carrier ring his bell and go to the letter-box expectin' to find a letter he was lookin' for, and find only a lot of printed politics. I met a man this very mornin' who told me he voted the Democratic State ticket last year just because the Republicans kept crammin' his letter-box with campaign documents.

What tells in holdin' your grip on your district is to go right down among the poor families and help

them in the different ways they need help. I've got a
regular system for this. If there's a fire in Ninth,
Tenth, or Eleventh Avenue, for example, any hour
of the day or night, I'm usually there with some of
my election district captains as soon as the fire-en-
gines. If a family is burned out I don't ask whether
they are Republicans or Democrats, and I don't refer
them to the Charity Organization Society, which
would investigate their case in a month or two and
decide they were worthy of help about the time they
are dead from starvation. I just get quarters for
them, buy clothes for them if their clothes were
burned up, and fix them up till they get things
runnin' again. It's philanthropy, but it's politics, too
—mighty good politics. Who can tell how many votes
one of these fires bring me? The poor are the most
grateful people in the world, and, let me tell you,
they have more friends in their neighborhoods than
the rich have in theirs.

If there's a family in my district in want I know
it before the charitable societies do, and me and my
men are first on the ground. I have a special corps to
look up such cases. The consequence is that the poor
look up to George W. Plunkitt as a father, come to
him in trouble—and don't forget him on election day.

Another thing, I can always get a job for a deservin' man. I make it a point to keep on the track of
jobs, and it seldom happens that I don't have a few

up my sleeve ready for use. I know every big employer in the district and in the whole city, for that matter, and they ain't in the habit of sayin' no to me when I ask them for a job.

And the children—the little roses of the district! Do I forget them? Oh, no! They know me, every one of them, and they know that a sight of Uncle George and candy means the same thing. Some of them are the best kind of vote-getters. I'll tell you a case. Last year a little Eleventh Avenue rosebud whose father is a Republican, caught hold of his whiskers on election day and said she wouldn't let go till he'd promise to vote for me. And she didn't.

ON "THE SHAME OF THE CITIES"

....

I'VE BEEN READIN' A BOOK BY Lincoln Steffens on "The Shame of the Cities." Steffens means well but, like all reformers, he don't know how to make distinctions. He can't see no difference between honest graft and dishonest graft and, consequent, he gets things all mixed up. There's the biggest kind of a difference between political looters and politicians who make a fortune out of politics by keepin' their eyes wide open. The looter goes in for himself alone without considerin' his organization or

39

his city. The politician looks after his own interests, the organization's interests, and the city's interests all at the same time. See the distinction? For instance, I ain't no looter. The looter hogs it. I never hogged. I made my pile in politics, but, at the same time, I served the organization and got more big improvements for New York City than any other livin' man. And I never monkeyed with the penal code.

The difference between a looter and a practical politician is the difference between the Philadelphia Republican gang and Tammany Hall. Steffens seems to think they're both about the same; but he's all wrong. The Philadelphia crowd runs up against the penal code. Tammany don't. The Philadelphians ain't satisfied with robbin' the bank of all its gold and paper money. They stay to pick up the nickels and pennies and the cop comes and nabs them. Tammany ain't no such fool. Why, I remember, about fifteen or twenty years ago, a Republican superintendent of the Philadelphia almshouse stole the zinc roof off the buildin' and sold it for junk. That was carryin' things to excess. There's a limit to everything, and the Philadelphia Republicans go beyond the limit. It seems like they can't be cool and moderate like real politicians. It ain't fair, therefore, to class Tammany men with the Philadelphia gang. Any man who undertakes to write political books should never for a moment lose sight of the distinction between honest graft and dishonest graft, which I explained in full in another talk. If he puts all kinds of graft on the same level, he'll make the fatal mistake that Steffens made and spoil his book.

A big city like New York or Philadelphia or Chicago might be compared to a sort of Garden of Eden, from a political point of view. It's an orchard full of beautiful apple trees. One of them has got a big sign on it, marked: "Penal Code Tree—Poison." The other trees have lots of apples on them for all. Yet, the fools go to the Penal Code Tree. Why? For the reason, I guess, that a cranky child refuses to eat good food and chews up a box of matches with relish. I never had any temptation to touch the Penal Code Tree. The other apples are good enough for me, and O Lord! how many of them there are in a big city!

Steffens made one good point in his book. He said he found that Philadelphia, ruled almost entirely by Americans, was more corrupt than New York, where the Irish do almost all the governin'. I could have told him that before he did any investigatin' if he had come to me. The Irish was born to rule, and they're the honestest people in the world. Show me the Irishman who would steal a roof off an almshouse! He don't exist. Of course, if an Irishman had the political pull and the roof was much worn, he might get the city authorities to put on a new one and get the contract for it himself, and buy the old roof at a bargain—but that's honest graft. It's goin' about the thing like a gentleman, and there's more money in it than in tearin' down an old roof and cartin' it to the junkman's—more money and no penal code.

One reason why the Irishman is more honest in politics than many Sons of the Revolution is that he is grateful to the country and the city that gave him protection and prosperity when he was driven by oppression from the Emerald Isle. Say, that sentence is fine, ain't it? I'm goin' to get some literary feller to work it over into poetry for next St. Patrick's Day dinner.

Yes, the Irishman is grateful. His one thought is to serve the city which gave him a home. He has this thought even before he lands in New York, for his friends here often have a good place in one of the city departments picked out for him while he is still in the old country. Is it any wonder that he has a tender spot in his heart for old New York when he is on its salary list the mornin' after he lands?

Now, a few words on the general subject of the so-called shame of cities. I don't believe that the government of our cities is any worse, in proportion to opportunities, than it was fifty years ago. I'll explain what I mean by "in proportion to opportunities." A half a century ago, our cities were small and poor. There wasn't many temptations lyin' around for politicians. There was hardly anything to steal, and hardly any opportunities for even honest graft. A city could count its money every night before goin' to bed, and if three cents was missin', all the fire-bells would be rung. What credit was there in bein' honest under them circumstances? It makes me tired to hear of old codgers back in the thirties or forties boastin' that they retired from politics without a dollar except what they earned in their profession or business. If they lived to-day, with all the existin' opportunities, they would be just the same as twentieth century politicians. There ain't any more honest people in the world just now than the convicts in Sing Sing. Not one of them steals anything. Why? Because they can't. See the application?

Understand, I ain't defendin' politicians of to-day who steal. The politician who steals is worse than a thief. He is a fool. With the grand opportunities all around for the man with a political pull, there's no excuse for stealin' a cent. The point I want to make is that if there is some stealin' in politics, it don't mean that the politicians of 1905 are, as a class, worse than them of 1835. It just means that the old-timers had nothin' to steal, while the politicians now are surrounded by all kinds of temptations and some of them naturally—the fool ones—buck up against the penal code.

INGRATITUDE IN POLITICS

THERE'S NO CRIME SO MEAN AS
ingratitude in politics, but every great statesman
from the beginnin' of the world has been up against
it. Caesar had his Brutus; that king of Shakspere's
—Leary, I think you call him—had his own daugh-
ters go back on him; Platt had his Odell, and I've
got my "The" McManus. It's a real proof that a
man is great when he meets with political ingratitude. Great men have a tender, trustin' nature. So
have I, outside of the contractin' and real estate

business. In politics I have trusted men who have told me they were my friends, and if traitors have turned up in my camp—well, I only had the same experience as Caesar, Leary, and the others. About my Brutus. McManus, you know, has seven brothers and they call him "The" because he is the boss of the lot, and to distinguish him from all other McManuses. For several years he was a political bushwhacker. In campaigns he was sometimes on the fence, sometimes on both sides of the fence, and sometimes under the fence. Nobody knew where to find him at any particular time, and nobody trusted him—that is, nobody but me. I thought there was some good in him after all and that, if I took him in hand, I could make a man of him yet.

I did take him in hand, a few years ago. My friends told me it would be the Brutus-Leary business all over again, but I didn't believe them. I put my trust in "The." I nominated him for the Assembly, and he was elected. A year afterwards, when I was runnin' for re-election as Senator, I nominated him for the Assembly again on the ticket with me. What do you think happened? We both carried the Fifteenth Assembly District, but he ran away ahead of me. Just think! Ahead of me in my own district! I was just dazed. When I began to recover, my election district captains came to me and said that McManus had sold me out with the idea of knockin' me out of the

Senatorship, and then tryin' to capture the leadership of the district. I couldn't believe it. My trustin' nature couldn't imagine such treachery.

I sent for McManus and said, with my voice tremblin' with emotions: "They say you have done me dirt, 'The.' It can't be true. Tell me it ain't true."

"The" almost wept as he said he was innocent.

"Never have I done you dirt, George," he declared. "Wicked traitors have tried to do you. I don't know just who they are yet, but I'm on their trail, and I'll find them or abjure the name of 'The' McManus. I'm goin' out right now to find them."

Well, "The" kept his word as far as goin' out and findin' the traitors was concerned. He found them all right—and put himself at their head. Oh, no! He didn't have to go far to look for them. He's got them gathered in his club-rooms now, and he's doin' his best to take the leadership from the man that made him. So you see that Caesar and Leary and me's in the same boat, only I'll come out on top while Caesar and Leary went under.

Now let me tell you that the ingrate in politics never flourishes long. I can give you lots of examples. Look at the men who done up Roscoe Conkling when he resigned from the United States Senate and went to Albany to ask for a re-election! What's become of them? Passed from view like a movin' picture. Who took Conkling's place in the Senate? Twenty dollars

even that you can't remember his name without looking in the almanac. And poor old Platt! He's down
and out now and Odell is in the saddle, but that
don't mean that he'll always be in the saddle. His
enemies are workin' hard all the time to do him, and I
wouldn't be a bit surprised if he went out before the
next State campaign.

The politicians who make a lastin' success in politics are the men who are always loyal to their friends,
even up to the gate of State prison, if necessary;
men who keep their promises and never lie. Richard
Croker used to say that tellin' the truth and stickin'
to his friends was the political leader's stock in trade.
Nobody ever said anything truer, and nobody lived
up to it better than Croker. That is why he remained
leader of Tammany Hall as long as he wanted to.
Every man in the organization trusted him. Sometimes he made mistakes that hurt in campaigns, but
they were always on the side of servin' his friends.

It's the same with Charles F. Murphy. He has always stood by his friends even when it looked like
he would be downed for doin' so. Remember how he
stuck to McClellan in 1903 when all the Brooklyn
leaders were against him, and it seemed as if Tammany was in for a grand smash-up! It's men like
Croker and Murphy that stay leaders as long as they
live; not men like Brutus and McManus.

Now I want to tell you why political traitors, in

New York City especially, are punished quick. It's because the Irish are in a majority. The Irish, above all people in the world, hates a traitor. You can't hold them back when a traitor of any kind is in sight and, rememberin' old Ireland, they take particular delight in doin' up a political traitor. Most of the voters in my district are Irish or of Irish descent; they've spotted "The" McManus, and when they get a chance at him at the polls next time, they won't do a thing to him.

The question has been asked: Is a politician ever justified in goin' back on his district leader? I answer: "No; as long as the leader hustles around and gets all the jobs possible for his constituents." When the voters elect a man leader, they make a sort of a contract with him. They say, although it ain't written out: "We've put you here to look out for our interests. You want to see that this district gets all the jobs that's comin' to it. Be faithful to us, and we'll be faithful to you."

The district leader promises and that makes a solemn contract. If he lives up to it, spends most of his time chasin' after places in the departments, picks up jobs from railroads and contractors for his followers, and shows himself in all ways a true statesman, then his followers are bound in honor to uphold him, just as they're bound to uphold the Constitution of the United States. But if he only looks after his own interests or shows no talent for scenting out jobs or ain't got the nerve to demand and get his share of the good things that are goin', his followers may be absolved from their allegiance and they may up and swat him without bein' put down as political ingrates.

RECIPROCITY IN PATRONAGE

WHENEVER TAMMANY IS whipped at the polls, the people set to predictin' that the organization is goin' to smash. They say we can't get along without the offices and that the district leaders are goin' to desert wholesale. That was what was said after the throwdowns in 1894 and 1901. But it didn't happen, did it? Not one big Tammany man deserted, and to-day the organization is stronger than ever.

Reciprocity in Patronage

How was that? It was because Tammany has more than one string to its bow.

I acknowledge that you can't keep an organization together without patronage. Men ain't in politics for nothin'. They want to get somethin' out of it.

But there is more than one kind of patronage. We lost the public kind, or a greater part of it in 1901, but Tammany has an immense private patronage that keeps things goin' when it gets a setback at the polls.

Take me, for instance. When Low came in, some of my men lost public jobs, but I fixed them all right. I don't know how many jobs I got for them on the surface and elevated railroads—several hundred.

I placed a lot more on public works done by contractors, and no Tammany man goes hungry in my district. Plunkitt's O.K. on an application for a job is never turned down, for they all know that Plunkitt and Tammany don't stay out long. See!

Let me tell you, too, that I got jobs from Republicans in office—Federal and otherwise. When Tammany's on top I do good turns for the Republicans. When they're on top they don't forget me.

Me and the Republicans are enemies just one day in the year—election day. Then we fight tooth and nail. The rest of the time it's live and let live with us.

On election day I try to pile up as big a majority as I can against George Wanmaker, the Republican

leader of the Fifteenth. Any other day George and I
are the best of friends. I can go to him and say:
"George, I want you to place this friend of mine."
He says: "All right, Senator." Or vice versa.

You see, we differ on tariffs and currencies and all
them things, but we agree on the main proposition
that when a man works in politics, he should get
something out of it.

The politicians have got to stand together this
way or there wouldn't be any political parties in a
short time. Civil service would gobble up everything,
politicians would be on the bum, the republic would
fall and soon there would be the cry of "Vevey le
roi!"

The very thought of this civil service monster
makes my blood boil. I have said a lot about it already, but another instance of its awful work just
occurs to me.

Let me tell you a sad but true story. Last Wednesday a line of carriages wound into Calvary Cemetery.
I was in one of them. It was the funeral of a young
man from my district—a bright boy that I had great
hopes of.

When he went to school, he was the most patriotic
boy in the district. Nobody could sing the "Star
Spangled Banner" like him, nobody was as fond of
waving a flag, and nobody shot off as many fire-
crackers on the Fourth of July. And when he grew

up he made up his mind to serve his country in one of the city departments. There was no way of gettin' there without passin' a civil service examination. Well, he went down to the civil service office and tackled the fool questions. I saw him next day—it was Memorial Day, and soldiers were marchin' and flags flyin' and people cheerin'.

Where was my young man? Standin' on the corner, scowlin' at the whole show. When I asked him why he was so quiet, he laughed in a wild sort of way and said: "What rot all this is!"

Just then a band came along playing "Liberty." He laughed wild again and said: "Liberty? Rats!"

I don't guess I need to make a long story of it.

From the time that young man left the civil service office he lost all patriotism. He didn't care no more for his country. He went to the dogs.

He ain't the only one. There's a gravestone over some bright young man's head for every one of them infernal civil service examinations. They are underminin' the manhood of the nation and makin' the Declaration of Independence a farce. We need a new Declaration of Independence—independence of the whole fool civil service business.

I mention all this now to show why it is that the politicians of two big parties help each other along, and why Tammany men are tolerably happy when not in power in the city. When we win I won't let any deservin' Republican in my neighborhood suffer from hunger or thirst, although, of course, I look out for my own people first.

Now, I've never gone in for non-partizan business, but I do think that all the leaders of the two parties should get together and make an open, non-partizan fight against civil service, their common enemy. They could keep up their quarrels about imperialism and free silver and high tariff. They don't count for much alongside of civil service, which strikes right at the root of the government.

The time is fast coming when civil service or the politicians will have to go. And it will be here sooner than they expect if the politicians don't unite, drop all them minor issues for a while and make a stand against the civil service flood that's sweepin' over the country like them floods out West.

BROOKLYNITES NATURAL-BORN HAYSEEDS

☞

SOME PEOPLE ARE WONDERIN' why it is that the Brooklyn Democrats have been sidin' with David B. Hill and the up-State crowd. There's no cause for wonder. I have made a careful study of the Brooklynite, and I can tell you why. It's because a Brooklynite is a natural-born hayseed, and can never become a real New Yorker. He can't be trained into it. Consolidation didn't make him a New Yorker, and nothin' on earth can. A man born in Germany can settle down and become a good New

Yorker. So can an Irishman; in fact, the first word an Irish boy learns in the old country is "New York," and when he grows up and comes here, he is at home right away. Even a Jap or a Chinaman can become a New Yorker, but a Brooklynite never can.

And why? Because Brooklyn don't seem to be like any other place on earth. Once let a man grow up amidst Brooklyn's cobblestones, with the odor of Newton Creek and Gowanus Canal ever in his nostrils, and there's no place in the world for him except Brooklyn. And even if he don't grow up there; if he is born there and lives there only in his boyhood and then moves away, he is still beyond redemption. In one of my speeches in the Legislature, I gave an example of this, and it's worth repeatin' now. Soon after I became a leader on the West Side, a quarter of a century ago, I came across a bright boy, about seven years old, who had just been brought over from Brooklyn by his parents. I took an interest in the boy, and when he grew up I brought him into politics. Finally, I sent him to the Assembly from my district. Now remember that the boy was only seven years old when he left Brooklyn, and was twenty-three when he went to the Assembly. You'd think he had forgotten all about Brooklyn, wouldn't you? I did, but I was dead wrong. When that young fellow got into the Assembly he paid no attention to bills or debates about New York City. He didn't even show any interest in his own district. But just let Brooklyn be mentioned, or a bill be introduced about Gowanus Canal, or the Long Island Railroad, and he was all attention. Nothin' else on earth interested him.

The end came when I caught him—what do you think I caught him at? One mornin' I went over from the Senate to the Assembly chamber, and there I found my young man readin'—actually readin' a Brooklyn newspaper! When he saw me comin' he tried to hide the paper, but it was too late. I caught him dead to rights, and I said to him: "Jimmy, I'm afraid New York ain't fascinatin' enough for you. You had better move back to Brooklyn after your present term." And he did. I met him the other day crossin' the Brooklyn Bridge, carryin' a hobby-horse under one arm, and a doll's carriage under the other, and lookin' perfectly happy.

McCarren and his men are the same way. They can't get it into their heads that they are New Yorkers, and just tend naturally towards supportin' Hill and his hayseeds against Murphy. I had some hopes of McCarren till lately. He spends so much of his time over here and has seen so much of the world that I thought he might be an exception, and grow out of his Brooklyn surroundings, but his course at Albany shows that there is no exception to the rule. Say, I'd rather take a Hottentot in hand

to bring up as a good New Yorker than undertake
the job with a Brooklynite. Honest, I would.

And, by the way, come to think of it, is there
really any up-State Democrats left? It has never
been proved to my satisfaction that there is any. I
know that some up-State members of the State committee call themselves Democrats. Besides these, I
know at least six more men above the Bronx who
make a livin' out of professin' to be Democrats, and
I have just heard of some few more. But if there is
any real Democrats up the State, what becomes of
them on election day? They certainly don't go near
the polls or they vote the Republican ticket. Look at
the last three State elections! Roosevelt piled up
more than 100,000 majority above the Bronx; Odell
piled up about 160,000 majority the first time he
ran and 131,000 the second time. About all the
Democratic votes cast were polled in New York City.
The Republicans can get all the votes they want up
the State. Even when we piled up 123,000 majority
for Coler in the city in 1902, the Republicans went
it 8000 better above the Bronx.

That's why it makes me mad to hear about up-
State Democrats controllin' our State convention,
and sayin' who we shall choose for President. It's
just like Staten Island undertakin' to dictate to a
New York City convention. I remember once a Syra-
cuse man came to Richard Croker at the Democratic

Club, handed him a letter of introduction and said: "I'm lookin' for a job in the Street Cleanin' Department; I'm backed by a hundred up-State Democrats." Croker looked hard at the man a minute and then said: "Up-State Democrats! Up-State Democrats! I didn't know there was any up-State Democrats. Just walk up and down a while till I see what an up-State Democrat looks like."

Another thing. When a campaign is on, did you ever hear of an up-State Democrat makin' a contribution? Not much. Tammany has had to foot the whole bill, and when any of Hill's men came down to New York to help him in the campaign, we had to pay their board. Whenever money is to be raised, there's nothin' doin' up the State. The Democrats there—always providin' that there is any Democrats there—take to the woods. Supposin' Tammany turned over the campaigns to the Hill men and then held off, what would happen? Why, they would have to hire a shed out in the suburbs of Albany for a headquarters, unless the Democratic National Committee put up for the campaign expenses. Tammany's got the votes and the cash. The Hill crowd's only got hot air.

TAMMANY LEADERS
NOT BOOKWORMS

....

YOU HEAR A LOT OF TALK about the Tammany district leaders bein' illiterate men. If illiterate means havin' common sense, we plead guilty. But if they mean that the Tammany leaders ain't got no education and ain't gents they don't know what they're talkin' about. Of course, we ain't all bookworms and college professors. If we were, Tammany might win an election once in four thousand years. Most of the leaders are plain American citizens, of the people and near to the people,

and they have all the education they need to whip
the dudes who part their name in the middle and
to run the City Government. We've got bookworms,
too, in the organization. But we don't make them
district leaders. We keep them for ornaments on
parade days.

Tammany Hall is a great big machine, with ever
part adjusted delicate to do its own particular work.
It runs so smooth that you wouldn't think it was a
complicated affair, but it is. Every district leader is
fitted to the district he runs and he wouldn't exactly
fit any other district. That's the reason Tammany
never makes the mistake the Fusion outfit always
makes of sendin' men into the districts who don't
know the people, and have no sympathy with their
peculiarities. We don't put a silk stockin' on the
Bowery, nor do we make a man who is handy with
his fists leader of the Twenty-ninth. The Fusionists
make about the same sort of a mistake that a repeater made at an election in Albany several years
ago. He was hired to go to the polls early in a half-
dozen election districts and vote on other men's
names before these men reached the polls. At one
place, when he was asked his name by the poll clerk,
he had the nerve to answer "William Croswell
Doane."

"Come off. You ain't Bishop Doane," said the poll
clerk.

"The hell I ain't, you————!" yelled the repeater.

Now, that is the sort of bad judgment the Fusionists are guilty of. They don't pick men to suit the work they have to do.

Take me, for instance. My district, the Fifteenth, is made up of all sorts of people, and a cosmopolitan is needed to run it successful. I'm a cosmopolitan. When I get into the silk-stockin' part of the district, I can talk grammar and all that with the best of them. I went to school three winters when I was a boy, and I learned a lot of fancy stuff that I keep for occasions. There ain't a silk stockin' in the district who ain't proud to be seen talkin' with George Washington Plunkitt, and maybe they learn a thing or two from their talks with me. There's one man in the district, a big banker, who said to me one day: "George, you can sling the most vigorous English I ever heard. You remind me of Senator Hoar of Massachusetts." Of course, that was puttin' it on too thick; but say, honest, I like Senator Hoar's speeches. He once quoted in the United States Senate some of my remarks on the curse of civil service, and, though he didn't agree with me altogether, I noticed that our ideas are alike in some things, and we both have the knack of puttin' things strong, only he put on more frills to suit his audience.

As for the common people of the district, I am at home with them at all times. When I go among them,

I don't try to show off my grammar, or talk about the Constitution, or how many volts there is in electricity or make it appear in any way that I am better educated than they are. They wouldn't stand for that sort of thing. No; I drop all monkey-shines. So you see, I've got to be several sorts of a man in a single day, a lightnin' change artist, so to speak. But I am one sort of man always in one respect: I stick to my friends high and low, do them a good turn whenever I get a chance, and hunt up all the jobs going for my constituents. There ain't a man in New York who's got such a scent for political jobs as I have. When I get up in the mornin' I can almost tell every time whether a job has become vacant over night, and what department it's in and I'm the first man on the ground to get it. Only last week I turned up at the office of Water Register Savage at 9 A.M. and told him I wanted a vacant place in his office for one of my constituents. "How did you know that O'Brien had got out?" he asked me. "I smelled it in the air when I got up this mornin'," I answered. Now, that was the fact. I didn't know there was a man in the department named O'Brien, much less that he had got out, but my scent led me to the Water Register's office, and it don't often lead me wrong.

A cosmopolitan ain't needed in all the other districts, but our men are just the kind to rule. There's

Dan Finn, in the Battery district, bluff, jolly Dan, who is now on the bench. Maybe you'd think that a court justice is not the man to hold a district like that, but you're mistaken. Most of the voters of the district are the janitors of the big office buildings on lower Broadway and their helpers. These janitors are the most dignified and haughtiest of men. Even I would have trouble in holding them. Nothin' less than a judge on the bench is good enough for them. Dan does the dignity act with the janitors, and when he is with the boys he hangs up the ermine in the closet and becomes a jolly good fellow.

Big Tom Foley, leader of the Second District, fits in exactly, too. Tom sells whisky, and good whisky, and he is able to take care of himself against a half dozen thugs if he runs up against them on Cherry Hill or in Chatham Square. Pat Ryder and Johnnie Ahearn of the Third and Fourth Districts are just the men for the places. Ahearn's constituents are about half Irishmen and half Jews. He is as popular with one race as with the other. He eats corned beef and kosher meat with equal nonchalance, and it's all the same to him whether he takes off his hat in the church or pulls it down over his ears in the synagogue.

The other downtown leaders, Barney Martin of the Fifth, Tim Sullivan of the Sixth, Pat Keahon

of the Seventh, Florrie Sullivan of the Eighth, Frank
Goodwin of the Ninth, Julius Harburger of the
Tenth, Pete Dooling of the Eleventh, Joe Scully of
the Twelfth, Johnnie Oakley of the Fourteenth, and
Pat Keenan of the Sixteenth are just built to suit
the people they have to deal with. They don't go in
for literary business much downtown, but these men
are all real gents, and that's what the people want
—even the poorest tenement dwellers. As you go
farther uptown you find rather different kind of district leaders. There's Victor Dowling who was until
lately the leader of the Twenty-fourth. He's a lulu.
He knows the Latin grammar backward. What's
strange, he's a sensible young fellow, too. About once
in a century we come across a fellow like that in
Tammany politics. James J. Martin, leader of the
Twenty-seventh, is also something of a hightoner,
and publishes a law paper, while Thomas E. Rush,
of the Twenty-ninth, is a lawyer, and Isaac Hop-
per, of the Thirty-first, is a big contractor. The
downtown leaders wouldn't do uptown, and vice versa. So, you see, these fool critics don't know what
they're talkin' about when they criticise Tammany
Hall, the most perfect political machine on earth.

DANGERS OF THE
DRESS-SUIT IN
POLITICS

. . . .

☞

PUTTIN' ON STYLE DON'T PAY
in politics. The people won't stand for it. If you've
got an achin' for style, sit down on it till you have
made your pile and landed a Supreme Court Justiceship with a fourteen-year term at $17,500 a year,
or some job of that kind. Then you've got about all
you can get out of politics, and you can afford to
wear a dress-suit all day and sleep in it all night if
you have a mind to. But, before you have caught
onto your life meal-ticket, be simple. Live like your

66

neighbors even if you have the means to live better. Make the poorest man in your district feel that he is your equal, or even a bit superior to you.

Above all things, avoid a dress-suit. You have no idea of the harm that dress-suits have done in politics. They are not so fatal to young politicians as civil service reform and drink, but they have scores of victims. I will mention one sad case. After the big Tammany victory in 1897, Richard Croker went down to Lakewood to make up the slate of offices for Mayor Van Wyck to distribute. All the district leaders and many more Tammany men went down there, too, to pick up anything good that was goin'. There was nothin' but dress-suits at dinner at Lakewood, and Croker wouldn't let any Tammany men go to dinner without them. Well, a bright young West Side politician, who held a three thousand dollar job in one of the departments, went to Lakewood to ask Croker for something better. He wore a dress-suit for the first time in his life. It was his undoin'. He got stuck on himself. He thought he looked too beautiful for anything, and when he came home he was a changed man. As soon as he got to his house every evenin' he put on that dress-suit and set around in it until bedtime. That didn't satisfy him long. He wanted others to see how beautiful he was in a dress-suit; so he joined dancin' clubs and began goin' to all the balls that was given in town. Soon he began to neglect his family. Then he took to drinkin', and didn't pay any attention to his political work in the district. The end came in less than a year. He was dismissed from the department and went to the dogs. The other day I met him rigged out almost like a hobo, but he still had a dress-suit vest on. When I asked him what he was doin', he said: "Nothin' at present, but I got a promise of a job enrollin' voters at Citizens' Union headquarters." Yes, a dress-suit had brought him that low!

I'll tell you another case right in my own Assembly District. A few years ago I had as one of my lieutenants a man named Zeke Thompson. He did fine work for me and I thought he had a bright future. One day he came to me, said he intended to buy an option on a house, and asked me to help him out. I like to see a young man acquirin' property and I had so much confidence in Zeke that I put up for him on the house.

A month or so afterwards I heard strange rumors. People told me that Zeke was beginnin' to put on style. They said he had a billiard-table in his house and had hired Jap servants. I couldn't believe it. The idea of a Democrat, a follower of George Washington Plunkitt in the Fifteenth Assembly District havin' a billiard-table and Jap servants! One mornin' I called at the house to give Zeke a chance to clear himself. A Jap opened the door for me. I saw the billiard-table. Zeke was guilty! When I got over the shock, I said to Zeke: "You are caught with the goods on. No excuses will go. The Democrats of this district ain't used to dukes and princes and we wouldn't feel comfortable in your company. You'd overpower us. You had better move up to the Nineteenth or Twenty-seventh District, and hang a silk stocking on your door." He went up to the Nineteenth, turned Republican, and was lookin' for an Albany job the last I heard of him.

Now, nobody ever saw me puttin' on any style. I'm the same Plunkitt I was when I entered politics forty years ago. That is why the people of the district have confidence in me. If I went into the stylish business, even I, Plunkitt, might be thrown down in the district. That was shown pretty clearly in the senatorial fight last year. A day before the election, my enemies circulated a report that I had ordered a $10,000 automobile and a $125 dress-suit. I sent out contradictions as fast as I could, but I wasn't able to stamp out the infamous slander before the votin' was over, and I suffered some at the polls. The people wouldn't have minded much if I had been accused of robbin' the city treasury, for they're used to slanders of that kind in campaigns, but the automobile and the dress-suit were too much for them.

Another thing that people won't stand for is showin' off your learnin'. That's just puttin' on style in another way. If you're makin' speeches in a campaign, talk the language the people talk. Don't try to show how the situation is by quotin' Shakspere. Shakspere was all right in his way, but he didn't know anything about Fifteenth District politics. If you know Latin and Greek and have a hankerin' to work them off on somebody, hire a stranger to come to your house and listen to you for a couple of hours; then go out and talk the language of the Fifteenth to the people. I know it's an awful temptation, the hankerin' to show off your learnin'. I've felt it myself, but I always resist it. I know the awful consequences.

On Municipal Ownership

....

☞

        I AM FOR MUNICIPAL OWNER-ship on one condition: that the civil service law be repealed. It's a grand idea—the city ownin' the railroads, the gas works and all that. Just see how many thousands of new places there would be for the workers in Tammany! Why, there would be almost enough to go around, if no civil service law stood in the way. My plan is this: first get rid of that infamous law, and then go ahead and by degrees get municipal ownership.

Some of the reformers are sayin' that municipal

ownership won't do because it would give a lot of patronage to the politicians. How those fellows mix things up when they argue! They're givin' the strongest argument in favor of municipal ownership when they say that. Who is better fitted to run the railroads and the gas plants and the ferries than the men who make a business of lookin' after the interests of the city? Who is more anxious to serve the city? Who needs the jobs more?

Look at the Dock Department! The city owns the docks, and how beautiful Tammany manages them! I can't tell you how many places they provide for our workers. I know there is a lot of talk about dock graft, but that talk comes from the outs. When the Republicans had the docks under Low and Strong, you didn't hear them sayin' anything about graft, did you? No; they just went in and made hay while the sun shone. That's always the case. When the reformers are out they raise the yell that Tammany men should be sent to jail. When they get in, they're so busy keepin' out of jail themselves that they don't have no time to attack Tammany.

All I want is that municipal ownership be postponed till I get my bill repealin' the civil service law before the next legislature. It would be all a mess if every man who wanted a job would have to run up against a civil service examination. For instance, if a man wanted a job as motorman on a surface car, it's ten to one that they would ask him: "Who wrote the Latin grammar, and, if so, why did he write it? How many years were you at college? Is there any part of the Greek language you don't know? State all you don't know, and why you don't know it. Give a list of all the sciences with full particulars about each one and how it came to be discovered. Write out word for word the last ten decisions of the United States Supreme Court and show if they conflict with the last ten decisions of the police courts of New York City."

Before the would-be motorman left the civil service room, the chances are he would be a raving lunatic. Anyhow I wouldn't like to ride on his car. Just here I want to say one last final word about civil service. In the last ten years I have made an investigation which I've kept quiet till this time. Now I have all the figures together, and I'm ready to announce the result. My investigation was to find out how many civil service reformers and how many politicians were in state prisons. I discovered that there was forty per cent more civil service reformers among the jail-birds. If any legislative committee wants the detailed figures, I'll prove what I say. I don't want to give the figures now, because I want to keep them to back me up when I go to Albany to get the civil service law repealed. Don't you think that when I've had my inning, the civil service law will go down, and the people will see that the politicians are all right, and that they ought to have the job of runnin' things when municipal ownership comes?

One thing more about municipal ownership. If the city owned the railroads, etc., salaries would be sure to go up. Higher salaries is the cryin' need of the day. Municipal ownership would increase them all along the line and would stir up such patriotism as New York City never knew before. You can't be patriotic on a salary that just keeps the wolf from the door. Any man who pretends he can will bear watchin'. Keep your hand on your watch and pocketbook when he's about. But, when a man has a good fat salary, he finds himself hummin' "Hail Columbia," all unconscious and he fancies, when he's ridin' in a trolley-car, that the wheels are always sayin': "Yankee Doodle Came to Town." I know how it is myself. When I got my first good job from the city I bought up all the fire-crackers in my district to salute this glorious country. I couldn't wait for the Fourth of July. I got the boys on the block to fire them off for me, and I felt proud of bein' an American. For a long time after that I use to wake up nights singin' the "Star Spangled Banner."

TAMMANY THE ONLY LASTIN' DEMOCRACY

I'VE SEEN MORE THAN ONE hundred "Democracies" rise and fall in New York City in the last quarter of a century. At least a half dozen new so-called Democratic organizations are formed every year. All of them go in to down Tammany and take its place, but they seldom last more than a year or two, while Tammany's like the everlastin' rocks, the eternal hills and the blockades on the "L" road—it goes on forever.

I recall off-hand the County Democracy, which

was the only real opponent Tammany has had in
my time, the Irving Hall Democracy, the New York
State Democracy, the German-American Democracy,
the Protection Democracy, the Independent County
Democracy, the Greater New York Democracy, the
Jimmy O'Brien Democracy, the Delicatessen Dealers' Democracy, the Silver Democracy, and the
Italian Democracy. Not one of them is livin' to-day,
although I hear somethin' about the ghost of the
Greater New York Democracy bein' seen on Broadway once or twice a year.

In the old days of the County Democracy, a new
Democratic organization meant some trouble for
Tammany—for a time anyhow. Nowadays a new
Democracy means nothin' at all except that about
a dozen bone-hunters have got together for one campaign only to try to induce Tammany to give them
a job or two, or in order to get in with the reformers
for the same purpose. You might think that it would
cost a lot of money to get up one of these organizations and keep it goin' for even one campaign, but,
Lord bless you! it costs next to nothin'. Jimmy
O'Brien brought the manufacture of "Democracies"
down to an exact science, and reduced the cost of
production so as to bring it within the reach of all.
Any man with $50 can now have a "Democracy" of
his own.

I've looked into the industry, and can give rock-bottom figures. Here's the items of cost of a new "Democracy":

A dinner to twelve bone-hunters.........	$12.00
A speech on Jeffersonian Democracy......	00.00
A proclamation of principles (typewriting)	2.00
Rent of a small room one month for head-quarters........................	12.00
Stationery.............................	2.00
Twelve second-hand chairs..............	6.00
One second-hand table..................	2.00
Twenty-nine cuspidors..................	9.00
Sign-painting.........................	5.00
Total.............................	$50.00

Is there any reason for wonder then, that "Democracies" spring up all over when a municipal campaign is comin' on? If you land even one small job, you get a big return on your investment. You don't have to pay for advertisin' in the papers. The New York papers tumble over one another to give columns to any new organization that comes out against Tammany. In describin' the formation of a "Democracy" on the $50 basis, accordin' to the items I give, the papers would say somethin' like this: "The organization of the Delicatessen Democracy last night threatens the existence of Tammany Hall. It is a grand move for a new and pure De-

mocracy in this city. Well may the Tammany leaders
be alarmed; Panic has already broke loose in Fourteenth Street. The vast crowd that gathered at the
launching of the new organization, the stirrin'
speeches and the proclamation of principles mean
that, at last, there is an uprisin' that will end Tammany's career of corruption. The Delicatessen
Democracy will open in a few days spacious headquarters where all true Democrats may gather and
prepare for the fight."

Say, ain't some of the papers awful gullible about
politics? Talk about come-ons from Iowa or Texas—
they ain't in it with the childlike simplicity of these
papers.

It's a wonder to me that more men don't go into
this kind of manufacturin' industry. It has bigger
profits generally than the green-goods business and
none of the risks. And you don't have to invest as
much as the green-goods men. Just see what good
things some of these "Democracies" got in the last
few years! The New York State Democracy in 1897,
landed a Supreme Court Justiceship for the man
who manufactured the concern—a fourteen-year
term at $17,500 a year, that is $245,000. You see,
Tammany was rather scared that year and was
bluffed into givin' this job to get the support of
the State Democracy which, by the way, went out of
business quick and prompt the day after it got this

big plum. The next year the German Democracy landed a place of the same kind. And then see how the Greater New York Democracy worked the game on the reformers in 1901! The men who managed this concern were former Tammanyites who had lost their grip; yet they made the Citizens' Union innocents believe that they were the real thing in the way of reformers, and that they had 100,000 votes back of them. They got the Borough President of Manhattan, the President of the Board of Aldermen, the Register and a lot of lesser places. It was the greatest bunco game of modern times.

And then, in 1894, when Strong was elected mayor, what a harvest it was for all the little "Democracies" that was made to order that year! Every one of them got somethin' good. In one case, all the nine men in an organization got jobs payin' from $2000 to $5000. I happen to know exactly what it cost to manufacture that organization. It was $42.04. They left out the stationery, and had only twenty-three cuspidors. The extra four cents was for two postage stamps.

The only reason I can imagine why more men don't go into this industry is because they don't know about it. And just here it strikes me that it might not be wise to publish what I've said. Perhaps if it gets to be known what a snap this manufacture of "Democracies" is, all the green-goods men, the bunco-steerers, and the young Napoleons of finance, will go into it and the public will be humbugged more than it has been. But, after all, what difference would it make? There's always a certain number of suckers and a certain number of men lookin' for a chance to take them in, and the suckers are sure to be took one way or another. It's the everlastin' law of demand and supply.

CONCERNING GAS IN POLITICS

:
:
:
:
:
:

☞ :

SINCE THE EIGHTY-CENT GAS bill was defeated in Albany, everybody's talkin' about senators bein' bribed. Now, I wasn't in the Senate last session, and I don't know the ins and outs of everything that was done, but I can tell you that the legislators are often hauled over the coals when they are all on the level. I've been there and I know. For instance, when I voted in the Senate in 1904, for the Remsen Bill that the newspapers called the "Astoria Gas Grab Bill," they didn't do a thing to me. The papers kept up a howl about all the supporters of the bill bein' bought up by the Consolidated Gas Company, and the Citizens' Union did me the honor to call me the commander-in-chief of the "Black Horse Cavalry."

The fact is that I was workin' for my district all this time, and I wasn't bribed by nobody. There's several of these gas-houses in the district, and I wanted to get them over to Astoria for three reasons: First, because they're nuisances; second, because there's no votes in them for me any longer; third, because—well, I had a little private reason which I'll explain further on. I needn't explain how they're nuisances. They're worse than open sewers. Still, I might have stood that if they hadn't degenerated so much in the last few years.

Ah, gas-houses ain't what they used to be! Not very long ago, each gas-house was good for a couple of hundred votes. All the men employed in them were Irishmen and Germans who lived in the district. Now, it is all different. The men are dagoes who live across in Jersey and take no interest in the district. What's the use of havin ill-smellin' gas-houses if there's no votes in them?

Now, as to my private reason. Well, I'm a business man and go in for any business that's profitable and honest. Real estate is one of my specialties. I know the value of every foot of ground in my district, and

I calculated long ago that if them gas-houses was removed, surroundin' property would go up 100 per cent. When the Remsen Bill, providin' for the removal of the gas-houses to Queens County came up, I said to myself: "George, hasn't your chance come?" I answered: "Sure." Then I sized up the chances of the bill. I found it was certain to pass the Senate and the Assembly, and I got assurances straight from headquarters that Governor Odell would sign it. Next I came down to the city to find out the mayor's position. I got it straight that he would approve the bill, too.

Can't you guess what I did then? Like any sane man who had my information, I went in and got options on a lot of the property around the gas-houses. Well, the bill went through the Senate and the Assembly all right and the mayor signed it, but Odell backslided at the last minute and the whole game fell through. If it had succeeded, I guess I would have been accused of graftin'. What I want to know is, what do you call it when I got left and lost a pot of money?

I not only lost money, but I was abused for votin' for the bill. Wasn't that outrageous? They said I was in with the Consolidated Gas Company and all other kinds of rot, when I was really only workin' for my district and tryin' to turn an honest penny on the side. Anyhow I got a little fun out of the business. When the Remsen Bill was up, I was tryin' to put through a bill of my own, the Spuyten Duyvil Bill, which provided for fillin' in some land under water that the New York Central Railroad wanted. Well, the Remsen managers were afraid of bein' beaten and they went around offerin' to make trades with senators and assemblymen who had bills they were anxious to pass. They came to me and offered six votes for my Spuyten Duyvil Bill in exchange for my vote on the Remsen Bill. I took them up in a hurry, and they felt pretty sore afterwards when they heard I was goin' to vote for the Remsen Bill anyhow.

A word about that Spuyten Duyvil Bill, I was criticized a lot for introducin' it. They said I was workin' in the interest of the New York Central, and was goin' to get the contract for fillin' in. The fact is, that the fillin' in was a good thing for the city, and if it helped the New York Central, too, what of it? The railroad is a great public institution, and I was never an enemy of public institutions. As to the contract, it hasn't come along yet. If it does come, it will find me at home at all proper and reasonable hours, if there is a good profit in sight.

The papers and some people are always ready to find wrong motives in what us statesmen do. If we bring about some big improvement that benefits the city and it just happens, as a sort of coincidence, that we make a few dollars out of the improvement, they say we are grafters. But we are used to this kind of ingratitude. It falls to the lot of all statesmen, especially Tammany statesmen. All we can do is to bow our heads in silence and wait till time has cleared our memories.

Just think of mentionin' dishonest graft in connection with the name of George Washington Plunkitt, the man who gave the city its magnificent chain of parks, its Washington Bridge, its Speedway, its Museum of Natural History, its One Hundred and Fifty-fifth Street Viaduct and its West Side Courthouse! I was the father of the bills that provided for all these; yet, because I supported the Remsen and Spuyten Duyvil bills, some people have questioned my honest motives. If that's the case, how can you expect legislators to fare who are not the fathers of the parks, the Washington Bridge, the Speedway and the Viaduct?

Now, understand; I ain't defendin' the senators who killed the eighty-cent gas bill. I don't know why they acted as they did; I only want to impress the idea to go slow before you make up your mind that a man, occupyin' the exalted position that I held for so many years, has done wrong. For all I know, these senators may have been as honest and high-minded about the gas bill as I was about the Remsen and Spuyten Duyvil bills.

PLUNKITT'S FONDEST DREAM

. . . .

👉

THE TIME IS COMIN' AND though I'm no youngster, I may see it, when New York City will break away from the State and become a state itself. It's got to come. The feelin' between this city and the hayseeds that make a livin' by plunderin' it is every bit as bitter as the feelin' between the North and South before the war. And, let me tell you, if there ain't a peaceful separation before long, we may have the horrors of civil war right here in New York State. Why, I know a

lot of men in my district who would like nothin' better to-day than to go out gunnin' for hayseeds!

New York City has got a bigger population than
most of the states in the Union. It's got more wealth
than any dozen of them. Yet the people here, as I
explained before, are nothin' but slaves of the Albany gang. We have stood the slavery a long, long
time, but the uprisin' is near at hand. It will be a
fight for liberty, just like the American Revolution.
We'll get liberty peacefully if we can; by cruel war
if we must.

Just think how lovely things would be here if we
had a Tammany Governor and Legislature meetin',
say in the neighborhood of Fifty-ninth Street, and
a Tammany Mayor and Board of Aldermen doin'
business in City Hall! How sweet and peaceful everything would go on! The people wouldn't have to
bother about nothin'. Tammany would take care of
everything for them in its nice quiet way. You
wouldn't hear of any conflicts between the state and
city authorities. They would settle everything pleasant and comfortable at Tammany Hall, and every
bill introduced in the Legislature by Tammany would
be sure to go through. The Republicans wouldn't
count.

Imagine how the city would be built up in a short
time! At present we can't make a public improvement of any consequence without goin' to Albany

for permission, and most of the time we get turned
down when we go there. But, with a Tammany Governor and Legislature up at Fifty-ninth Street, how
public works would hum here! The Mayor and Aldermen could decide on an improvement, telephone
the Capitol, have a bill put through in a jiffy and—
there you are. We could have a state constitution,
too, which would extend the debt limit so that we
could issue a whole lot more bonds. As things are
now, all the money spent for docks, for instance, is
charged against the city in calculatin' the debt limit,
although the Dock Department provides immense
revenues. It's the same with some other departments.
This humbug would be dropped if Tammany ruled
at the Capitol and the City Hall, and the city would
have money to burn.

Another thing—the constitution of the new state
wouldn't have a word about civil service, and if any
man dared to introduce any kind of a civil service
bill in the Legislature, he would be fired out the window. Then we would have government of the people
by the people who were elected to govern them.
That's the kind of government Lincoln meant. O
what a glorious future for the city! Whenever I
think of it I feel like goin' out and celebratin', and
I'm really almost sorry that I don't drink.

You may ask what would become of the up-State
people if New York City left them in the lurch and

went into the State business on its own account. Well, we wouldn't be under no obligation to provide for them; still I would be in favor of helpin' them along for a while until they could learn to work and earn an honest livin', just like the United States Government looks after the Indians. These hayseeds have been so used to livin' off of New York City that they would be helpless after we left them. It wouldn't do to let them starve. We might make some sort of an appropriation for them for a few years, but it would be with the distinct understandin' that they must get busy right away and learn to support themselves. If, after, say five years, they weren't self-supportin', we could withdraw the appropriation and let them shift for themselves. The plan might succeed and it might not. We'd be doin' our duty anyhow.

Some persons might say: "But how about it if the hayseed politicians moved down here and went in to get control of the government of the new state?" We could provide against that easy by passin' a law that these politicians couldn't come below the Bronx without a sort of passport limitin' the time of their stay here, and forbiddin' them to monkey with politics here. I don't know just what kind of a bill would be required to fix this, but with a Tammany Constitution, Governor, Legislature and Mayor, there would be no trouble in settlin' a little matter of that sort.

Say, I don't wish I was a poet, for if I was, I guess I'd be livin' in a garret on no dollars a week instead of runnin' a great contractin' and transportation business which is doin' pretty well, thank you; but, honest, now, the notion takes me sometimes to yell poetry of the red-hot-hail-glorious-land kind when I think of New York City as a state by itself.

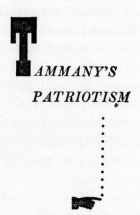

TAMMANY'S PATRIOTISM

TAMMANY'S THE MOST PATRI-
otic organization on earth, not withstandin' the fact
that the civil service law is sappin' the foundations
of patriotism all over the country. Nobody pays any
attention to the Fourth of July any longer except
Tammany and the small boy. When the Fourth comes,
the reformers, with Revolutionary names parted in
the middle, run off to Newport or the Adirondacks
to get out of the way of the noise and everything
that reminds them of the glorious day. How different

it is with Tammany! The very constitution of the Tammany Society requires that we must assemble at the wigwam on the Fourth, regardless of the weather, and listen to the readin' of the Declaration of Independence and patriotic speeches.

You ought to attend one of these meetin's. They're a liberal education in patriotism. The great hall upstairs is filled with five thousand people, suffocatin' from heat and smoke. Every man Jack of these five thousand knows that down in the basement there's a hundred cases of champagne and two hundred kegs of beer ready to flow when the signal is given. Yet that crowd stick to their seats without turnin' a hair while, for four solid hours, the Declaration of Independence is read, long-winded orators speak, and the glee club sings itself hoarse.

Talk about heroism in the battlefield! That comes and passes away in a moment. You ain't got time to be anything but heroic. But just think of five thousand men sittin' in the hottest place on earth for four long hours, with parched lips and gnawin' stomachs, and knowin' all the time that the delights of the oasis in the desert were only two flights downstairs! Ah, that is the highest kind of patriotism, the patriotism of long sufferin' and endurance. What man wouldn't rather face a cannon for a minute or two than thirst for four hours, with champagne and beer almost under his nose?

And then see how they applaud and yell when patriotic things are said! As soon as the man on the platform starts off with "when, in the course of human events," word goes around that it's the Declaration of Independence, and a mighty roar goes up. The Declaration ain't a very short document and the crowd has heard it on every Fourth but they give it just as fine a send-off as if it was brand new and awful excitin'. Then the "long talkers" get in their work, that is two or three orators who are good for an hour each. Heat never has any effect on these men. They use every minute of their time. Sometimes human nature gets the better of a man in the audience and he begins to nod, but he always wakes up with a hurrah for the Declaration of Independence.

The greatest hero of the occasion is the Grand Sachem of the Tammany Society who presides. He and the rest of us Sachems come on the stage wearin' stove-pipe hats, accordin' to the constitution, but we can shed ours right off, while the Grand Sachem is required to wear his hat all through the celebration. Have you any idea what that means? Four hours under a big silk hat in a hall where the heat registers 110 and the smoke 250! And the Grand Sachem is expected to look pleasant all the time and say nice things when introducin' the speakers! Often his hand goes to his hat, unconscious like, then he catches himself up in time and looks around like a man who is in the tenth story of a burnin' buildin' seekin' a way to escape. I believe that Fourth-of-July silk hat shortened the life of one of our Grand Sachems, the late Supreme Court Justice Smyth, and I know that one of our Sachems refused the office of Grand Sachem because he couldn't get up sufficient patriotism to perform this four-hour hat act. You see, there's degrees of patriotism just as there's degrees in everything else.

You don't hear of the Citizens' Union people holdin' Fourth-of-July celebrations under a five-pound silk hat, or any other way, do you? The Cits take the Fourth like a dog I had when I was a boy. That dog knew as much as some Cits and he acted just like them about the glorious day. Exactly forty-eight hours before each Fourth of July, the dog left our house on a run and hid himself in the Bronx woods. The day after the Fourth he turned up at home as regular as clockwork. He must have known what a dog is up against on the Fourth. Anyhow, he kept out of the way. The name-parted-in-the-middle aristocrats act in just the same way. They don't want to be annoyed with fire-crackers and the Declaration of Independence, and when they see the Fourth comin' they hustle off to the woods like my dog.

Tammany don't only show its patriotism at

Fourth-of-July celebrations. It's always on deck when the country needs its services. After the Spanish-American War broke out, John J. Scannell, the Tammany leader of the Twenty-fifth District, wrote to Governor Black offerin' to raise a Tammany regiment to go to the front. If you want proof, go to Tammany Hall and see the beautiful set of engrossed resolutions about this regiment. It's true that the Governor didn't accept the offer, but it showed Tammany's patriotism. Some enemies of the organization have said that the offer to raise the regiment was made after the Governor let it be known that no more volunteers were wanted, but that's the talk of envious slanderers.

Now, a word about Tammany's love for the American flag. Did you ever see Tammany Hall decorated for a celebration? It's just a mass of flags. They even take down the window shades and put flags in place of them. There's flags everywhere except on the floors. We don't care for expense where the American flag is concerned, especially after we have won an election. In 1904 we originated the custom of givin' a small flag to each man as he entered Tammany Hall for the Fourth-of-July celebration. It took like wild-fire. The men waved their flags whenever they cheered and the sight made me feel so patriotic that I forgot all about civil service for a while. And the good work of the flags didn't stop there.

The men carried them home and gave them to the children, and the kids got patriotic, too. Of course, it all cost a pretty penny, but what of that? We had won at the polls the precedin' November, had the offices and could afford to make an extra investment in patriotism.

O*N THE USE OF MONEY IN POLITICS*

THE CIVIL SERVICE GANG IS
always howlin' about candidates and office-holders
puttin' up money for campaigns and about corporations chippin' in. They might as well howl about
givin' contributions to churches. A political organization has to have money for its business as well as
a church, and who has more right to put up than
the men who get the good things that are goin'?
Take, for instance, a great political concern like
Tammany Hall. It does missionary work like a

church, it's got big expenses and it's got to be supported by the faithful. If a corporation sends in a check to help the good work of the Tammany Society, why shouldn't we take it like other missionary societies? Of course, the day may come when we'll reject the money of the rich as tainted, but it hadn't come when I left Tammany Hall at 11:25 A.M. to-day.

Not long ago some newspapers had fits because the Assemblyman from my district said he had put up $500 when he was nominated for the Assembly last year. Every politician in town laughed at these papers. I don't think there was even a Citizens' Union man who didn't know that candidates of both parties have to chip in for campaign expenses. The sums they pay are accordin' to their salaries and the length of their terms of office, if elected. Even candidates for the Supreme Court have to fall in line. A Supreme Court Judge in New York County gets $17,500 a year, and he's expected, when nominated, to help along the good cause with a year's salary. Why not? He has fourteen years on the bench ahead of him, and ten thousand other lawyers would be willin' to put up twice as much to be in his shoes. Now, I ain't sayin' that we sell nominations. That's a different thing altogether. There's no auction and no regular biddin'. The man is picked out and somehow he gets to understand what's expected of him in the way of a contribution, and he ponies up—all from gratitude to the organization that honored him, see?

Let me tell you an instance that shows the difference between sellin' nominations and arrangin' them in the way I described. A few years ago a Republican district leader controlled the nomination for Congress in his Congressional district. Four men wanted it. At first the leader asked for bids privately, but decided at last that the best thing to do was to get the four men together in the back room of a certain saloon and have an open auction. When he had his men lined up, he got on a chair, told about the value of the goods for sale, and asked for bids in regular auctioneer style. The highest bidder got the nomination for $5000. Now, that wasn't right at all. These things ought to be always fixed up nice and quiet.

As to office-holders, they would be ingrates if they didn't contribute to the organization that put them in office. They needn't be assessed. That would be against the law. But they know what's expected of them, and if they happen to forget they can be reminded polite and courteous. Dan Donegan, who used to be the Wiskinkie of the Tammany Society, and received contributions from grateful office-holders, had a pleasant way of remindin'. If a man forgot his duty to the organization that made him, Dan would call on the man, smile as sweet as you please

99

and say: "You haven't been round at the Hall lately, have you?" If the man tried to slide around the question, Dan would say: "It's gettin' awful cold." Then he would have a fit of shiverin' and walk away. What could be more polite and, at the same time, more to the point? No force, no threats—only a little shiverin' which any man is liable to even in summer.

Just here, I want to charge one more crime to the infamous civil service law. It has made men turn ungrateful. A dozen years ago, when there wasn't much civil service business in the city government, and when the administration could turn out almost any man holdin' office, Dan's shiver took effect every time and there was no ingratitude in the city departments. But when the civil service law came in and all the clerks got lead-pipe cinches on their jobs, ingratitude spread right away. Dan shivered and shook till his bones rattled, but many of the city employees only laughed at him. One day, I remember, he tackled a clerk in the Public Works Department, who used to give up pretty regular, and, after the usual question, began to shiver. The clerk smiled. Dan shook till his hat fell off. The clerk took ten cents out of his pocket, handed it to Dan and said: "Poor man! Go and get a drink to warm yourself up." Wasn't that shameful? And yet, if it hadn't been for the civil service law, that clerk would be contributin' right along to this day.

On the Use of Money in Politics

The civil service law don't cover everything, however. There's lots of good jobs outside its clutch, and the men that get them are grateful every time. I'm not speakin' of Tammany Hall alone, remember! It's the same with the Republican Federal and State office-holders, and every organization that has or has had jobs to give out—except, of course, the Citizens' Union. The Cits held office only a couple of years and, knowin' that they would never be in again, each Cit office-holder held on for dear life to every dollar that came his way.

Some people say they can't understand what becomes of all the money that's collected for campaigns. They would understand fast enough if they were district leaders. There's never been half enough money to go around. Besides the expenses for meetin's, bands and all that, there's the bigger bill for the district workers who get men to the polls. These workers are mostly men who want to serve their country but can't get jobs in the city departments on account of the civil service law. They do the next best thing by keepin' track of the voters and seein' that they come to the polls and vote the right way. Some of these deservin' citizens have to make enough on registration and election days to keep them the rest of the year. Isn't it right that they should get a share of the campaign money?

Just remember that there's thirty-five Assembly

districts in New York County, and thirty-six district leaders reachin' out for the Tammany dough-bag for somethin' to keep up the patriotism of ten thousand workers, and you wouldn't wonder that the cry for more, more, is goin' up from every district organization now and forevermore. Amen.

THE SUCCESSFUL
POLITICIAN
DOES NOT DRINK

I HAVE EXPLAINED HOW TO succeed in politics. I want to add that no matter how well you learn to play the political game, you won't make a lastin' success of it if you're a drinkin' man. I never take a drop of any kind of intoxicatin' liquor. I ain't no fanatic. Some of the saloon-keepers are my best friends, and I don't mind goin' into a saloon any day with my friends. But as a matter of business I leave whisky and beer and the rest of that stuff alone. As a matter of business, too, I take for my lieutenants in my district men who don't drink. I tried the other kind for several years, but it didn't pay. They cost too much. For instance, I had a young man who was one of the best hustlers in town. He knew every man in the district, was popular everywhere and could induce a half-dead man to come to the polls on election day. But, regularly, two weeks before election, he started on a drunk, and I had to hire two men to guard him day and night and keep him sober enough to do his work. That cost a lot of money, and I dropped the young man after a while.

Maybe you think I'm unpopular with the saloon-keepers because I don't drink. You're wrong. The most successful saloon-keepers don't drink themselves and they understand that my temperance is a business proposition, just like their own. I have a saloon under my headquarters. If a saloon-keeper gets into trouble, he always knows that Senator Plunkitt is the man to help him out. If there is a bill in the Legislature makin' it easier for the liquor dealers, I am for it every time. I'm a one of the best friends the saloon men have—but I don't drink their whisky. I won't go through the temperance lecture dodge and tell you how many bright young men I've seen fall victims to intemperance, but I'll tell you that I could name dozens—young men who had started on the road to statesmanship, who could carry their districts every time, and who could turn out any vote you wanted at the primaries. I honestly believe that drink is the greatest curse of the day, except, of course, civil service, and that it has driven more young men to ruin than anything except civil service examinations.

Look at the great leaders of Tammany Hall! No regular drinkers among them. Richard Croker's strongest drink was vichy. Charlie Murphy takes a glass of wine at dinner sometimes, but he don't go beyond that. A drinkin' man wouldn't last two weeks as leader of Tammany Hall. Nor can a man manage an assembly district long if he drinks. He's got to have a clear head all the time. I could name ten men who, in the last few years, lost their grip in their districts because they began drinkin'. There's now thirty-six district leaders in Tammany Hall, and I don't believe a half-dozen of them ever drink anything except at meals. People have got an idea that because the liquor men are with us in campaigns, our district leaders spend most of their time leanin' against bars. There couldn't be a wronger idea. The district leader makes a business of politics, gets his livin' out of it, and, in order to succeed, he's got to keep sober just like in any other business.

Just take as examples, "Big Tim" and "Little Tim" Sullivan. They're known all over the country as the Bowery leaders and, as there's nothin' but

saloons on the Bowery, people might think that they
are hard drinkers. The fact is that neither of them
has ever touched a drop of liquor in his life or even
smoked a cigar. Still they don't make no pretences
of being better than anybody else, and don't go
around deliverin' temperance lectures. Big Tim made
money out of liquor—sellin' it to other people. That's
the only way to get good out of liquor.

Look at all the Tammany heads of city departments! There's not a real drinkin' man in the lot. Oh,
yes, there are some prominent men in the organization who drink sometimes, but they are not the men
who have power. They're ornaments, fancy speakers
and all that, who make a fine show behind the foot-
lights, but ain't in it when it comes to directin' the
city government and the Tammany organization.
The men who sit in the executive committee-room at
Tammany Hall and direct things are men who celebrate on apollinaris or vichy. Let me tell you what I
saw on election night in 1897, when the Tammany
ticket swept the city: Up to 10 P.M. Croker, John F.
Carroll, Tim Sullivan, Charlie Murphy, and myself
sat in the committee-room receivin' returns. When
nearly all the city was heard from and we saw that
Van Wyck was elected by a big majority, I invited
the crowd to go across the street for a little celebration. A lot of small politicians followed us, expectin'
to see magnums of champagne opened. The waiters

in the restaurant expected it, too, and you never saw a more disgusted lot of waiters when they got our orders. Here's the orders: Croker, vichy and bicarbonate of soda; Carroll, seltzer lemonade; Sullivan, apollinaris; Murphy, vichy; Plunkitt, ditto. Before midnight we were all in bed, and next mornin' we were up bright and early attendin' to business, while other men were nursin' swelled heads. Is there anything the matter with temperance as a pure business proposition?

Bosses Preserve the Nation

WHEN I RETIRED FROM THE Senate, I thought I would take a good, long rest, such a rest as a man needs who has held office for about forty years, and has held four different offices in one year and drawn salaries from three of them at the same time. Drawin' so many salaries is rather fatiguin', you know, and, as I said, I started out for a rest; but when I seen how things were goin' in New York State, and how a great big black shadow hung

108

over us, I said to myself: 'No rest for you, George. Your work ain't done. Your country still needs you and you mustn't lay down yet."

What was the great big black shadow? It was the primary election law, amended so as to knock out what are called the party bosses by lettin' in everybody at the primaries and givin' control over them to state officials. Oh, yes, that is a good way to do up the so-called bosses, but, have you ever thought what would become of the country if the bosses were put out of business, and their places were taken by a lot of cart-tail orators and college graduates? It would mean chaos. It would be just like takin' a lot of dry-goods clerks and settin' them to run express trains on the New York Central Railroad. It makes my heart bleed to think of it. Ignorant people are always talkin' against party bosses, but just wait till the bosses are gone! Then, and not until then, will they get the right sort of epitaphs, as Patrick Henry or Robert Emmet said.

Look at the bosses of Tammany Hall in the last twenty years. What magnificent men! To them New York City owes pretty much all it is to-day. John Kelly, Richard Croker, and Charles F. Murphy— what names in American history compares with them, except Washington and Lincoln? They built up the grand Tammany organization, and the organization built up New York. Suppose the city had to depend for the last twenty years on irresponsible concerns like the Citizens' Union, where would it be now? You can make a pretty good guess if you recall the Strong and Low administrations when there was no boss, and the heads of departments were at odds all the time with each other, and the Mayor was at odds with the lot of them. They spent so much time in arguin' and makin' grand-stand play, that the interests of the city were forgotten. Another administration of that kind would put New York back a quarter of a century.

Then see how beautiful a Tammany city government runs, with a so-called boss directin' the whole shootin' match! The machinery moves so noiseless that you wouldn't think there was any. If there's any differences of opinion, the Tammany leader settles them quietly, and his orders go every time. How nice it is for the people to feel that they can get up in the mornin' without bein' afraid of seein' in the papers that the Commissioner of Water Supply has sand-bagged the Dock Commissioner, and that the Mayor and heads of the departments have been taken to the police court as witnesses! That's no joke. I remember that, under Strong, some commissioners came very near sandbaggin' one another.

Of course, the newspapers like the reform administration. Why? Because these administrations, with their daily rows, furnish as racy news as prize-fights or divorce cases. Tammany don't care to get in the papers. It goes right along attendin' to business quietly and only wants to be let alone. That's one reason why the papers are against us.

Some papers complain that the bosses get rich while devotin' their lives to the interests of the city. What of it? If opportunities for turnin' an honest dollar comes their way, why shouldn't they take advantage of them, just as I have done? As I said, in another talk, there is honest graft and dishonest graft. The bosses go in for the former. There is so much of it in this big town that they would be fools to go in for dishonest graft.

Now, the primary election law threatens to do away with the boss and make the city government a menagerie. That's why I can't take the rest I counted on. I'm goin' to propose a bill for the next session of the legislature repealin' this dangerous law, and leavin' the primaries entirely to the organizations themselves, as they used to be. Then will return the good old times, when our district leaders could have nice comfortable primary elections at some place selected by themselves and let in only men that they approved of as good Democrats. Who is a better judge of the Democracy of a man who offers his vote than the leader of the district? Who is better equipped to keep out undesirable voters?

The men who put through the primary law are

111

the same crowd that stand for the civil service blight
and they have the same objects in view—the destruction of governments by party, the downfall of the
constitution and hell generally.

CONCERNING EXCISE

ALTHOUGH I'M NOT A DRINKIN' man myself, I mourn with the poor liquor dealers of New York City, who are taxed and oppressed for the benefit of the farmers up the state. The Raines liquor law is infamous. It takes away nearly all the profits of the saloon-keepers, and then turns in a large part of the money to the State treasury to relieve the hayseeds from taxes. Ah, who knows how many honest, hard-workin' saloon-keepers have been driven to untimely graves by this law! I know personally of a half-dozen who committed suicide because they couldn't pay the enormous license fee, and I have heard of many others. Every time there is an increase of the fee, there is an increase in the suicide record of the city. Now, some of these Republican hayseeds are talkin' about makin' the liquor tax $1500, or even $2000 a year. That would mean the suicide of half of the liquor dealers in the city.

Just see how these poor fellows are oppressed all around! First, liquor is taxed in the hands of the manufacturer by the United States Government; second, the wholesale dealer pays a special tax to the government; third, the retail dealer is specially taxed by the United States Government; fourth, the retail dealer has to pay a big tax to the State government.

Now, liquor dealing is criminal or it ain't. If it's criminal, the men engaged in it ought to be sent to prison. If it ain't criminal, they ought to be protected and encouraged to make all the profit they honestly can. If it's right to tax a saloon-keeper $1000, it's right to put a heavy tax on dealers in other beverages—in milk, for instance—and make the dairymen pay up. But what a howl would be raised if a bill was introduced in Albany to compel the farmers to help support the State government! What would be said of a law that put a tax of, say $60 on a grocer, $150 on a dry-goods man, and $500 more if he includes the other goods that are kept in a country store?

If the Raines law gave the money extorted from the saloon-keepers to the city, there might be some excuse for the tax. We would get some benefit from it, but it gives a big part of the tax to local option localities where the people are always shoutin' that liquor-dealin' is immoral. Ought these good people be subjected to the immoral influence of money taken from the saloons—tainted money? Out of respect for the tender consciences of these pious people, the Raines law ought to exempt them from all contamination from the plunder that comes from the saloon traffic. Say, mark that sarcastic. Some people who ain't used to fine sarcasm might think I meant it.

The Raines people make a pretense that the high license fee promotes temperance. It's just the other way around. It makes more intemperance and, what is as bad, it makes a monopoly in dram-shops. Soon the saloons will be in the hands of a vast trust, and any stuff can be sold for whisky or beer. It's gettin' that way already. Some of the poor liquor dealers in my district have been forced to sell wood alcohol for whisky, and many deaths have followed. A half-dozen men died in a couple of days from this kind of whisky which was forced down their throats by the high liquor tax. If they raise the tax higher, wood alcohol will be too costly, and I guess some dealers will have

115

to get down to kerosene oil and add to the Rockefeller millions.

The way the Raines law divides the different classes of licenses is also an outrage. The sumptuous hotel-saloons, with $10,000 paintin's and bricky-brac and Oriental splendors gets off easier than a shanty on the rocks, by the water's edge in my district where boatmen drink their grog, and the only ornaments is a three-cornered mirror nailed to the wall, and a chromo of the fight between Tom Hyer and Yankee Sullivan. Besides, a premium is put on places that sell liquor not to be drunk on the premises, but to be taken home. Now, I want to declare that from my experience in New York City, I would rather see rum sold in the dram-shops unlicensed, provided the rum is swallowed on the spot, than to encourage, by a low tax, "bucket-shops" from which the stuff is carried into the tenements at all hours of the day and night and make drunkenness and debauchery among the women and children. A "bucket-shop" in the tenement district means a cheap, so-called distillery, where raw spirits, poisonous colorin' matter and water are sold for brandy and whisky at ten cents a quart, and carried away in buckets and pitchers; I have always noticed that there are many undertakers wherever the "bucket-shop" flourishes, and they have no dull seasons.

I want it understood that I'm not an advocate of

116

the liquor dealers or of drinkin'. I think every man would be better off if he didn't take any intoxicatin' drink at all, but as men will drink, they ought to have good stuff without impoverishin' themselves by goin' to fancy places and without riskin' death by goin' to poor places. The State should look after their interests as well as the interests of those who drink nothin' stronger than milk.

Now, as to the liquor dealers themselves. They ain't the criminals that cantin' hypocrites say they are. I know lots of them and I know that, as a rule, they're good honest citizens who conduct their business in a straight, honorable way. At a convention of the liquor dealers a few years ago, a big city city official welcomed them on behalf of the city and said: "Go on elevatin' your standard higher and higher. Go on with your good work. Heaven will bless you!" That was puttin' it just a little strong, but the sentiment was all right and I guess the speaker went a bit further than he intended in his enthusiasm over meetin' such a fine set of men and, perhaps, dinin' with them.

A PARTING WORD ON THE FUTURE OF THE DEMOCRATIC PARTY IN AMERICA

THE DEMOCRATIC PARTY OF the nation ain't dead, though it's been givin' a life-like imitation of a corpse for several years. It can't die while it's got Tammany for its backbone. The trouble is that the party's been chasin' after theories and stayin' up nights readin' books instead of study-in' human nature and actin' accordin', as I've ad-vised in tellin' how to hold your district. In two Presidential campaigns, the leaders talked themselves red in the face about silver bein' the best money and gold bein' no good, and they tried to prove it out of books. Do you think the people cared for all that guff? No. They heartily indorsed what Richard Croker said at the Hoffman House one day in 1900. "What's the use of discussin' what's the best kind of money?" said Croker. "I'm in favor of all kinds of money—the more the better." See how a real Tammany statesman can settle in twenty-five words a problem that monopolized two campaigns!

Then imperialism. The Democratic party spent all its breath on that in the last national campaign. Its position was all right, sure, but you can't get people excited about the Philippines. They've got too much at home to interest them; they're too busy makin' a livin' to bother about the niggers in the Pacific. The party's got to drop all them put-you-to-sleep issues and come out in 1908 for somethin' that will wake the people up; somethin' that will make it worth while to work for the party.

There's just one issue that would set this country on fire. The Democratic party should say in the first plank of its platform: "We hereby declare, in national convention assembled, that the paramount issue now, always and forever, is the abolition of the iniquitous and villainous civil service laws which are destroyin' all patriotism, ruinin' the country and takin' away good jobs from them that earn them.

119

We pledge ourselves, if our ticket is elected, to repeal those laws at once and put every civil service reformer in jail."

Just imagine the wild enthusiasm of the party, if that plank was adopted, and the rush of Republicans to join us in restorin' our country to what it was before this college professor's nightmare, called civil service reform, got hold of it! Of course, it would be all right to work in the platform some stuff about the tariff and sound money and the Philippines, as no platform seems to be complete without them, but they wouldn't count. The people would read only the first plank and then hanker for election day to come to put the Democratic party in office.

I see a vision. I see the civil service monster lyin' flat on the ground. I see the Democratic party standin' over it with foot on its neck and wearin' the crown of victory. I see Thomas Jefferson lookin' out from a cloud and sayin': "Give him another sockdologer; finish him." And I see millions of men wavin' their hats and singin' "Glory Hallelujah!"

STRENUOUS LIFE OF THE TAMMANY DISTRICT LEADER

☞

NOTE: *This chapter is based on extracts from Plunkitt's Diary and on my daily observation of the work of the district leader.*—W.L.R.

THE LIFE OF THE TAMMANY district leader is strenuous. To his work is due the wonderful recuperative power of the organization.

One year it goes down in defeat and the prediction is made that it will never again raise its head. The district leader, undaunted by defeat, collects his scattered forces, organizes them as only Tammany knows how to organize, and in a little while the organization is as strong as ever.

No other politician in New York or elsewhere is exactly like the Tammany district leader or works as he does. As a rule, he has no business or occupation other than politics. He plays politics every day and night in the year, and his headquarters bears the inscription, "Never closed."

Everybody in the district knows him. Everybody knows where to find him, and nearly everybody goes to him for assistance of one sort or another, especially the poor of the tenements.

He is always obliging. He will go to the police courts to put in a good word for the "drunks and disorderlies" or pay their fines, if a good word is not effective. He will attend christenings, weddings, and funerals. He will feed the hungry and help bury the dead.

A philanthropist? Not at all. He is playing politics all the time.

Brought up in Tammany Hall, he has learned how to reach the hearts of the great mass of voters. He does not bother about reaching their heads. It is his belief that arguments and campaign literature have never gained votes.

He seeks direct contact with the people, does them

good turns when he can, and relies on their not forgetting him on election day. His heart is always in his work, too, for his subsistence depends on its results.

If he holds his district and Tammany is in power, he is amply rewarded by a good office and the opportunities that go with it. What these opportunities are has been shown by the quick rise to wealth of so many Tammany district leaders. With the examples before him of Richard Croker, once leader of the Twentieth District; John F. Carroll, formerly leader of the Twenty-ninth; Timothy ("Dry Dollar") Sullivan, late leader of the Sixth, and many others, he can always look forward to riches and ease while he is going through the drudgery of his daily routine.

This is a record of a day's work by Plunkitt:

2 A.M.: Aroused from sleep by the ringing of his door bell; went to the door and found a bartender, who asked him to go to the police station and bail out a saloon-keeper who had been arrested for violating the excise law. Furnished bail and returned to bed at three o'clock.

6 A.M.: Awakened by fire engines passing his house. Hastened to the scene of the fire, according to the custom of the Tammany district leaders, to give assistance to the fire sufferers, if needed. Met several of his election district captains who are always under orders to look out for fires, which are considered

great vote-getters. Found several tenants who had been burned out, took them to a hotel, supplied them with clothes, fed them, and arranged temporary quarters for them until they could rent and furnish new apartments.

8:30 A.M.: Went to the police court to look after his constituents. Found six "drunks." Secured the discharge of four by a timely word with the judge, and paid the fines of two.

9 A.M.: Appeared in the Municipal District Court. Directed one of his district captains to act as counsel for a widow against whom dispossess proceedings had been instituted and obtained an extension of time. Paid the rent of a poor family about to be dispossessed and gave them a dollar for food.

11 A.M.: At home again. Found four men waiting for him. One had been discharged by the Metropolitan Railway Company for neglect of duty, and wanted the district leader to fix things. Another wanted a job on the road. The third sought a place on the Subway and the fourth, a plumber, was looking for work with the Consolidated Gas Company. The district leader spent nearly three hours fixing things for the four men, and succeeded in each case.

3 P.M.: Attended the funeral of an Italian as far as the ferry. Hurried back to make his appearance at the funeral of a Hebrew constituent. Went conspicu-

ously to the front both in the Catholic church and the synagogue, and later attended the Hebrew confirmation ceremonies in the synagogue.

7 P.M.: Went to district headquarters and presided over a meeting of election district captains. Each captain submitted a list of all the voters in his district, reported on their attitude toward Tammany, suggested who might be won over and how they could be won, told who were in need, and who were in trouble of any kind and the best way to reach them. District leader took notes and gave orders.

8 P.M.: Went to a church fair. Took chances on everything, bought ice-cream for the young girls and the children. Kissed the little ones, flattered their mothers and took their fathers out for something down at the corner.

9 P.M.: At the club-house again. Spent $10 on tickets for a church excursion and promised a subscription for a new church-bell. Bought tickets for a base-ball game to be played by two nines from his district. Listened to the complaints of a dozen push-cart peddlers who said they were persecuted by the police and assured them he would go to Police Headquarters in the morning and see about it.

10:30 P.M.: Attended a Hebrew wedding reception and dance. Had previously sent a handsome wedding present to the bride.

12 P.M.: In bed.

That is the actual record of one day in the life of Plunkitt. He does some of the same things every day, but his life is not so monotonous as to be wearisome.

Sometimes the work of a district leader is exciting, especially if he happens to have a rival who intends to make a contest for the leadership at the primaries. In that case, he is even more alert, tries to reach the fires before his rival, sends out runners to look for "drunks and disorderlies" at the police stations, and keeps a very close watch on the obituary columns of the newspapers.

A few years ago there was a bitter contest for the Tammany leadership of the Ninth District between John C. Sheehan and Frank J. Goodwin. Both had had long experience in Tammany politics and both understood every move of the game.

Every morning their agents went to their respective headquarters before seven o'clock and read through the death notices in all the morning papers. If they found that anybody in the district had died, they rushed to the homes of their principals with the information and then there was a race to the house of the deceased to offer condolences, and, if the family were poor, something more substantial.

On the day of the funeral there was another contest. Each faction tried to surpass the other in the number and appearance of the carriages it sent to the funeral, and more than once they almost came to blows at the church or in the cemetery.

On one occasion the Goodwinites played a trick on their adversaries which has since been imitated in other districts. A well-known liquor dealer who had a considerable following died, and both Sheehan and Goodwin were eager to become his political heir by making a big showing at the funeral.

Goodwin managed to catch the enemy napping. He went to all the livery stables in the district, hired all the carriages for the day, and gave orders to two hundred of his men to be on hand as mourners.

Sheehan had never had any trouble about getting all the carriages that he wanted, so he let the matter go until the night before the funeral. Then he found that he could not hire a carriage in the district.

He called his district committee together in a hurry and explained the situation to them. He could get all the vehicles he needed in the adjoining district, he said, but if he did that, Goodwin would rouse the voters of the Ninth by declaring that he (Sheehan), had patronized foreign industries.

Finally, it was decided that there was nothing to do but to go over to Sixth Avenue and Broadway for carriages. Sheehan made a fine turnout at the funeral, but the deceased was hardly in his grave before Goodwin raised the cry of "Protection to home industries," and denounced his rival for patronizing

127

livery-stable keepers outside of his district. The cry had its effect in the primary campaign. At all events, Goodwin was elected leader.

A recent contest for the leadership of the Second District illustrated further the strenuous work of the Tammany district leaders. The contestants were Patrick Divver, who had managed the district for years, and Thomas F. Foley.

Both were particularly anxious to secure the large Italian vote. They not only attended all the Italian christenings and funerals, but also kept a close lookout for the marriages in order to be on hand with wedding presents.

At first, each had his own reporter in the Italian quarter to keep track of the marriages. Later, Foley conceived a better plan. He hired a man to stay all day at the City Hall marriage bureau, where most Italian couples go through the civil ceremony, and telephone to him at his saloon when anything was doing at the bureau.

Foley had a number of presents ready for use and, whenever he received a telephone message from his man, he hastened to the City Hall with a ring or a watch or a piece of silver and handed it to the bride with his congratulations. As a consequence, when Divver got the news and went to the home of the couple with his present, he always found that Foley had been ahead of him. Toward the end of the campaign, Divver also stationed a man at the marriage bureau and then there were daily foot races and fights between the two heelers.

Sometimes the rivals came into conflict at the death-bed. One night a poor Italian peddler died in Roosevelt Street. The news reached Divver and Foley about the same time, and as they knew the family of the man was destitute, each went to an undertaker and brought him to the Roosevelt Street tenement.

The rivals and the undertakers met at the house and an altercation ensued. After much discussion the Divver undertaker was selected. Foley had more carriages at the funeral, however, and he further impressed the Italian voters by paying the widow's rent for a month, and sending her half a ton of coal and a barrel of flour.

The rivals were put on their mettle toward the end of the campaign by the wedding of a daughter of one of the original Cohens of the Baxter Street region. The Hebrew vote in the district is nearly as large as the Italian vote, and Divver and Foley set out to capture the Cohens and their friends.

They stayed up nights thinking what they would give the bride. Neither knew how much the other was prepared to spend on a wedding present, or what form it would take; so spies were employed by both sides to keep watch on the jewelry stores, and the jewelers of the district were bribed by each side to impart the desired information.

At last Foley heard that Divver had purchased a set of silver knives, forks and spoons. He at once bought a duplicate set and added a silver tea service. When the presents were displayed at the home of the bride, Divver was not in a pleasant mood and he charged his jeweler with treachery. It may be added that Foley won at the primaries.

One of the fixed duties of a Tammany district leader is to give two outings every summer, one for the men of his district and the other for the women and children, and a beefsteak dinner and a ball every winter. The scene of the outings is, usually, one of the groves along the Sound.

The ambition of the district leader on these occasions is to demonstrate that his men have broken all records in the matter of eating and drinking. He gives out the exact number of pounds of beef, poultry, butter, etc., that they have consumed and professes to know how many potatoes and ears of corn have been served.

According to his figures, the average eating record of each man at the outing is about ten pounds of beef, two or three chickens, a pound of butter, a half peck of potatoes, and two dozen ears of corn. The drinking records, as given out, are still more phenomenal. For some reason, not yet explained, the district leader thinks that his popularity will be greatly increased if he can show that his followers can eat and drink more than the followers of any other district leader.

The same idea governs the beefsteak dinners in the winter. It matters not what sort of steak is served or how it is cooked; the district leader considers only the question of quantity, and when he excels all others in this particular, he feels, somehow, that he is a bigger man and deserves more patronage than his associates in the Tammany Executive Committee.

As to the balls, they are the events of the winter in the extreme East Side and West Side society. Mamie and Maggie and Jennie prepare for them months in advance, and their young men save up for the occasion just as they save for the summer trips to Coney Island.

The district leader is in his glory at the opening of the ball. He leads the cotillion with the prettiest woman present—his wife, if he has one, permitting— and spends almost the whole night shaking hands with his constituents. The ball costs him a pretty penny, but he has found that the investment pays.

By these means the Tammany district leader reaches out into the homes of his district, keeps watch not only on the men, but also on the women and children; knows their needs, their likes and dislikes, their troubles and their hopes, and places himself in a position to use his knowledge for the benefit of his organization and himself. Is it any wonder that scandals do not permanently disable Tammany and that it speedily recovers from what seems to be crushing defeat?

A NOTE ON THE TYPE

This book was set on the Linotype in Scotch, *a type-face that has been in continuous service for more than one hundred years. It is usually considered that the style of "modern face" followed in our present-day cuttings of Scotch was developed in the foundry of Alexander Wilson and Sons of Glasgow early in the nineteenth century. The new Wilson patterns were made to meet the requirements of the new fashion in printing that had been set going at the beginning of the century by the "modern" types of Didot in France and of Bodoni in Italy. It is to be observed that the* modern *in these matters is a modernity of* A.D. *1800, not of today. The "modernist" type-faces of today are quite another story.*

The book was composed, printed and bound by H. Wolff, New York, and was designed by Marshall Lee.